STUDY GUIDE

Christine Stamm-Griffin

to accompany

ON COOKING
A Textbook of Culinary Fundamentals

Fifth Edition

Sarah R. Labensky
Alan M. Hause
Priscilla A. Martel

PRENTICE HALL

Boston   Columbus   Indianapolis   New York   San Francisco   Upper Saddle River
Amsterdam   Cape Town   Dubai   London   Madrid   Milan   Munich   Paris   Montreal   Toronto
Delhi   Mexico City   Sao Paulo   Sydney   Hong Kong   Seoul   Singapore   Taipei   Tokyo

Editor in Chief: Vernon Anthony
Senior Acquisitions Editor: William Lawrensen
Development Editor: Sonya Kottcamp
Editorial Assistant: Lara Dimmick
Director of Marketing: David Gesell
Senior Marketing Manager: Leigh Ann Sims
Assistant Marketing Manager: Alicia Wozniak
Marketing Assistant: Les Roberts
Senior Managing Editor: Joellen Gohr

Associate Managing Editor: Alexandrina Benedicto Wolf
Senior Operations Supervisor: Pat Tonneman
Operations Specialist: Deidra Skahill
Cover Design: John Christiana
Cover Art: Yuri Arcurs/iStockphoto.com
Printer/Binder: Edwards Brothers, Inc.
Cover Printer: Lehigh-Phoenix Color
Text Font: Times Roman

Figures in this book are from *On Cooking: A Textbook of Culinary Fundamentals,* Fifth Edition, copyright © 2011 by Pearson Education.

10 9 8 7 6 5 4

Prentice Hall
is an imprint of

ISBN 10: 0-13-510889-6
ISBN 13: 978-0-13-510889-5

CONTENTS

Chapter 1   **Professionalism, 1**
Chapter 2   **Food Safety and Sanitation, 7**
Chapter 3   **Menus and Recipes, 15**
Chapter 4   **Tools and Equipment, 23**
Chapter 5   **Knife Skills, 35**
Chapter 6   **Flavors and Flavorings, 39**
Chapter 7   **Dairy Products, 49**
Chapter 8   **Mise en Place, 55**
Chapter 9   **Principles of Cooking, 61**
Chapter 10   **Stocks and Sauces, 69**
Chapter 11   **Soups, 79**
Chapter 12   **Principles of Cookery, 85**
Chapter 13   **Beef, 91**
Chapter 14   **Veal, 99**
Chapter 15   **Lamb, 107**
Chapter 16   **Pork, 115**
Chapter 17   **Poultry, 121**
Chapter 18   **Game, 129**
Chapter 19   **Fish and Shellfish, 135**
Chapter 20   **Eggs and Breakfast, 143**
Chapter 21   **Vegetables, 151**
Chapter 22   **Potatoes, Grains and Pasta, 157**
Chapter 23   **Healthy Cooking, 165**
Chapter 24   **Salads and Salad Dressings, 173**
Chapter 25   **Fruits, 179**
Chapter 26   **Sandwiches, 185**
Chapter 27   **Charcuterie, 189**
Chapter 28   **Hors d'oeuvre and Canapés, 197**
Chapter 29   **Principles of the Bakeshop, 205**
Chapter 30   **Quick Breads, 213**
Chapter 31   **Yeast Breads, 217**
Chapter 32   **Pies, Pastries and Cookies, 223**
Chapter 33   **Cakes and Frostings, 229**
Chapter 34   **Custards, Creams, Frozen Desserts and Dessert Sauces, 235**
Chapter 35   **Plate Presentation, 241**
Chapter 36   **Buffet Presentation, 245**

Answer Key, 249

To Linda Cullen, beloved friend, chef, and educator,
whose heart and soul will forever be reflected in the students she taught.
Without Linda's collaboration, this study guide would never have become a reality.
Thank you, Linda, for touching us all in your own special way.
I appreciate it more now than when we first started this project and wish you were here
so I could remind you how special you are in so many ways.

vi

About the Author

Dr. Christine Stamm-Griffin is an experienced culinarian and professor at Johnson & Wales University in Providence, Rhode Island. During her twenty years teaching at Johnson & Wales she has written and taught a variety of culinary and service courses in the associate and baccalaureate degree programs. She has taught at the Providence, Rhode Island; Miami, Florida; and Denver, Colorado, campuses. In addition to serving as a member of the opening team for the Johnson & Wales University Denver campus, where she taught for eight years, she is a primary author of Johnson & Wales' 1997 edition of the university's *Culinary Fundamentals* textbook.

Christine has earned an AOS degree in culinary arts, a BS degree in food service management, and a MS degree in management technology. She completed her Ed.D. in curriculum and teaching from Boston University's School of Education in 2001. In addition, she is certified as an executive chef and culinary educator by the American Culinary Federation. She has achieved acclaim, winning several national and international gold awards in food show competitions such as Hotelympia in London, England; Chef Ireland; the Culinary Olympics in Frankfurt, Germany; and the New England Chapters of the American Culinary Federation. Outside teaching she serves as a food service consultant with Yum! Inc. Christine also conducts professional lectures on topics in culinary arts, culinary nutrition, and education.

Christine resides in Massachusetts with her husband, Jim; her daughter, Haley, and her son, Jonah.

Chapter 1

PROFESSIONALISM

TEST YOUR KNOWLEDGE

The practice sets provided here have been designed to test your comprehension of the information found in this chapter. It is recommended that you read this chapter completely before attempting these questions.

1A. Terminology

Fill in each blank space with the correct definition.

1. Brigade _____

2. Gourmand _____

3. Nouvelle cuisine _____

4. Sous chef _____

5. Grande cuisine _____

6. Fernand Point _____

7. Classic cuisine _____

8. Executive chef _____

9. Dining room manager _____

10. Marie-Antoine Carême _____

11. Line cooks _____

12. Auguste Escoffier _____

13. Pastry chef _____

14. Area chef _____

15. Head waiter _____

16. Cuisine bourgeoisie _____

17. New American cuisine _____

18. Fusion cuisine _____

19. Restaurateur _____

20. Molecular gastronomy _____

1B.   Fill in the Blank

Fill in the blanks provided with the response that correctly completes the statement.

1.   Another term used for the area where guests are generally not allowed, such as the kitchen, is

_____.

2.   A type of service that tends to be more formal by using two waiters (a captain and a waiter) is called

_____.

3.   Another term for the area where guests are welcome and serviced, such as the dining room, is known
as the _____.

4.   The style of table service in which the waiter serves the entrée, vegetables, and carbohydrate—such as
potatoes—from a platter onto a guest's plate is called _____.

5.   The name of the front-of-the-house employee who makes sure the tables are properly set, foods are
delivered in a timely fashion to the proper tables, and the guests' needs are met is _____

_____.

6.   In _____ service, one waiter takes the order and brings the food to the table.

7.   Another term used for the position of the dining room attendant, who clears plates and refills water
glasses at various tables in the dining room, is _____.

8.   Another name for the sommelier is _____ , the one responsible for all aspects of
wine service.

9.   A tool delivered to professional kitchens everywhere by the use of modern computer technology that
enables chefs to communicate more effectively and source and order foods from a world of suppliers is
called _____.

1C.   Short Answer

Provide a short response that correctly answers each of the following questions.

1.   The introduction of the cast-iron stove provided several advantages to the 19th-century cooking
professional. List three (3) such advantages.

a.   _____

b.   _____

c.   _____

2.   Many food preservation and storage techniques were developed in the 19th century. List three (3) such
preservation and storage techniques.

a.   _____

b.   _____

c.   _____

3. What is the reasoning behind the design of each the following elements of the professional chef's uniform?

    a. Neckerchief: _____

    b. Black-and-white checked trousers: _____

    c. White double-breasted jacket: _____

    d. Apron: _____

4. List three (3) ways a professional chef can show pride in performing his or her job.

    a. _____

    b. _____

    c. _____

1D. Defining Professionalism

A student chef should try to develop six basic attributes in readiness for his or her role as a professional chef. Fill in the blank with the term that best matches the definition given on the right. (Term choices: knowledge, skill, taste, judgment, dedication, and pride)

Term	Definition
1. _____	The ability to make sound decisions such as what items to include on the menu; what, how much, and when to order food; and approving finished items for service, all of which can be learned only through experience.
2. _____	The desire to continually strive for the utmost professionalism and quality in spite of the physical and psychological strains of being a chef.
3. _____	A chef's ability to prepare flavorful and attractive foods that appeal to all senses and to the desires of his or her clientele.
4. _____	The desire to show high self-esteem for one's personal and professional accomplishments by means of such details as professional appearance and behavior.
5. _____	An ability developed through practical, hands-on experience that can be perfected only with extended experience.
6. _____	The understanding of a base of information that enables a chef to perform each aspect of the job.

1E. Noteworthy Chefs

Match each of the chefs in List A with the major culinary claim to fame he or she is known for in List B. Each choice in List B can be used only once.

List A	List B
_____ 1. Alice Waters	a. Trained by Fernand Point; pioneers of nouvelle cuisine
_____ 2. Boulanger	b. One of first to offer a menu listing available dishes during fixed hours of operation.
_____ 3. Fernand Point	c. The father of nouvelle cuisine
_____ 4. Auguste Escoffier	d. Exhibited culinary skill in grande cuisine in some of Europe's finest hotels
_____ 5. Paul Bocuse, Roger Vergé	e. Prepared meals consisting of dozens of courses of elaborately prepared and presented foods
_____ 6. Antonin Carême	f. An experimental Spanish chef who believes that "creativity means not copying"
_____ 7. Ferran Adrià	g. First known to offer a variety of foods prepared on premises to customers whose primary interest was dining
	h. Served fresh American food, simply prepared

1F. Matching

Match each of the terms in List A with the appropriate duty/responsibility in List B. Each choice in List B can be used only once.

List A	List B
_____ 1. Saucier	a. Sautéed items and most sauces
_____ 2. Friturier	b. Chocolate éclairs
_____ 3. Potager	c. Caesar salad
_____ 4. Garde manger	d. All vegetable and starch dishes
_____ 5. Rotisseur	e. Stocks and soups
_____ 6. Poissonier	f. Grilled veal tenderloin
_____ 7. Glacier	g. Roast pork au jus
_____ 8. Grillardin	h. Ground beef
_____ 9. Boucher	i. French fries
_____ 10. Boulanger	j. Steamed asparagus with hollandaise sauce
_____ 11. Entremetier	k. French bread
_____ 12. Commis	l. Poached sole with caper sauce
	m. Apprentices

4

1G. Chapter Review

For each statement, circle either True or False to indicate the correct answer. If an answer is false, then explain why.

1. Aside from quickly preparing foods to order, a short-order cook may serve much the same role as a tournant, having mastered many cooking stations.
   True   False _____

2. Today most well-run foodservice operations use the formal kitchen brigade system as the means for organizing the kitchen staff.
   True   False _____

3. Most new concerns that affect the foodservice industry, such as nutrition and sanitation, are brought about by the government.
   True   False _____

4. It was not until the early 1900s that advances in transportation efficiency improved to the point where the foodservice industry finally began to expand.
   True   False _____

5. A regional cuisine is composed of recipes based on local ingredients, traditions, and practices.
   True   False _____

6. The process of cooking can be described as transferring energy from the heat source to the food to alter the food's molecular structure.
   True   False _____

7. Most consumers choose a restaurant or foodservice establishment because it provides quality service and food for a price they are willing to pay.
   True   False _____

8. Escoffier is credited with developing the kitchen brigade system used in large restaurant kitchens.
   True   False _____

9. Although sun-drying, salting, smoking, pickling, and fermenting are effective means of preserving foods, they were passed up for newer technologies because of the labor intensity of preparation.
   True   False _____

10. As chefs of classical cuisine, Carême, Point, and Escoffier also practiced gastronomy.
    True   False _____

11. Dining in the European or Western style by proceeding through a meal course by course enables diners to simultaneously satisfy all five major groups of taste: sweet, salty, bitter, sour, and spicy.
    True   False _____

12. Escoffier's most important contribution to culinary arts was *Le Guide Culinaire*, an extensive book of classic garnishes for the professional chef.
    True   False _____

13. The farm-to-table movement, in which chefs focus on using locally raised or grown ingredients, also encourages them to use more seasonal ingredients while preserving local agriculture and heirloom varieties.
    True   False _____

1H.   Putting It All Together

Provide a short response for each of the following questions. These questions are designed to help you connect the bigger concepts presented in this chapter and/or text.

1.   What is the value of learning about the evolution of the culinary profession?

2.   Although Chef Gaston Lenôtre is known for his advancement of the baking and pastry profession, as an owner he was exceptionally entrepreneurial. Compare and contrast in detail what Lenôtre did differently from other famous chefs like Carême and Escoffier, hypothesizing whether the different era in which he lived played any role in these differences.

3.   Explain what impact the use of modern technologies has had on the production of raw food ingredients. In developing your answer, consider touching on the following:
   *   switch from organic to chemical fertilizers and pesticides (and the resurgence of organic produce production)
   *   rise of traditional hybridization techniques as well as genetic engineering
   *   advancements in animal husbandry and aquaculture
   *   commercially raised foods that were once available only in the wild
   *   modern preservation and transportation methods.

Chapter 2

FOOD SAFETY AND SANITATION

TEST YOUR KNOWLEDGE

The practice sets provided here have been designed to test your comprehension of the information found in this chapter. It is recommended that you read this chapter completely before attempting these questions.

2A. Terminology

Fill in each blank space with the correct definition.

1. Clean _____

2. Contamination

    a. Direct contamination _____

    b. Cross-contamination _____

3. Toxins

4. Intoxication _____

5. Microorganisms _____

6. Bacteria

    a. Aerobic _____

    b. Anaerobic _____

    c. Facultative _____

7. Molds _____

8. Chemical contaminants _____

9. Atmosphere _____

10. Infection _____

11. Acid/alkali balance _____

12. Potentially hazardous foods (PHF) _____

13. Toxin-mediated infection _____

14. Trichinosis _____

15. Temperature danger zone (TDZ) _____

16. Virus _____

17. Parasites _____

18. Anisakiasis _____

19. Time/temperature controlled for safety (TCS) foods _____

20. Tasting spoons _____

21. Water activity _____

22. Hazard Analysis Critical Control Points (HACCP) _____

2B. Multiple Choice

For each of the following, choose the one correct response.

1. Which of the following is **not** a necessity for bacteria to survive and reproduce?

   a. food
   b. time
   c. moisture
   d. sunlight
   e. temperature

2. The federal government enacted legislation designed to reduce hazards in the work area and therefore reduce accidents. This legislation is called:

   a. Safe Jobs for Working Americans Act (SJWAA)
   b. Occupational Hazards Prevention Policy (OHPP)
   c. Safety and Health for Working Americans (SHWA)
   d. Occupational Safety and Health Act (OSHA)
   e. Safe and Fast Employees (SAFE)

3. Which of the following is **not** an important step in proper hand washing?

   a. Use hot running water to thoroughly wet hands and forearms.
   b. Apply antibacterial soap and rub hands and arms briskly with lather for at least 10 seconds.
   c. Scrub between fingers and under nails with a nail brush.
   d. Rinse thoroughly with hot running water.
   e. Reapply soap and scrub hands and forearms for another 5–10 seconds, then rinse again in hot water.

4. To defrost frozen foods, pull the product from the freezer and:

   a. microwave on high in a plastic pan deep enough to catch the moisture.
   b. thaw at room temperature in a pan deep enough to catch the moisture.
   c. thaw in a warming oven on a roasting rack.
   d. thaw under refrigeration in a pan deep enough to catch the moisture.
   e. thaw under warm running water.

5. Foods that are considered acidic have a pH of:

   a.   7.0
   b.   8.5 to 10.0
   c.   0.0 to below 4.6
   d.   10.0 to 12.0
   e.   13.0 to 14.0

6. Which of the following factors is most easily controlled by food service workers, therefore limiting bacterial growth?

   a.   food
   b.   time
   c.   moisture
   d.   temperature
   e.   pH

2C. Chapter Review

For each statement, circle either True or False to indicate the correct answer. If an answer is false, then explain why.

1. The time-temperature principle is one of the best rules to follow to control the growth of bacteria.
   True   False _____

2. The first thing that should be done when a pest infestation is discovered is to try to find the source.
   True   False _____

3. A contaminated food will have an unusual odor.
   True   False _____

4. When cooling semisolid foods, they may be placed in any size container providing they are refrigerated at 40°F (4°C) or below.
   True   False _____

5. Food handlers are a major cause of the spread of bacteria.
   True   False _____

6. A dish can be clean without being sanitary.
   True   False _____

7. The acronym HACCP stands for Hazard Analysis Critical Control Points.
   True   False _____

8. Vinyl or plastic gloves are important to food handlers because they eliminate the need to wash hands frequently.
   True   False _____

9. Hepatitis A is a parasite that often enters shellfish through polluted waters, is carried by humans, and is often transmitted either by cross-contamination or by infected food handlers practicing poor personal hygiene.
   True   False _____

10. The high internal temperatures reached during cooking (165° F–212°F [74°C–100°C]) kill most of the bacteria that can cause food-borne illnesses.
    True   False _____

11. Reducing a food's water activity level to below 0.85A$_W$ kills all microorganisms.
    True   False _____

12. One can make an effective sanitizing solution that lasts for up to 2 hours by combining 1 gallon of lukewarm water with 1 tablespoon of chlorine bleach.
    True   False _____

13. If home cooks follow proper health procedures, most cases of illnesses caused by *E. coli* and salmonella could be avoided.
    True   False _____

14. The steps for the two-tasting-spoon method for sampling foods for finishing touches involves dipping the first spoon into the food product, tasting, discarding the first spoon, then repeating the process with the second spoon.
    True   False _____

15. Tomatoes or mixtures of cut tomatoes that are not acidified or modified by processing can be considered PHF/TCS and should be handled as such.
    True   False _____

16. Garlic-in-oil mixtures that are not acidified or otherwise processed are PHF/TCS and should be handled as such.
    True   False _____

2D. HACCP Overview

1. Number the following HACCP steps (1–8) to indicate the order in which they should be considered in the flow of a food service operation. (1 indicates the first step, 8 the last step.)

    _____   a. Selecting menu and recipes
    _____   b. Holding and service
    _____   c. Storing
    _____   d. Receiving
    _____   e. Preparing
    _____   f. Cooling leftovers
    _____   g. Cooking
    _____   h. Reheating

2. Which statement is **false** regarding HACCP?

    a. HACCP is a rigorous system of self-inspection that ensures that food service standards are followed.
    b. Law mandates that all food service operations establish and maintain a HACCP system.
    c. HACCP identifies what actions can be taken to reduce or prevent each risk or hazard.
    d. Hazards must be prioritized, and correction of critical concerns should take priority.
    e. The most effective HACCP programs are formalized and the employees trained to understand them.

3. Which statement is **false** regarding HACCP?

   a. It focuses on the flow of food through the food service facility.
   b. It is a rigorous system of sanitary inspection conducted by the health department.
   c. It is an effective and efficient method for managing and maintaining sanitary conditions in a food service operation.
   d. It is a system that should be followed on a daily basis.
   e. An establishment should maintain written charts for recording times and temperatures once they've been checked throughout the day.

4. Which **two** statements are **true** about the HACCP system?

   a. HACCP is best applied only to institutional food service establishments.
   b. Staff should fully check and record time/temperature information in written logs.
   c. All personnel must be constantly aware and responsive to the system, the risks, problems, and solutions.
   d. HACCP monitors areas where a mistake can result in the transmission, growth, or survival of viruses, fungi, parasites, or putrefactive bacteria.
   e. A well-designed HACCP program completely eliminates the possibility of food-borne illness ever occurring.

2E. Food-Borne Diseases Review

This section provides a review of information regarding food-borne diseases. Fill in the blanks provided with the response that correctly completes each portion of the statement. Following is a definition of each of the points needing answers for each question.

Organism: What type of organism causes the disease? Is it a bacterium, parasite, virus, fungus, mold, or yeast?
Form: Especially relevant to bacteria, what form does it take? Is it a cell, a toxin, or a spore?
Source: In what foods might this organism be found, or what is the source of the contaminant?
Prevention: How can an outbreak of this disease be avoided?

1. Botulism

Organism: _____
Form: _____
Source: _____
Prevention: _____

2. Hepatitis A

Organism: _____
Source: _____
Prevention: _____

3. Strep

Organism: _____
Form: _____
Source: _____
Prevention: _____

4. Perfringens or CP

Organism: _____
Form: _____
Source: _____
Prevention: _____

5. Norwalk virus

Organism: _____
Source: _____
Prevention: _____

6. Salmonella

Organism: _____
Form: _____
Source: _____
Prevention: _____

7. *E. coli* or 0157

Organism: _____
Form: _____
Source: _____
Prevention: _____

8. Trichinosis

Organism: _____
Source: _____
Prevention: _____

9. Anisakiasis

Organism: _____
Source: _____
Prevention: _____

10. Listeriosis

Organism: _____
Form: _____
Source: _____
Prevention: _____

11. Staphylococcus

Organism: _____
Form: _____
Source: _____
Prevention: _____

2F. Matching

Match each of the food categories in List A with the appropriate internal cooking temperature in List B. Some answers in List B may be used more than once.

List A

_____ 1. Pork, ham, bacon
_____ 2. Poultry/wild game, whole/ground
_____ 3. Stuffing, stuffed foods, or
         casseroles
_____ 4. Fish, shellfish
_____ 5. Beef, pork, veal or lamb roasts
_____ 6. Commercial game
_____ 7. Egg dishes

_____ 8. Beef, veal, lamb steaks or chops
_____ 9. Ground beef, veal, pork, or lamb
_____ 10. Eggs

_____ 11. Ratites and injected meats
_____ 12. Any PHF/TCS, cooked in
         microwave

List B

a. 165°F/74°C for 15 seconds
b. Cook until opaque and firm and shells open
c. 155°F/63°C for 15 seconds

d. 145°F/63°C for 4 minutes
e. 170°F/76°C for 15 seconds
f. 145°F/63°C for 15 seconds; shells should open
g. 145°F/63°C for 15 seconds OR till yolk and white are
    firm
h. 160°F/71°C
i. 175°F/63°C for 15 seconds
j. 155°F/63°C for 15 seconds; if the dish is uncooked,
    use only pasteurized product
k. 145°F/63°C for 15 seconds
l. 165°F/74°C; let stand for 2 minutes

Chapter 3

MENUS AND RECIPES

TEST YOUR KNOWLEDGE

The practice sets provided here have been designed to test your comprehension of the information found in this chapter. It is recommended that you read this chapter completely before attempting these questions.

3A. Terminology

Fill in each blank space with the correct definition.

1. Course _____

2. Entrée _____

3. Static (or fixed) menu _____

4. Cycle menu _____

5. Market menu _____

6. Hybrid menu _____

7. California menu _____

8. À la carte _____

9. Semi à la carte _____

10. Table d'hôte / Prix fixe _____

11. Tasting menu _____

12. Recipe _____

13. Standardized recipe _____

14. Weight _____

15. Volume _____

16. Count _____

17. U.S. system _____

18. Metric system _____

29. Yield/yield percentage _____

20. Conversion factor _____

21. As-purchased costs or prices _____

22. Unit costs or prices _____

23. Total recipe cost _____

24. Cost per portion _____

25. Selling price _____

26. Portion size _____

27. Nutritional statements _____

28. Parstock _____

29. Menu language _____

30. Trim _____

3B. Units of Measure

Fill in the blanks for the following conversions.

1. 1 lb. = _____ oz.
2. 1 oz. = _____ g
3. 1 lb. = _____ g = _____ kg
4. 1 kg = _____ g
5. 1 g = _____ oz.
6. 1 kg = _____ oz. = _____ lb.
7. 1 c. = _____ tbsp. = _____ fl. oz.
8. 2 pt. = _____ qt. = _____ fl. oz.
9. 2 qt. = _____ gal. = _____ pt.
10. 2 c. = _____ tbsp. = _____ fl. oz.
11. ½ c. = _____ tbsp. = _____ tsp.
12. 2 c. = _____ pt. = _____ qt.
13 2 fl. oz. = _____ c. = _____ tbsp. = _____ tsp.
14. 1 gal. = _____ fl. oz. = _____ qt. = _____ c.
15. 1.5 qt. = _____ pt. = _____ gal.

3C. Conversion Factors

Solve the following math problems by calculating the new conversion factors for each example. Round all answers to the nearest hundredth decimal point.

1. The original recipe for tartar sauce yields 1 gallon, but you need to prepare 2½ gallons.
   Conversion factor: _____

2. A Chicken Marsala recipe yields 50 portions; however, you're expecting a party of only 35.
   Conversion factor: _____

3. You need to make 7 gallons of beef barley soup, but your recipe yields 12 gallons.
   Conversion factor: _____

4. A recipe for lasagna that yields 8 portions must be increased to yield enough for 20 guests.
   Conversion factor: _____

5. Alone for the evening, you want to make 1 portion of veal paprika from a recipe that originally yielded 4 portions.
   Conversion factor: _____

6. The broccoli polonaise recipe yields 8 pounds, but you need only 6 pounds.
   Conversion factor: _____

7. Twenty-five pounds (8 ounces per serving) of beef stew is the original yield of the recipe, but you need to produce only 15 pounds.
   Conversion factor: _____
   How many portions will 15 pounds of beef stew yield? _____

8. As a part of your mise en place for Sunday brunch you're required to make 5 gallons of pancake batter but the original recipe yields only 2 quarts.
   Conversion factor: _____

3D. Conversion Problems

When making large recipe changes, some additional problems may occur. Give a brief description of how each of the following elements can cause a problem during the conversion process.

1. Equipment: _____

2. Evaporation: _____

3. Recipe errors: _____

4. Time: _____

3E. Recipe Conversion

The following recipe presently yields 32 6-oz portions. Calculate the conversion factors and convert the quantities in the recipe to yield 28 6-ounce portions and 84 3-ounce portions.
   • Remember to convert new yields back into pounds, ounces, and quarts or cups.
   • Round all answers to the nearest hundredth decimal point.

Cream of Broccoli Soup

Old Yield: 6 qt. (6 lt), 32 portions, 6 oz. each	Conversion Factor I: _____	Yield I: 28 portions, 6 oz. each _____	Conversion Factor II: _____	Yield II: 84 portions, 3 oz. each _____
Butter	3½ oz.	_____		_____
Onion	12 oz.	_____		_____
Celery	2½ oz.	_____		_____
Broccoli	3 lb.	_____		_____
Chicken velouté	4 qt.	_____		_____
Chicken stock	2 qt.	_____		_____
Heavy cream	24 oz.	_____		_____
Broccoli florets	8 oz.	_____		_____

3F. Unit Costs

Solve the following math problems by calculating the unit costs for each ingredient. Round all answers to the nearest hundredth decimal point.

1. One case of milk costs $38.25. There are nine (9) half gallons in each case. How much does one (1) cup cost?
   Answer: $ _____

2. One case of English muffins costs $18.00. There are six (6) packages of twelve (12) muffins in each case. How much does one (1) English muffin cost?
   Answer: $ _____

3. One case of olive oil costs $78.00. There are six (6) gallons per case. How much does one (1) quart cost?
   Answer: $ _____

4. Five (5) pounds of sliced American cheese cost $12.00. If one slice weighs ½ ounce, how much do two (2) slices cost?
   Answer: $ _____

5. One case of cooking wine costs $18.08. If four (4) gallons of wine are in each case, what is the cost per ounce of cooking wine?
   Answer: $ _____

6. One case of disposable chef hats costs $14.42 and contains twenty-five (25) hats. What is the unit cost of each hat?
   Answer: $ _____

7. Twelve rolls of commercial-grade paper towels come in one case costing $23.58. What is the cost per roll of paper towels?
   Answer: $ _____

8. One case of heavy cream containing two (2) gallons of product costs $32.16. What is the cost per quart of cream?
   Answer: $ _____

3G. Cost per Portion

Solve the following math problems by calculating the cost per portion of food product. Round all answers to the nearest hundredth decimal point.

1. Sandwich sales for one week are $1,462.50, and 325 sandwiches are sold. How much did each sandwich sell for, assuming each sold for the same dollar amount?
   Answer: $ _____

2. The ingredient costs for producing 30 portions of New England boiled dinner are as follows: potatoes, $15.75; carrots, $12.25; turnips, $10.60; cabbage, $9.85; corned beef, $75.50. What is the cost to produce each dinner?
   Answer: $ _____

3. One dozen eggs cost $1.00 and the buffet cook uses 3 eggs per omelet. What is the cost for the eggs needed in one omelet?
Answer: $ _____

4. In one day a restaurant sells 68 bowls of soup. Sales for soup total $51.00. What is the price per bowl of soup for each customer?
Answer: $ _____

5. The cost to purchase 25 pounds of ground beef is $56.25. Assuming that 8-ounce hamburgers are made from the full 25 pounds of meat:

    a. What is the cost per pound for the ground meat?   Answer: $ _____
    b. What is the cost for the meat used to make each burger?   Answer: $ _____

6. A chef purchases a 9¼-pound pork loin for $35.61. As she trims the loin to portion 5-ounce chops, she loses ½ pound of the yield to waste.

    a. What was the cost per pound of meat remaining for portioning?   Answer: $ _____
    b. What is the weight of the meat that is available for portioning?   Answer: $ _____
    c. How many chops did the trimmed pork loin yield?   Answer: $ _____
    d. What was the final cost for each pork chop?   Answer: $ _____

7. One case of lettuce contains 28 heads and costs $17.92. Assuming each portion of lettuce for the house salad costs $0.16:

    a. What is the cost per head of lettuce?   Answer: $ _____
    b. Approximately how many portions will the case yield?   Answer: $ _____

8. In making an ice cream sundae, one gallon of premium vanilla fudge swirl ice cream costs $12.00 and yields 16 portions. One quart of chocolate sauce costs $3.30 and is portioned in 2-ounce increments. One quart of maraschino cherries costs $10.60 and yields approximately 90 cherries, one per portion. What is the total cost of ingredients to produce two sundaes?
Answer: $ _____

3H. Controlling Food Cost

Briefly describe the impact the following areas have on the operational costs of a restaurant:

1. Menu: _____

2. Purchasing: _____

3. Receiving: _____

4. Storing: _____

5. Issuing: _____

6. Standard portions: _____

7. Waste: _____

8. Sales and service: _____

3I. Chapter Review

For each statement, circle either True or False to indicate the correct answer. If an answer is false, then explain why.

1. The following order of courses is an example of a typical meal at a North American restaurant: appetizer, soup, or salad followed by an entrée and finished with a dessert, fruit, or cheese course.
    True   False _____

2. Portion or balance scales are commonly used in commercial kitchens to accurately determine volumes of ingredients.
    True   False _____

3. The weight and volume of water, butter, eggs, and milk are the same.
    True   False _____

4. Static (fixed), cycle, market, and hybrid menus can be purchased á la carte, semi á la carte, and/or table d'hôte.
    True   False _____

5. In the European tradition a palate cleanser such as a cheese course may be served after the entrée and before the dessert.
    True   False _____

6. Volume measurements are generally less accurate than measuring by weight.
    True   False _____

7. Figuring the portion cost of everything on a plate served to the guest is the primary thing one has to worry about in order to determine the selling price.
    True   False _____

8. A guest orders a plate of chicken à la russe with appropriate accompaniments, which add up to a total cost of $2.56 to prepare. If the chef is trying to run his kitchen at a 32% food cost, the minimum selling price should be $9.20.
    True   False _____

9. In general, nutritional data is not required for menu items that do not carry a nutritional content or health claim.
    True   False _____

10. Food safety laws dictate that all temperature-controlled foods (such as PHF/TCS foods) must be cooked to the minimum internal temperature unless a customer requests otherwise.
    True   False _____

3J. Putting It All Together

Provide a short response for each of the following questions. These questions are designed to help you connect the bigger concepts presented in this chapter and/or text.

1. What benefits exist for guests when the chef of a restaurant offers a tasting menu? What benefits exist for the chef/establishment?

2. What impact can straying from following accurate measurements have on the accuracy of costing standardized recipes? Would the results be similar or different if the chef also varied in his or her portion control techniques?

3. What would the results likely be if a chef did not know how to accurately convert recipes to meet varying production needs?

Chapter 4

TOOLS AND EQUIPMENT

TEST YOUR KNOWLEDGE

The practice sets provided here have been designed to test your comprehension of the information found in this chapter. It is recommended that you read this chapter completely before attempting these questions.

4A. Terminology

Fill in each blank space with the correct definition.

1. Carbon steel _____

2. Stainless steel _____

3. High-carbon stainless steel _____

4. Ceramic _____

5. Bird's-beak knife _____

6. Scimitar _____

7. Tang _____

8. Baster _____

9. Whetstone _____

10. Vertical cutter/mixer _____

11. Flat top _____

12. Griddles _____

13. Salamander _____

14. Rotisserie _____

15. Insulated carriers _____

16. Chafing dishes _____

17. Heat lamps _____

18. Work stations _____

19. Work sections _____

20. P.A.S.S. _____

21. Convection oven _____

22. Tare _____

4B. Equipment Identification

Identify each of the following items and give a use for each.

Hand Tools:

1. Name of item: _____
    Major use: _____

2. Name of item: _____
    Major use: _____

3. Name of item: _____
    Major use: _____

4. Name of item: _____
    Major use: _____

5. Name of item: _____
    Major use: _____

24

Knives:

6. Name of item: _____
    Major use: _____

7. Name of item: _____
    Major use: _____

8. Name of item: _____
    Major use: _____

9. Name of item: _____
    Major use: _____

10. Name of item: _____
    Major use: _____

11. Name of item: _____
    Major use: _____

Cookware:

12. Name of item: _____
     Major use: _____

13. Name of item: _____
     Major use: _____

14. Name of item: _____
     Major use: _____

15. Name of item: _____
     Major use: _____

16. Name of item: _____
     Major use: _____

17. Name of item: _____
     Major use: _____

18. Name of item: _____
     Major use: _____

19. Name of item: _____
     Major use: _____

20. Name of item: _____
    Major use: _____

21. Name of item: _____
    Major use: _____

22. Name of item: _____
    Major use: _____

Processing Equipment:

23. Name of item: _____
    Major use: _____

24. Name of item: _____
    Major use: _____

Heavy Equipment:

25. Name of item: _____
    Major use: _____

26. Name of item: _____
    Major use: _____

27. Name of item: _____
     Major use: _____

28. Name of item: _____
     Major use: _____

29. Name of item: _____
     Major use: _____

4C. Short Answer

Provide a short response that correctly answers each of the following questions.

1. List three (3) of the six (6) requirements for NSF certification of kitchen tools and equipment.

   a. _____

   b. _____

   c. _____

2. Describe four (4) important criteria for evaluation of equipment for kitchen use.

   a. _____

   b. _____

   c. _____

   d. _____

3. List and describe the three (3) types of metals used in the production of knife blades.

   a. _____

   b. _____

   c. _____

4. Provide four (4) characteristics of the sous vide technique.

   a. _____

   b. _____

   c. _____

   d. _____

5. Describe the four (4) basic steps required to calibrate a stem-type thermometer.

   a. _____

   b. _____

   c. _____

   d. _____

4D. Matching

Match each of the terms in List A with the appropriate description in List B. Each choice in List B can be used only once.

List A	List B
_____ 1. Mandoline	a. Can be used for food up to 400°F/204°C
_____ 2. Refrigerator	b. The metal used most commonly for knife blades
_____ 3. Candy thermometer	c. A metal that holds and distributes heat very well but is also quite heavy
_____ 4. Salamander	d. Food is placed on a revolving spit
_____ 5. Copperware	e. An overhead broiler used to brown the top of foods
_____ 6. Rotisserie	f. A loosely woven cotton fabric used to strain liquids
_____ 7. Cast iron	g. The metal that is the most effective conductor of heat for cookware
_____ 8. Cheesecloth	h. Used for food storage; may be walk-in or reach-in
_____ 9. Tilting skillet	i. A manually operated slicer used for small quantities of fruit and vegetables
_____ 10. Aluminum	j. A piece of equipment that can be used for frying or braising
	k. A metal that changes color when in contact with acid foods

4E. Fill in the Blank

Fill in each blank space with the response that correctly completes the statement.

1. A _____ knife is used for general-purpose cutting of fruits and vegetables.

2. On a chef's knife, the part of the blade found inside the handle is called the _____.

3. A flat metal cooking surface often used by short-order cooks and fast-food operations is known as a _____.

4. A _____ _____ is a large, heavy piece of equipment used primarily to chop large quantities of foods to a uniform size (but not shape).

5. _____ spoons should be used when cooking foods on nonstick surfaces.

6. Another name for a butcher knife is a _____.

7. _____ knives have an asymmetrical blade that is flat on one side and beveled to a sharp edge on the other side.

8. A _____ thermometer is the best to purchase and use to ensure accurate temperatures and minimize the chance for cross-contamination.

4F. Chapter Review

For each statement, circle either True or False to indicate the correct answer. If an answer is false, then explain why.

1. Stem-type thermometers should be thrown away if they have been dropped.
    True   False _____

2. Ventilation hoods should be cleaned and inspected by the hotel/restaurant maintenance staff.
    True   False _____

3. Some handmade imported pottery may contain lead in the glaze.
    True   False _____

4. Class B fire extinguishers are the only ones used for fires caused by oil or grease.
    True   False _____

5. High-carbon stainless steel discolors when it comes into contact with acidic foods.
    True   False _____

6. A steam kettle cooks more slowly than a pot sitting on a stove.
    True   False _____

7. Most equipment manufacturers voluntarily submit their designs to NSF for certification to show that they are suitable for use in professional food service operations.
    True   False _____

8. Seamless plastic or rubber parts on food service equipment are important to prevent cracking or splitting over extended use.
    True   False _____

9. A fire extinguisher rated Class B would be best to eliminate a grease or oil fire.
    True   False _____

10. Silicone bakeware is good only for baking; putting it in the freezer destroys its flexibility.
    True   False _____

11. Although pans lined with a polymer such as Silverstone or Teflon provide a slippery, non-reactive finish that keeps food from sticking, thus enabling the chef to use less fat in the cooking process, the great deal of care required to keep this coating from chipping, scratching, or peeling may not make it an appropriate pan to have in a commercial kitchen.
    True   False _____

12. Induction burners are portable and favorable because they maintain a safer and cooler cooking environment; however, they will not likely become a regular part of the commercial kitchen.
    True   False _____

13. The size and design of each work station in a kitchen is determined primarily by the menu.
    True   False _____

14. The anti-griddle resembles a traditional griddle, but instead of cooking food, it freezes food by searing it with extreme cold on the outside, allowing foods such as purées to have two temperatures: cold on the outside and warm on the inside.
    True   False _____

4G. Putting It All Together

Provide a short response for each of the following questions. These questions are designed to help you connect the bigger concepts presented in this chapter and/or text.

1. In Chapter 1, Professionalism, you learned about numerous chefs whose work has advanced the culinary profession into what it is today. Contrast Alexis Soyer's contributions—discussed in this chapter—with those found in Chapter 1.

2. What food safety and sanitation principles might you need to follow/be careful of when storing food in an insulated carrier?

3. Based on your knowledge of food safety and sanitation, describe some steps you can take to avoid chemical contamination of food products in your establishment.

Chapter 5

KNIFE SKILLS

TEST YOUR KNOWLEDGE

The practice sets provided here have been designed to test your comprehension of the information found in this chapter. It is recommended that you read this chapter completely before attempting these questions.

5A. Terminology

Fill in each blank space with the correct definition.

1. Grip _____

2. Whetstone _____

3. Steel _____

4. Uniformity _____

5. Chiffonade _____

6. Rondelles/rounds _____

7. Diagonals _____

8. Oblique or roll cut _____

9. Lozenges _____

10. Butterfly _____

11. Julienne _____

12. Bâtonnet _____

13. Brunoise _____

14. Small dice _____

15. Medium dice _____

16. Large dice _____

17. Paysanne _____

18. Gaufrette _____

19. Parisienne _____

20. Tourner _____

21. Roll cut _____

22. Oblique cut _____

23. Chop _____

24. Mince _____

5B. Knife Safety

Briefly describe the eight (8) basic steps for knife safety.

1. _____

2. _____

3. _____

4. _____

5. _____

6. _____

7. _____

8. _____

5C. Cuts of Vegetables

Using a ruler, draw the following cuts of vegetables to scale and describe their dimensions. On the lines provided, describe any similarities between the strips and the cubes of vegetables.

_____

_____

_____

1. Julienne

4. Brunoise

2. Batonnet

5. Small dice

3. Paysanne

6. Medium dice

5D. Fill in the Blank

Fill in each blank space with the response that correctly completes the statement.

1. There are two safe methods of cutting. In one, the _____ _____ acts as the fulcrum; in the other, the _____ acts as the fulcrum.

2. Parsley and garlic should be chopped with one hand flat on the _____ of the knife, using a _____ motion.

3. When cutting food, always cut _____ from yourself and never cut on surfaces made of _____ , _____ , or _____ .

4. When using a whetstone, start by placing the _____ of the knife on the stone. Start sharpening on the _____ side of the stone and finish with the _____ side.

5. To dice an onion, cut it in half through the root and then make incisions toward the _____ of the onion, without cutting through it. Then turn the onion half in the opposite direction and complete the dice holding the incisions together while cutting against them in the appropriate width to achieve the size of the dice desired.

5E. Dicing an Onion

Describe the five (5) steps necessary to dice an onion.

1. _____

2. _____

3. _____

4. _____

5. _____

5F. Chapter Review

For each statement, circle either True or False to indicate the correct answer. If an answer is false, then explain why.

1. A sharp knife is more dangerous than a dull one.
   True   False _____

2. *Tourner* means "to turn" in French.
   True   False _____

3. A steel is used to sharpen knives.
   True   False _____

4. Bâtonnets are also referred to as allumettes.
   True   False _____

5. A whetstone should be moistened with a mixture of water and mineral oil.
   True   False _____

6. Paysanne can be a half-inch dice that has been cut in half.
   True   False _____

7. One should not attempt to catch a falling knife.
   True   False _____

8. Knives should not be washed in the dishwasher.
   True   False _____

5G. Putting It All Together

Provide a short response for each of the following questions. These questions are designed to help you connect the bigger concepts presented in this chapter and/or text.

1. In Chapter 1 you learned about professionalism. How would applying excellent knife skills to menu preparation help differentiate the quality of final foods/dishes of a professional chef from a practitioner?

2. In Chapter 2 you learned about food safety and sanitation. What are some practices you can employ to prevent cross-contamination of your knives during long hours of preparation?

Chapter 6

FLAVORS AND FLAVORINGS

TEST YOUR KNOWLEDGE

The practice sets provided here have been designed to test your comprehension of the information found in this chapter. It is recommended that you read the chapter completely before attempting these questions.

6A. Terminology

Fill in each blank space with the correct definition.

1. Herbs _____

2. Table salt _____

3. Shortenings _____

4. Spices _____

5. Capsaicin _____

6. Vinegar _____

7. Smoke point _____

8. Pickles _____

9. Flavorings _____

10. Rancid _____

11. Relish _____

12. Taste _____

13. Aroma _____

14. Mouth feel _____

15. Palate _____

16. Pungent _____

17. Astringent _____

18. Seasoning _____

19. Condiment _____

20. Flavor _____

21. Flavor profile _____

22. Flavor notes _____

23. Taste _____

24. Supertaster _____

25. Taste receptor cells _____

26. Nostrils _____

27. Olfactory bulb _____

28. Flash point _____

29. Brandy _____

30. Wine _____

31. Liqueur _____

32. Beer _____

33. Liquor _____

34. Flambéing _____

35. Vintner _____

36. Viniculture _____

37. Viticulture _____

38. Fermentation _____

6B. Discovering Tastes

Match each term in List A with the appropriate description in List B. Each choice in List B can be used only once.

	List A		List B
_____	1. Western definition of taste	a.	Maintaining the proper balance of tastes in a dish or during an entire meal assists in maintaining good health and fortune
_____	2. Sweet	b.	Found in acidic foods, it can vary in intensity but can be made more palatable by adding varying amounts of sweet
_____	3. Umami	c.	Helps finish a dish, heightening or enhancing other flavors; it may occur naturally in the food or be added by the cook
_____	4. Chinese five-taste scheme	d.	Based more on science, it identifies four tastes: sweet, sour, salty, bitter, and sometimes umami
_____	5. Bitter	e.	The practice of arranging tastes on a continuum, rating them as primary or secondary, including sweet, salty, bitter, pungent, harsh and astringent
_____	6. Salty	f.	Less preferred across cultures than other tastes, it is potent and easily unbalanced by other tastes like sour or salty
_____	7. Sour	g.	Literally means "delicious"; it occurs naturally in foods that contain amino acid glutamates such as soy sauce, cheese, meats, mushrooms, and tomatoes
_____	8. Ayurvedic medicine	h.	Created by naturally occurring sugars that can be enhanced by small amounts of sour, bitter, or salty tastes
		i.	The Indian way of creating dishes with the balance of six tastes that are based on the tastes of various herbs and spices

6C. Categorizing Flavorings

Place each item in the following list into the correct category.

paprika	oregano	lemon grass
cilantro	thyme	lavender
capers	ground mustard	coriander
black pepper	garlic	

Herbs:

1. _____

2. _____

3. _____

4. _____

5. _____

Spices:

6. _____

7. _____

8. _____

9. _____

10. _____

11. _____

6D. Herbs and Spices

For each of the following, choose the one correct response.

1. Which of the following is **not** one of the three guidelines to follow when experimenting with the use of different herbs and spices in various dishes?

    a. Flavorings should be added at the beginning of the preparation.
    b. Flavorings should not hide the taste or aroma of the primary ingredients.
    c. Flavorings should be combined in balance, so as not to overwhelm the palate.
    d. Flavorings should not be used to disguise poor quality or poorly prepared products.
    e. Flavorings should initially be used by following guidelines provided in books such as this one.

2. Which spice does the following description identify?
    Thin layers of bark that are peeled from branches of small evergreen trees and dried in the sun. This pale brown spice is most commonly purchased ground because it is difficult to grind.

    a. nutmeg
    b. allspice
    c. cinnamon
    d. mace
    e. fennel

3. Which spice does the following description identify?
    Hand-picked, dried stigmas of a type of crocus that are the most expensive spice in the world.

    a. turmeric
    b. saffron
    c. poppy seeds
    d. juniper
    e. cloves

4. Which herb does the following description identify?
    Hollow, thin, grasslike stems that have a mild onion flavor and bright green color.

    a. chervil
    b. lemongrass
    c. dill
    d. chives
    e. cilantro

5. Which herb does the following description identify?
    A flowering herb commonly used as a flavoring in Mediterranean cooking and having a flavor similar to thyme, only sweeter. The wild version of this herb is known as oregano.

    a. cilantro
    b. lemon thyme
    c. rosemary
    d. marjoram
    e. bay leaf

6. Which spice does the following description identify?
   Round and beige seeds from the cilantro plant that have a sweet, spicy flavor and strong aroma.

   a. coriander
   b. cardamom
   c. fenugreek
   d. cumin
   e. ginger

7. Which spice does the following description identify?
   A root that comes from a tall, flowering tropical plant and has a fiery yet sweet flavor, with hints of lemon and rosemary. It is used extensively in Asian cookery.

   a. turmeric
   b. cloves
   c. ginger
   d. caraway
   e. fennel

8. Which herb does the following description identify?
   Commonly used in Mediterranean cuisines, it has a strong, warm, and slightly peppery flavor with a hint of cloves. It is available in a variety of "flavors"—cinnamon, garlic, lemon, and chocolate.

   a. garlic chives
   b. sweet basil
   c. rosemary
   d. oregano
   e. cilantro

9. Which herb does the following description identify?
   Typically used in poultry dishes, with fatty meats or brewed as a beverage, its strong balsamic/camphor flavor does not blend well with other herbs.

   a. savory
   b. tarragon
   c. thyme
   d. sage
   e. parsley

10. Which spice does the following description identify?
    Perhaps the world's oldest spice; is a small, crescent-shaped brown seed with the peppery flavor of rye.

    a. caraway
    b. cardamom
    c. coriander
    d. mustard
    e. cumin

11. Which herb does the following description identify?
A member of the parsley family that has delicate blue-green, feathery leaves and whose flavor is similar to parsley, only with a hint of anise.

    a. fennel
    b. dill
    c. tarragon
    d. chervil
    e. basil

12. Which spice does the following description identify?
An American combination of spices—oregano, cumin, garlic, and other flavorings—intended for use in Mexican dishes.

    a. paprika
    b. chile powder
    c. commercial chilli powder
    d. grains of paradise
    e. herbes de Provence

13. Which spice does the following description identify?
The dried green leaf of the sassafras plant used by Choctaw Indians as a thickener and flavoring in Cajun and Creole cuisines.

    a. garlic
    b. paprika
    c. horseradish
    d. filé powder
    e. bay

14. Which spice does the following description identify?
A pale green root with a strong aroma and sharp cleansing flavor with herbal overtones that is similar to, but hotter than, the unrelated horseradish root. Often accompanies sushi.

    a. turmeric
    b. galangal
    c. wasabi
    d. ginger
    3. garlic

15. Which herb does the following description identify?
Tough, glossy leaves with a sweet balsamic aroma and peppery flavor also known as sweet laurel.

    a. epazote
    b. bay
    c. sage
    d. lavender
    e. rosemary

6E. Short Answer

Provide a short response that correctly answers each of the following questions.

1. Even though umami is a relatively new addition to the list of basic tastes for Westerners, it has been part of what country's cuisine focus and taste profile for years?

2. Name the three areas in the mouth where taste receptors can be found.

    a. _____

    b. _____

    c. _____

3. Taste compounds require _____ in order to be dissolved in the mouth so that they can then stimulate the taste receptors.

4. There are two ways that we smell foods, which enhance our ability to taste, and both are enabled by olfactory bulbs located in two different places. In simple terms, not the complex ones provided in vocabulary in the text, explain where the sense organs are that enable us to smell.

    a. _____

    b. _____

5. During food preparation, a chef must take into account several factors affecting one's perception of flavors. Next to the factor listed on the left, write the rule that a chef should follow.

    a. Temperature: _____

    b. Consistency: _____

    c. Presence of contrasting tastes: _____

    d. Presence of fats: _____

    e. Color: _____

6. Considering some of the things that can compromise one's perception of taste, why might food preparation be more challenging to a chef in a nursing home compared to a chef in a restaurant (who serves numerous guests of a variety of different age groups and healthfulness)?

    _____

    _____

    _____

7. Describe the process of making sparkling wines, including both the first and second stages of production.

    _____

    _____

    _____

8. Explain what caused an unusually large number of French vintners to relocate throughout Europe, Australia, and North America in the late 1800s.

    _____

    _____

    _____

    _____

9. List and explain the four guidelines a chef should use when matching beer and food.

    a. _____

    b. _____

    c. _____

    d. _____

10. Fill in the missing information on international flavor principles in the following table:

Country	Common Flavors
China, general	General: Northern: Southern: Western:
Eastern Europe	(Jewish)
Eastern and Northern Europe	General:
France	General: Northern: Southern:
Greece	
India	Northern: Southern:
Italy	General: Northern: Southern:
Japan	
Mexico	
Spain	
Thailand	

6F. Chapter Review

For each statement, circle either True or False to indicate the correct answer. If an answer is false, then explain why.

1. *Ketchup* originally referred to any salty extract from fish, fruits, or vegetables.
    True   False _____

2. In terms of making beverages, the term *steeping* means mixing hot water with ground coffee.
    True   False _____

3. When preparing a recipe that calls for fresh herbs, the rule to follow when fresh herbs are unavailable is to use more dried herbs than the fresh variety asked for in the recipe.
    True   False _____

4. Mustard never really spoils; its flavor just fades away.
    True   False _____

5. Vegetable oils are cholesterol free, are virtually odorless, and have a neutral flavor.
    True   False _____

6. Olive oil is extracted from a fruit.
    True   False _____

7. Distilled vinegar is made from white wine and is completely clear with a stronger vinegar flavor and higher acid content than most vinegars.
    True   False _____

8. Salt is used as a basic seasoning universally, and its flavor can be tasted and smelled easily.
    True   False _____

9. Every culture tends to combine a small number of flavoring ingredients so frequently and so consistently that they become a definite part of that particular cuisine.
    True   False _____

10. Once ground, spices lose their flavors rapidly, so it is better to purchase them in their whole form, then grind them as needed.
    True   False _____

11. For thousands of years the only purpose for spices has been to season foods.
    True   False _____

12. One can experience certain taste qualities on only certain areas of the tongue. For example, sweetness can be experienced only on the tip.
    True   False _____

13. Pungent, hot, spicy, piquant, and astringent are not technically tastes because they are not detected solely by the taste buds.
    True   False _____

14. It is possible to scientifically measure one's ability to taste.
    True   False _____

15. Savory herbs such as dill and basil have no role in the bakeshop.
    True   False _____

16. All Champagnes are sparkling wines, but not all sparkling wines are Champagnes.
    True   False _____

17. The most popular red wine grape varietals of *Vitis vinifera* include Cabernet Sauvignon, Merlot, Chianti, Nebbiolo, and Pinot Noir.
    True   False _____

18. Some of the grapes used for white wines that are also noble include Chardonnay, Riesling, and Sauvignon Blanc.
    True   False _____

19. Alcohol contributes less to the flavor of a wine than the vintner's balance between the sugars and acids.
    True   False _____

20. Each grape varietal used to make a wine possesses a certain hallmark aroma and flavor, and therefore a Pinot Noir wine produced in California will be almost identical to one produced in Australia.
    True   False _____

21. Wines have an alcoholic content of 10–15% whereas fortified wines contain 18–22% by volume.
    True   False _____

22. The only rule about matching wine with food is that there are no absolute rules.
    True   False _____

23. The best types of wines to use for cooking are cooking wines.
    True   False _____

24. Unlike wine, beer does not improve with age and is best consumed as soon as possible after production.
    True   False _____

25. Of the two main categories of beers produced in the world, lagers are characteristically light, clear, and crisp, whereas ales are aromatic and cloudy.
    True   False _____

26. Both sumac and za'atar are spices whose application started in Middle Eastern cookery.
    True   False _____

27. Creole cooking can be found only in the southern United States.
    True   False _____

6G. Putting It All Together

Provide a short response for each of the following questions. These questions are designed to help you connect the bigger concepts presented in this chapter and/or text.

1. A repeat customer walks into a chef's restaurant. While greeting her, the chef learns that the customer's doctor has told her to cut back on the amount of meat she consumes each day because of her high cholesterol. The customer is frantic, as she loves the taste of meat and she cannot imagine missing that taste in her foods. What ingredients could the chef substitute that would still provide the meaty or delicious taste of meat while using less or no meat and therefore decreasing or eliminating the cholesterol and saturated fats?

2. *Mediterranean cooking* is a very general description of food characteristics. Provide a general description of what foods from this region are like and make a connection between the countries that influence this cooking style and the ways the warm climate of this region influence the characteristics of the cuisine.

Chapter 7

DAIRY PRODUCTS

TEST YOUR KNOWLEDGE

The practice sets provided here have been designed to test your comprehension of the information found in this chapter. It is recommended that you read this chapter completely before attempting these questions.

7A. Terminology

Fill in each blank space with the correct definition.

1. Cream cheese _____

2. Heavy whipping cream _____

3. Fondue _____

4. Dairy products _____

5. Nonfat milk _____

6. Half-and-half _____

7. Whipped butter _____

8. Skim milk _____

9. Buttermilk _____

10. Salted butter _____

11. Low-fat milk _____

12. Evaporated milk _____

13. Yogurt _____

14. Light cream _____

15. Sour cream _____

16. Pasteurization _____

17. Homogenization _____

18. Bloomy rind _____

19. Washed rind _____

20. Natural cheese rind _____

21. Margarine _____

22. Crème fraîche _____

7B. Comparing Creams

Match each type of cream in List A with the appropriate fat content in List B. Each choice in List B can be used only once.

List A	List B
_____ 1. Light whipping cream	a. Not less than 36% milkfat
_____ 2. Light cream	b. 10–18% milkfat
_____ 3. Half-and-half	c. 16%-23% milk fat
_____ 4. Heavy (whipping) cream	d. 18% to less than 30% milkfat
	e. 30–36% milkfat

7C. Cheese Identification

Match each cheese variety in List A with the appropriate letter definition in List B. Each choice in List B can be used only once.

List A

_____ 1. Mozzarella

_____ 2. American cheddar

_____ 3. Parmigiano-Reggiano

_____ 4. Gruyère

_____ 5. Boursin

_____ 6. Roquefort

_____ 7. Chèvre

_____ 8. Brie

_____ 9. Feta

_____ 10. Havarti

_____ 11. Ricotta

_____ 12. Monterey Jack

_____ 13. Gorgonzola

_____ 14. Mascarpone

_____ 15. Colby

_____ 16. Camembert

_____ 17. Pecorino-Romano

List B

a. A French semisoft blue-veined sheep's-milk cheese containing 45% fat

b. A hard cow's-milk cheese containing 32–35% fat and produced exclusively near Parma, Italy

c. A cheddarlike cow's-milk cheese from California containing 50% fat

d. A fresh, soft, Italian cow's-milk cheese similar to cottage cheese, containing 4–10% fat

e. A fresh, firm, Italian cow's-milk cheese very mild in flavor that can become elastic when cooked

f. A French, rindless, soft, triple-cream cow's-milk cheese usually flavored with garlic, herbs, or peppers

g. A firm cow's-milk cheese made primarily in New York, Wisconsin, Vermont, and Oregon, containing 45–50% fat

h. A well-known mild Wisconsin cheddar containing 45–50% fat

i. A sharp-flavored, hard sheep's-milk cheese from central and southern Italy containing 35% fat

j. A milder French or Belgian soft rind-ripened cheese made from cow's milk, containing 45% fat

k. A semi-soft cow's-milk cheese from Piedmont, Italy containing 45% fat.

l. A soft French rind-ripened cheese made with cow's milk and containing 60% fat

m. A firm Swiss cow's-milk cheese that is highly flavorful, sweet, and nutty and aged up to 12 months

n. A fresh, soft, Italian cow's-milk cheese originally from Lombardy, Italy, containing 70–75% fat

o. A fresh, soft, American, cow's milk cheese containing 35% fat.

p. A semisoft, Italian, blue-veined cow's-milk cheese containing 48% fat

q. A pale yellow Danish cow's-milk cheese with many small, irregular holes, often made with herbs and spices

r. A fresh Italian or Greek sheep and/or goat's-milk cheese that is white and flaky from pickling in brine

s. A soft, creamy goat's-milk cheese with a short shelf life

7D. Milk Products

For each of the following, choose the correct response(s).

1. Milk products should be kept refrigerated at or below:

   a. 30°F.
   b. 35°F.
   c. 40°F.
   d. 45°F.

2. Aside from increasing the shelf life of cream, the process of ultrapasteurization:

   a. reduces the whipping properties.
   b. thickens the consistency.
   c. causes the cream to stay whipped for longer periods of time.
   d. concentrates the fat content.

3. Which of the following is **false** regarding concentrated or condensed milk products?

   a. They do not require refrigeration once opened.
   b. They are produced by using a vacuum to remove all or part of the water from whole milk.
   c. They have a high concentration of milkfat and milk solids.
   d. They have an extended shelf life.

4. Grades of milk are assigned based on:

   a. the clarity of color and distribution of fat globules.
   b. bacterial count; no fewer than 20 and no more than 30 per gallon earns a Grade A.
   c. bacterial count; the lower the count, the higher the grade.
   d. the flavor of the milk as determined by the breed and feed of the animal.

5. Which one of the following is **false** regarding homogenization?

   a. Homogenization breaks the fat globules in the whole milk into a smaller size and permanently disperses them.
   b. Homogenization is not required but is commonly performed on commercial products.
   c. Homogenization results in a milk product with a whiter color and richer taste.
   d. Homogenization increases the shelf life of the milk product.

6. Pasteurization requires holding the milk at a temperature of:

   a. 140°F for 15 seconds.
   b. 161°F for 15 seconds.
   c. 275°F for a very short time.
   d. 280°F–300°F for 2 to 6 seconds.

7. Evaporated milk, sweetened condensed milk, and dry milk powders are examples of:

    a. canned milk products.
    b. concentrated milk products.
    c. cultured dairy products.
    d. substandard milk products.

8. Which of the following is **true** about sweetened condensed milk?

    a. It contains between 60% and 65% sugar.
    b. It can be substituted for whole milk or evaporated milk.
    c. It is concentrated like evaporated milk by removing 60% of the water.
    d. It has a brilliant white color and faint flavor of caramel.

9. Dairy products are naturally high in all of the following **except**:

    a. carbohydrates.
    b. vitamins.
    c. proteins.
    d. minerals.

10. What **two** products become separated when an enzyme, such as rennet, is used to coagulate milk proteins in cheese production?

    a. liquid fats
    b. solid curds
    c. liquid whey
    d. water

11. In order to produce 3 pounds of ricotta cheese using the recipe found in this chapter, the conversion factor would be:

    a. 5.
    b. 0.16.
    c. 7.5.
    d. 6.

12. According to the recipe found in this chapter, 4 quarts of milk and 12 fluid ounces of fresh lime juice will yield how much ricotta cheese?

    a. 30 ounces
    b. 1½ pounds
    c. 2 pounds
    d. 40 ounces

13. Which one of the following choices **does not** equal 4 quarts?

    a. 1 gallon
    b. 8 pints
    c. 136 ounces
    d. 16 cups

14. Twelve fluid ounces are equal to:

    a. 1 pint.
    b. 1 cup.
    c. ½ cup.
    d. 1½ cups.

15. Fresh limes cost $2.50 per pound, and on the average, 8 limes weigh 1 pound. While squeezing the fresh lime juice for the ricotta cheese recipe, the chef uses 16 limes. What is the cost of the lime juice?

    a. $2.50
    b. $4.50
    c. $5.00
    d. $4.25

7E. Chapter Review

For each statement, circle either True or False to indicate the correct answer. If an answer is false, then explain why.

1. Milk products processed by ultra-high-temperature (UHT) processing can be stored without refrigeration for at least 3 months.
   True   False _____

2. Margarine contains cholesterol.
   True   False _____

3. Coffee whiteners, imitation sour cream, and whipped topping mixes are made from nondairy products.
   True   False _____

4. All grades of milk must be pasteurized before retail sale.
   True   False _____

5. The lack of moisture in dry milk powder prevents the growth of microorganisms.
   True   False _____

6. Seasoning butter with salt changes the butter's flavor and extends its shelf life.
   True   False _____

7. Both butter and margarine contain about 80% fat and 16% water.
   True   False _____

8. Yogurt is a good example of a health or diet food.
   True   False _____

9. Margarine is a dairy product that serves as a good substitute for butter.
   True   False _____

10. Aside from excess moisture, processed cheese foods are equal in quality to natural cheeses.
    True   False _____

11. One pound of whole butter that is clarified will result in 12 ounces of clarified butter.
    True   False _____

12. Natural cheeses contain cholesterol.
    True   False _____

13. Imitation and artificial dairy products may be useful for people who have allergies or are on a restricted diet.
    True   False _____

14. Fluid milk is a potentially hazardous food and should be kept refrigerated at 45°F/5°C.
    True   False _____

15. Freezing cultured milk products is generally not recommended.
    True   False _____

16. Dry milk powder and sweetened condensed milk are both examples of concentrated milks.
    True   False _____

17. The Food and Drug Administration does not allow the manufacture and distribution of raw-milk cheeses in the United States.
    True   False _____

18. The best way to reheat a serving of macaroni and cheese for service would be over low heat, stirring frequently, making sure not to cook it for too long in order to prevent scorching and separating of the cheese.
    True   False _____

7F. Putting It All Together

Provide a short response for each of the following questions. These questions are designed to help you connect the bigger concepts presented in this chapter and/or text.

1. Which would add more creamy texture to a poulette sauce if used as a final addition to the sauce, by whisking small pieces in at the end: traditional (American-style) whole butter or European-style whole butter? Why?

2. Why do low-fat milks and lower-fat creams contain smaller quantities of cholesterol than their full-fat counterparts?

Chapter 8

MISE EN PLACE

TEST YOUR KNOWLEDGE

The practice sets provided here have been designed to test your comprehension of the information found in this chapter. It is recommended that you read this chapter completely before attempting these questions.

8A. Terminology

Fill in each blank space with the correct definition.

1. Mise en place _____

2. Expiration dates _____

3. Mass _____

4. Volume _____

5. Clarification _____

6. Steeping _____

7. Clarification _____

8. Sachet _____

9. Meal _____

10. Fresh bread crumbs _____

11. Standard breading procedure _____

12. Onion piquet _____

13. Blanching _____

14. Dry bread crumbs _____

15. Battering _____

16. Rub/wet rub _____

17. Paste _____

18. Bouquet garni _____

19. Marinate _____

20. Shocked/refreshed _____

8B. Short Answer

Provide a short response that correctly answers each of the following questions.

1. How can one keep his or her hands from becoming coated with breading during the standard breading procedure?

   _____

   _____

2. What is the procedure for battering foods?

   a. _____

   b. _____

   c. _____

3. If 1 pound of butter costs $2.69 and approximately 80% of the whole butter is fat, 16% is water, and 4% is milk solids, what cost proportion (of the $2.69) does each component represent?

   Fat: _____

   Water: _____

   Milk solids: _____

4. When preparing mise en place, a chef should consider more than what ingredients need to be prepped and should also include the following:

   a. _____

   b. _____

5. List, in proper sequence, the four (4) steps for the standard breading procedure.

   a. _____

   b. _____

   c. _____

   d. _____

6. If 1 pound of butter is made up of 80% fat, 16% water and 4% milk solids, how many ounces of the pound of whole butter does each component represent?

   a. Fat: _____

   b. Water: _____

   c. Milk solids: _____

8C. Multiple Choice

For each of the following, choose the one correct response.

1. If 1 pound of whole butter costs $2.69, what is the final cost to produce 1 pound of clarified butter?

    a. $2.69
    b. $3.36
    c. $2.02
    d. $0.67

2. Toasting nuts and spices does everything **except**:

    a. remove rancidity.
    b. brown them.
    c. make the flavor more pronounced.
    d. make them crispier and crunchier.

3. After processing dried bread crumbs, they should be passed through a tamis to:

    a. remove the crusts.
    b. enhance the flavor.
    c. remove foreign particles.
    d. ensure even size.

4. Which of the following is **not** an important consideration when determining mise en place needs?

    a. the person completing the final task
    b. thinking about each task and the most efficient way to complete it
    c. knowing how long before service to begin a task
    d. planning to eliminate unnecessary steps and conserving resources

5. Which technique is used to rehydrate dried fruits or mushrooms?

    a. clarifying
    b. steaming
    c. toasting
    d. steeping

6. Modern marinades impart flavor to foods but are also known for their ability to:

    a. clarify.
    b. color.
    c. tenderize.
    d. preserve.

7. Which of the following is a liquid with a medium viscosity made by combining milk, flour, seasonings, and baking powder?

    a. a slurry
    b. a roux
    c. a batter
    d. béchamel sauce

8. When considering whether to purchase a certain convenience product, the chef must determine all of the following **except**:

   a. whether he or she can properly store the product.
   b. the amount of employee time saved producing the product in-house.
   c. the cost of the convenience product.
   d. the quality and consistency of the convenience product.

9. All of the following are true statements regarding shocking or refreshing **except**:

   a. It quickly cools hot foods to a temperature below 41°F/4°C.
   b. It will occur more quickly in a plastic container.
   c. It should be conducted in a combination of water and ice.
   d. It helps maintain the delicate textures and doneness of blanched or parcooked foods.

10. Which of the following statements regarding marinating is **false**?

   a. The type of wine used in a wine-based marinade is not an important consideration for flavor.
   b. Cover the food completely with the marinade and refrigerate.
   c. Smaller pieces of food take less time to marinate than larger pieces.
   d. If there is not enough marinade to completely cover the food, heavy-duty plastic food storage bags may be used to keep the marinade in contact with the food product more completely.

8D. Chapter Review

For each statement, circle either True or False to indicate the correct answer. If an answer is false, then explain why.

1. A standard sachet consists of peppercorns, bay leaves, parsley stems, thyme, cloves, and optionally garlic.
   True   False _____

2. The only purpose for beer in a batter is flavor.
   True   False _____

3. Mise en place is a task that is important for only the back-of-the-house personnel to complete.
   True   False _____

4. A food's weight is equal to its volume.
   True   False _____

5. The composition of ghee is identical to clarified butter.
   True   False _____

6. Convenient location of sanitizing solution, hand towels, disposable gloves, and trash receptacles should be part of the mise en place planning process.
   True   False _____

7. Dried bread crumbs should be stored in a tightly closed plastic container in a cool, dry place.
   True   False _____

8. Breaded foods are usually cooked by roasting or stewing.
   True   False _____

9. How foods are prepped for mise en place is as important as the way they are stored (at proper temperatures) before the final preparation occurs.
   True   False   _____

10. You've just finished making fresh bread crumbs, and they're sticking together in clumps rather than being a smooth mixture of evenly chopped crumbs. Chances are the problem is your bread was stale.
    True   False   _____

11. Partially cooking vegetables as part of mise en place may be done to remove bitter flavors, loosen peels, soften firm foods, and shorten final cooking times.
    True   False   _____

12. A combination of water and ice will chill foods more rapidly than a container of only tap water or only ice.
    True   False   _____

8E. Putting It All Together

Provide a short response for each of the following questions. These questions are designed to help you connect the bigger concepts presented in this chapter and/or text.

1. Referring back to Chapter 4, Tools and Equipment, why are dried bread crumbs passed through a tamis after processing? In your answer, explain what a tamis is and the product that will result by using this piece of equipment.

2. When marinating raw meats in the refrigerator, aside from storing them in a covered container, where should they be placed on the shelving unit? Refer back to Chapter 2, Food Safety and Sanitation, if you need help answering this question.

Chapter 9

PRINCIPLES OF COOKING

TEST YOUR KNOWLEDGE

The practice sets provided here have been designed to test your comprehension of the information found in this chapter. It is recommended that you read the chapter completely before attempting these questions.

9A. Terminology

Fill in each blank space with the correct definition.

1. Convection

    a. Natural _____

    b. Mechanical _____

2. Coagulation _____

3. Gelatinization _____

4. Radiation _____

5. Conduction _____

6. Combination cooking methods _____

7. Hydrogenation _____

8. Infrared cooking _____

9. Caramelization _____

10. Moist-heat cooking methods _____

11. Microwave cooking _____

12. Evaporates _____

13. Melting _____

14. Dry-heat cooking methods _____

15. Poêléing _____

9B. Cooking Methods

Fill in each blank space with the response that correctly completes information about each cooking method.

	Cooking Method	Medium	Equipment
Ex:	Sautéing	Fat	Stove
1.	Stewing	_____	_____
2.	Deep-frying	_____	_____
3.	Broiling	_____	_____
4.	Poaching	_____	_____
5.	Grilling	_____	_____
6.	Simmering	_____	_____
7.	Baking	_____	_____
8.	Roasting	_____	_____
9.	Steaming	_____	_____
10.	Braising	_____	_____

9C. Smoking Points

Match each lipid in List A with its smoke point in List B. Each choice in List B can be used only once.

List A

_____ 1. Whole butter
_____ 2. Deep-fryer shortening
_____ 3. Corn oil
_____ 4. Lard
_____ 5. Peanut oil
_____ 6. Extra virgin olive oil
_____ 7. Clarified butter
_____ 8. Margarine

List B

a. 440°F/232°C
b. 450°F/232°C
c. 335°F–380°F/168°C–193°C
d. 410°F–430°F/210°C–221°C
e. 495°F/257°C
f. 260°F/127°C
g. 350°F–410°F/177°F–210°C
h. 370°F/188°C
i. 440°F/227°C

9D. Multiple Choice

For each of the following, choose the correct response(s).

1. Which of the following is the transfer of heat through a fluid?

    a. natural convection
    b. radiation
    c. conduction
    d. induction
    e. mechanical convection

2. Which of the following cooking techniques is an example of moist cooking?

    a. grilling
    b. sautéing
    c. deep-fat frying
    d. steaming
    e. broiling

3. The rounded shape of the wok used for stir-frying:

    a. makes it easier to pour liquids out of the wok.
    b. is designed to fit into the specially designed shape of the turbo gas burners.
    c. diffuses the heat and makes tossing and stirring easier.
    d. makes the cookware more durable.
    e. makes it easier to stack with other equipment.

4. Which of the following is an example of infrared cooking?

    a. broiling
    b. sautéing
    c. roasting
    d. baking
    e. braising

5. In pan-frying, how much fat or oil should be in the pan?

    a. just enough to coat the bottom of the pan
    b. 1 cup measure
    c. ½ to ⅔ of the way up on the product being cooked
    d. enough to completely cover the product
    e. 1/16–1/8 of the way up on the product

6. Which cooking technique is defined as "to briefly and partially cook a food in boiling water or hot liquid"?

    a. boiling
    b. blanching
    c. frying
    d. simmering
    e. poaching

7. Which one of the following does **not** describe convection heat transfer?

    a. the natural tendency of warm liquids and gases to rise while cooler ones fall
    b. fans or a stirring motion circulating heat
    c. a combination of conduction and a mixing of molecules in a fluid (air, water, or fat) moving from a warmer area to a cooler area
    d. energy transferred by waves of heat or light striking the food
    e. radiant waves penetrating the food, agitating water molecules and creating heat

8. A liquid thickened with a starch will begin to thicken gradually (depending on what starch was used) over what temperature range?

    a. 90°F–110°F
    b. 112°F–125°F
    c. 127°F–148°F
    d. 150°F–212°F
    e. 230°F–250°F

9. Which statement is **false** regarding deep-fat frying?

    a. Deep-frying in a saucepan is equally effective as using a commercial fryer.
    b. Foods deep-fried together should be of similar size and shape.
    c. Delicately flavored foods should be fried separately from foods with strong flavors.
    d. Vegetable oils are the most common type of lipid used for deep-frying.
    e. Foods that are deep-fried are often breaded or battered just prior to frying.

10. Which of the following **two** lipids are considered flavorful fats for frying but are inferior because they cannot be kept at the high cooking temperatures required for frying for long periods of time?

    a. peanut oil
    b. beef fat
    c. soybean oil
    d. pork fat (lard)
    e. canola oil

11. Which of the following is **not** important to consider when choosing the appropriate type of fat in which to fry foods?

    a. availability
    b. smoke point
    c. resistance to chemical breakdown
    d. flavor
    e. cost

12. Which of the following practices related to properly maintaining deep-fryer fat to maximize its life span is relatively unimportant?

    a. Strain and skim the fat regularly to remove food particles.
    b. Avoid salting the food over the fat.
    c. Store the fat in an airtight container when cool.
    d. Avoid exposing the fat to excessive moisture (water).
    e. Fry strongly flavored foods (such as fish) in separate fat from mild foods (such as potatoes).

9E. Short Answer

Provide a short response that correctly answers each of the following questions.

1. List the four (4) major differences between braising and stewing.

Braising

a. _____

b. _____

c. _____

d. _____

Stewing

a. _____

b. _____

c. _____

d. _____

2. List two recommendations on how to properly steam a food product.

a. _____

b. _____

3. In six (6) steps, explain how to properly sauté a chicken breast.

a. _____

b. _____

c. _____

d. _____

e. _____

f. _____

4. Describe the seven (7) steps necessary for correctly poaching a food item.

a. _____

b. _____

c. _____

d. _____

e. _____

f. _____

g. _____

9F. Matching

Match each cooking method in List A with the appropriate temperature in List B. Each choice in List B may be used only once.

List A	List B
_____ 1. Boiling	a. 160° F–180°F/71°C–82°C
_____ 2. Broiling	b. 185°F–205°F/85°C–96°C
_____ 3. Simmering	c. Up to 2000°F/1093°C
_____ 4. Poaching	d. 212°F/100°C or higher (at sea level)
_____ 5. Steaming	e. 212°F/100°C (at sea level)
_____ 6. Deep-fat frying	f. 212° F/100°C to 220° F/104°C
	g. 325°F–375°F/160°C–190°C

9G. Chapter Review

For each statement, circle either True or False to indicate the correct answer. If an answer is false, then explain why.

1. A microwave oven can be considered an acceptable replacement for traditional ovens.
    True   False _____

2. Sautéing is an example of the conduction heat transfer method.
    True   False _____

3. A wood-fired grill is an example of the convection heat transfer method.
    True   False _____

4. According to proper food safety guidelines, lasagna should be baked to an internal temperature of 160°F/71°C.
    True   False _____

5. Most proteins complete coagulation at 160°F–185°F/71°C–85°C.
    True   False _____

6. In broiling, the heat source comes from below the cooking surface.
    True   False _____

7. Deep-frying is an example of a combination cooking method.
    True   False _____

8. When creating crosshatch markings on a grilled steak, the meat should be rotated 90 degrees from the original position on the grill.
    True   False _____

9. Stir-frying is a variation in technique to sautéing except it uses more fat in the process.
    True   False _____

10. A court bouillon should be used when steaming foods in order to prevent flavor loss.
    True   False _____

11. Blanching means to partially cook a food product in a boiling liquid or hot fat.
    True   False _____

12. The process of stewing generally takes less time than braising because the food products are cut into smaller pieces.
    True   False _____

13. Cooking destroys harmful microorganisms and makes food easier to ingest and digest.
    True   False _____

14. The internal temperature of a roasted chicken breast should be 180°F/82°C.
    True   False _____

15. The swimming method is best to use when frying large quantities of food.
    True   False _____

16. Pastas are some of the few starches that can hold up to the rapid convection movement of boiling.
    True   False _____

17. Wire frying baskets should be filled with foods to be fried while hanging over the fat to prevent the possibility of dripping fat or water on the floor or work surfaces.
    True   False _____

18. Grilled double lamb chops should be cooked to an internal temperature of 145°F.
    True   False _____

9H.   Putting It All Together

Provide a short response for each of the following questions. These questions are designed to help you connect the bigger concepts presented in this chapter and/or text.

1. In Chapter 4, Tools and Equipment, we learned about different characteristics of metals and how some are better conductors of heat than others. Using that same concept, explain why a potato would cook faster in boiling water than baking in an oven of equal or higher temperature.

2. There are two ways to determine the doneness of a braised piece of meat. One requires you to think back to Chapter 2, Food Safety and Sanitation; the other clue is in this chapter. How can you tell when the meat is ready to serve?

Chapter 10

STOCKS AND SAUCES

TEST YOUR KNOWLEDGE

The practice sets provided here have been designed to test your comprehension of the information found in this chapter. It is recommended that you read the chapter before attempting these questions.

10A. Terminology

Fill in each blank space with the correct definition.

1. Stock _____

2. Sauce _____

3. Pan gravy _____

4. Fumet _____

5. Court bouillon _____

6. Mirepoix _____

    a. Standard _____

    b. White _____

7. Cartilage _____

8. Connective tissue _____

9. Collagen _____

10. Gelatin _____

11. Degrease/skim _____

12. Deglaze _____

13. Remouillage _____

14. Sweat _____

15. Mother or leading sauces _____

16. Small or compound sauces _____

17. Coulis _____

18. Beurre blanc and beurre rouge _____

69

19. Slurry _____

20. Reduction _____

21. Roux _____

    a. White _____

    b. Blond _____

    c. Brown _____

22. Temper _____

23. Béchamel _____

24. Velouté _____

25. Espagnole _____

26. Demi-glace _____

27. Tomato sauce _____

28. Hollandaise sauce _____

29. Jus lié _____

30. Gastrique _____

31. Emulsion _____

32. Glace de viande _____

33. Glaçage _____

34. Beurre noir and beurre noisette _____

35. Maitre d'hôtel _____

36. Chutney _____

37. Essence or tea _____

38. Flavored oil _____

39. Pesto _____

10B. Stock-Making Review

List the essential ingredients and describe in a step-by-step manner the cooking procedure for white stock, brown stock, and fish stock. Exact quantities are not important for this exercise. However, cooking times should be included and each step should be numbered for production purposes.

White Stock
Ingredients: *Procedure:*

_____

_____

_____

_____

_____

_____

_____

_____

_____

Brown Stock
Ingredients: *Procedure:*

_____

_____

_____

_____

_____

_____

_____

_____

Fish Stock
Ingredients: *Procedure:*

_____

_____

_____

_____

_____

_____

_____

_____

_____

_____

_____

10C. Mother Sauce Review

This section reviews the makeup of the five mother sauces. In the blank spaces, fill in the name of each sauce, the thickener used, and the liquid that forms the base of the sauce. For sauces that use a roux as a thickener, please specify the type of roux used.

Mother Sauce	Thickener	Liquid
1. _____	_____	_____
2. _____	_____	_____
3. _____	_____	_____
4. _____	_____	_____
5. _____	_____	_____

10D. Small Sauces

For each of the following small sauces, identify the leading sauce that forms its base and list the main ingredients or garnish that distinguishes it from the mother sauce.

Small Sauce	Mother Sauce	Ingredients Added
1. Cream sauce	_____	_____
2. Cheddar sauce	_____	_____
3. Mornay	_____	_____

Small Sauce	Mother Sauce	Ingredients Added
4. Nantua	_____	_____
5. Soubise	_____	_____
6. Allemande	_____	_____
7. Suprême	_____	_____
8. Bercy	_____	_____
9. Cardinal	_____	_____
10. Normandy	_____	_____
11. Aurora	_____	_____
12. Horseradish	_____	_____
13. Poulette	_____	_____
14. Albufera	_____	_____
15. Hungarian	_____	_____
16. Ivory	_____	_____
17. Bordelaise	_____	_____
18. Chasseur	_____	_____
19. Châteaubriand	_____	_____
20. Cherveuil	_____	_____
21. Madeira or port	_____	_____
22. Marchand de vin	_____	_____
23. Périgueux	_____	_____
24. Piquant	_____	_____
25. Poivrade	_____	_____
26. Robert	_____	_____
27. Creole	_____	_____
28. Milanaise	_____	_____
29. Spanish	_____	_____
30. Béarnaise	_____	_____

Small Sauce	Mother Sauce	Ingredients Added
31. Choron	_____	_____
32. Foyot	_____	_____
33. Grimrod	_____	_____
34. Maltaise	_____	_____
35. Mousseline	_____	_____

10E. Short Answer

Provide a short response that correctly answers each of the following questions.

1. List the seven (7) principles of stock making.

a. _____

b. _____

c. _____

d. _____

e. _____

f. _____

g. _____

2. List the essential ingredients and describe in a step-by-step manner the preparation of hollandaise sauce, using the classical method. Exact quantities are important for this exercise, and each step should be numbered for production purposes.

Ingredients: **Procedure:**

_____

_____

_____

_____

_____

_____

_____

_____

3. Give five (5) reasons why hollandaise sauce might separate.

a. _____

b. _____

c. _____

d. _____

e. _____

4. Briefly describe how each of the following thickening agents is combined with the liquid to form a sauce.

a. Roux _____

b. Cornstarch _____

c. Arrowroot _____

d. Beurre manié _____

e. Liaison _____

10F. Matching

Match each mother sauce in List A with the appropriate small sauces in List B.

List A

1. Espagnole: _____
   _____
   _____

2. Hollandaise: _____
   _____
   _____

3. Béchamel: _____
   _____
   _____

4. Velouté: _____
   _____
   _____

5. Tomato: _____
   _____
   _____

List B

a. Cream sauce
b. Maltaise
c. Suprême
d. Bordelaise
e. Creole
f. Mornay
g. Bercy
h. Milanaise
i. Choron
j. Nantua
k. Chasseur
l. Béarnaise
m. Cardinal
n. Robert
o. Spanish

10G.   Chapter Review

For each statement, circle either True or False to indicate the correct answer. If an answer is false, then explain why.

1. More roux is needed to thicken brown sauces than to thicken light sauces.
    True   False _____

2. To avoid lumps in sauces, add hot stock to hot roux.
    True   False _____

3. After adding a liaison to a sauce, simmer for 5 minutes.
    True   False _____

4. *Nappé* is a term used to describe the consistency of sauce.
    True   False _____

5. The combination of water and cornstarch is called slurry.
    True   False _____

6. A velouté is a roux-thickened sauce.
    True   False _____

7. Tempering is the gradual lowering of the temperature of a hot liquid by adding a cold liquid.
    True   False _____

8. A reduction method is sometimes used to thicken sauces.
    True   False _____

9. Compound sauces come from small sauces.
    True   False _____

10. Fish stock needs to simmer for 1 hour in order to extract flavor from the ingredients.
    True   False _____

11. La Varenne is credited with developing the modern system for classifying hundreds of classical sauces.
    True   False _____

12. Escoffier simplified Carême's extravagant list of sauces in the 19th century.
    True   False _____

13. Commercial bases and bouillon cubes or granules are all labor-saving convenience ingredients
    available to chefs.
    True   False _____

14. A court bouillon is derived from a nage.
    True   False _____

15. A chinois is the most appropriate piece of equipment through which to strain a finished stock.
    True   False _____

16. *Fond* is the French word for "stock" or "base."
    True   False _____

17. The quality of a stock is judged by its body, flavor, clarity, and color.
    True   False _____

18. The bones from young animals, such as mature beef bones, are the best source of collagen proteins that can enhance the body of a stock.
    True   False _____

19. Vegetable stocks have the same body as meat stocks.
    True   False _____

10H. Putting It All Together

Provide a short response for each of the following questions. These questions are designed to help you connect the bigger concepts presented in this chapter and/or text.

1. Referring back to Chapter 2, Food Safety and Sanitation, how can the layer of fat that solidifies on top of a chilled container of stock help preserve it?

2. This chapter talks about cooling and storing stock properly but gives few details in terms of the proper procedure. Refer to Chapter 2, Food Safety and Sanitation, to create a description of the process that should be followed, including size and shape of the containers and how quickly the stock should cool to a particular temperature. Also make note of how a cooling wand may be used to speed the cooling process.

Chapter 11

SOUPS

TEST YOUR KNOWLEDGE

The practice sets provided here have been designed to test your comprehension of the information found in this chapter. It is recommended that you read this chapter completely before attempting these questions.

11A. Terminology

Fill in each blank space with the correct definition.

1. Broth _____

2. Consommé/double consommé _____

3. Cream soup _____

4. Purée soup _____

5. Bisque _____

6. Chowder _____

7. Cold soup _____

8. Garnish _____

9. Tomato concassée _____

10. Clearmeat or clarification _____

11. Onion brûlée _____

12. Raft _____

13. Render _____

14. Scorch _____

11B. Short Answer

1. Briefly describe the six (6) steps in the preparation of a broth.

   a. _____

   b. _____

   c. _____

   d. _____

   e. _____

   f. _____

2. The procedure for making consommé is time tested. List the essential ingredients and describe the eight (8) steps necessary for the production of consommé.

   a. _____

   b. _____

   c. _____

   d. _____

   e. _____

   f. _____

   g. _____

   h. _____

3. Provide a reason for each of the following problems with consommé preparation.

   a. Cloudy _____

   b. Greasy _____

   c. Lacks flavor _____

   d. Lacks color _____

4. Describe the four (4) steps that can be taken to correct a cloudy consommé.

   a. _____

   b. _____

   c. _____

   d. _____

5. List four (4) steps that can be taken to prevent cream from curdling when it is added to cream soups.

   a. _____

   b. _____

   c. _____

   d. _____

6. List the essential ingredients of a cream soup and describe the seven (7) essential steps for its preparation.

   a. _____

   b. _____

      1. _____

      2. _____

      3. _____

   c. _____

   d. _____

   e. _____

   f. _____

   g. _____

11C. Soup Review

1. List the seven (7) common categories of soups and provide two (2) examples of each type. In addition, suggest an appropriate garnish for each soup.

Soup	Example	Garnish
a. _____	_____	_____
	_____	_____
b. _____	_____	_____
	_____	_____
c. _____	_____	_____
	_____	_____
d. _____	_____	_____
	_____	_____

e. _____ _____ _____

_____ _____

f. _____ _____ _____

_____ _____

g. _____ _____ _____

_____ _____

2. Compare and contrast the following soups. Explain what they have in common and what makes them different from each other.

a.   Beef broth   Beef consommé

Commonalities: _____

Differences: _____

b.   Cream of mushroom   Lentil soup

Commonalities: _____

Differences: _____

c.   Gazpacho   Cold consommé

Commonalities: _____

Differences: _____

11D. Chapter Review

For each statement, circle either True or False to indicate the correct answer. If an answer is false, then explain why.

1. A purée soup is usually chunkier than a cream soup.
    True   False _____

2. A cream soup is always finished with milk or cream.
    True   False _____

3. Cool consommé should be stirred immediately after the clearmeat is added and as it begins to heat.
    True   False _____

4. A broth is a consommé with vegetables added to it.
    True   False _____

5. Cream soups are thickened with a purée of vegetables that have been cooked in a stock.
    True   False _____

6. Bisques are generally made from shellfish, thickened with a roux, and prepared using a combination of cream and purée soup procedures.
   True   False _____

7. Cold soups should be served at room temperature.
   True   False _____

8. Once a consommé is clouded, it should be discarded.
   True   False _____

9. Cold soups need less seasoning than hot soups.
   True   False _____

10. A roux can be used as a thickener for cold soups.
    True   False _____

11. In the recipe for Fresh Peach and Yogurt Soup, twenty-four pounds of peaches are needed to make 3 gallons of the product.
    True   False _____

12. All chowders are hearty soups, contain milk or cream, and have chunks of the main ingredients.
    True   False _____

13. To control bacterial growth in cold soups—whether they've been cooked or not—they should be made in small batches and stored and served at or below 40°F/4°C.
    True   False _____

14. One of the biggest food safety challenges involved in cooling and reheating thick soups is that they scorch easily.
    True   False _____

15. In the recipe for Beef Consommé, the egg whites, ground beef, mirepoix, seasonings, and tomato product serve as the clearmeat ingredients.
    True   False _____

16. If only 3 quarts of Beef Broth are to be produced, the conversion factor would be 0.425.
    True   False _____

17. Puréeing large quantities of soup would be most efficiently achieved by using a vertical chopper/mixer.
    ·True   False _____

18. Adding a final liaison to a soup as a thickening agent is not appropriate if the soup will need to be brought back to a boil before serving.
    True   False _____

19. Vichyssoise contains two ingredients that are considered potentially hazardous food products.
    True   False _____

20. A chowder is an example of a soup that contains so many hearty, eye-appealing chunks that it may not need to be garnished at service.
    True   False _____

11E.   Putting It All Together

Provide a short response for each of the following questions. These questions are designed to help you connect the bigger concepts presented in this chapter and/or text.

1.   Refer back to Chapter 2, Food Safety and Sanitation. What are the potential food safety issues associated with uncooked cold soups?

2.   This chapter provides information about both cold and hot soups. Referring back to Chapter 6, Flavors and Flavorings, what is the rule about seasoning each soup based on its temperature?

3.   Referring back to the principles you learned in Chapter 3, Menus and Recipes, and using two of the soup recipes found in this chapter, estimate which would be more economical to produce: New England–Style Clam Chowder or Chilled Cherry Soup. Provide some specifics when explaining your answer.

Chapter 12

PRINCIPLES OF MEAT COOKERY

TEST YOUR KNOWLEDGE

The practice sets provided here have been designed to test your comprehension of the information found in this chapter. It is recommended that you read this chapter completely before attempting these questions.

12A. Terminology

1. Primal cuts _____

2. Subprimal cuts _____

3. Fabricated cuts _____

4. Marbling _____

5. Subcutaneous fat _____

6. Collagen _____

7. To butcher _____

8. Dress _____

9. Fabricate _____

10. Carve _____

11. Baste _____

12. Sear _____

13. Yield grades _____

14. Vacuum packaging _____

15. Portion control _____

16. Freezer burn _____

17. Carryover cooking _____

18. Fond _____

19. Cutlet _____

20. Scallop _____

21. Émincé _____

22. Paillard _____

23. Medallion _____

24. Mignonette _____

25. Noisette _____

26. Chop _____

27. Brown stew _____

28. White stew/fricassee _____

29. Blanquette _____

30. USDA inspection _____

31. USDA Prime _____

32. USDA Choice _____

33. USDA Select _____

34. USDA Standard _____

12B.   Fill in the Blank

Fill in each blank space with the response that correctly completes the statement.

1.   The quality of meat best cooked by dry-heat cooking methods is _____.

2.   The temperature at which a stew should be cooked once the meat is added to the sauce
     is _____ for a _____ period of time—or until the meat is tender.

3.   Very rare meats should feel soft and have a very red color, but well-cooked meats, in contrast, should
     feel _____ and have a _____ - _____ color.

4.   Sauté items are sometimes dredged in _____ before being placed in the hot pan.

5.   Some _____ cooking occurs when a roast item is removed from the oven and its internal
     temperature continues to rise. Allowing the meat to rest will help the meat _____ more
     juices.

6.   Covering the exterior surface of a piece of meat or other protein with fat before cooking is called
     barding, whereas inserting strips of fat into the meat is called _____.

7.   Marinating meats adds a distinctive flavor and breaks down the _____ _____ to
     help tenderize the meat.

8.   Ionizing radiation kills significant amounts of insects, _____, and _____ in
     meat.

9.   Dry-heat cooking methods are not recommended for _____ cuts of meat or those high in
     connective tissue.

10. The direction in which one should carve (or slice) a roast in order to make its texture most tender once it's cooked is _____ the grain.

12C. Matching

Match each stew in List A with the appropriate description in List B. Each choice in List B can be used only once.

	List A		List B
_____	1. Ragoût	a.	A spicy ragoût of ground or diced meat with vegetables, peppers, and sometimes beans
_____	2. Goulash	b.	A white stew usually made with white meat and garnished with onions and mushrooms
_____	3. Blanquette	c.	A brown ragoût made with root vegetables and lamb
_____	4. Fricassee	d.	A general term that refers to stews
_____	5. Navarin	e.	A Hungarian beef stew made with onions and paprika and garnished with potatoes
		f.	A white stew in which the meat is blanched and added to the sauce to finish the cooking process; the stew is finished with a liaison of cream and egg yolks

12D. Cooking Methods

Briefly describe each of the following methods of cooking and provide an example of a cut of meat used in each method.

Cooking Method	Description	Example
Grilling	_____	_____
Roasting	_____	_____
Sautéing	_____	_____
Pan-frying	_____	_____
Simmering	_____	_____
Braising	_____	_____
Stewing	_____	_____

12E.   Chapter Review

For each statement, circle either True or False to indicate the correct answer. If an answer is false, then explain why.

1. Fresh meats should be stored at 35°F–40°F.
   True   False _____

2. Green meats are meats that are allowed to turn moldy.
   True   False _____

3. Braising and stewing are combination cooking methods.
   True   False _____

4. The USDA stamp on whole carcasses of meat does not ensure their quality or tenderness.
   True   False _____

5. USDA Choice meat is used in the finest restaurants and hotels.
   True   False _____

6. Yield grades are used for beef, lamb, and pork.
   True   False _____

7. Wet aging occurs in a vacuum package.
   True   False _____

8. During dry aging, the meat may develop mold, which adds to the flavor of the meat.
   True   False _____

9. Under the correct conditions, vacuum-packed meat can be held for 2 to 3 weeks.
   True   False _____

10. Still-air freezing is the most common method of freezing meats in food service facilities.
    True   False _____

11. The fat cap on a piece of meat adds tenderness and is a principal factor in determining meat quality.
    True   False _____

12. Broiled chicken livers wrapped in bacon is an example of a barded meat product.
    True   False _____

13. In order to account for carryover cooking, an 8-pound roasted pork loin should be removed from the oven when the internal temperature is approximately 140°F.
    True   False _____

14. Roasting meats at a lower temperature, such as 300°F–325°F, may result in better yield and a slightly juicier final product.
    True   False _____

15. All meat produced for public consumption in the United States is subject to USDA inspection, which indicates a meat's quality and tenderness.
    True   False _____

16. Once Sautéed Veal Scallops with White Wine Lemon Sauce is converted to yield 10 portions, the amount of veal needed is 3.76 pounds.
    True   False _____

17. In order to account for carryover cooking, a steamship round should be removed from the oven when the internal temperature is approximately 145°F.
    True   False _____

18. The conversion factor to change New England Boiled Dinner from 12 portions to 30 is 0.40.
    True   False _____

19. A whole stuffed chicken would be benefit from being larded.
    True   False _____

20. Scallops wrapped in bacon is an example of the barding technique.
    True   False _____

21. Cattle that graze on grassland their entire lives and then are fed grain for the last 4 to 8 months before slaughter can still be marketed by restaurants as "grass-fed" on menus.
    True   False _____

22. Animals that are grass-fed tend to have meat that is more heavily marbled with fat because there is no way for the farmer to control how much the animal eats while it is out to pasture.
    True   False _____

23. A beef tenderloin graded USDA Prime will be more likely to cause a flare-up during grilling than one graded USDA Select.
    True   False _____

12F. Putting It All Together

Provide a short response for each of the following questions. These questions are designed to help you connect the bigger concepts presented in this chapter and/or text.

1. In Chapter 2, Food Safety and Sanitation, you learned about the importance of adhering to the time/temperature principles within the HACCP system. Relate the same principles to primary suppliers of raw meats that undergo the grading process; what would a chef's job be like if the primary suppliers don't follow HACCP closely?

2. This chapter includes a safety alert regarding proper internal temperatures to which various meats should be cooked in order to be considered safe for consumption. Based on your knowledge of food safety, why is it not recommended that beef or fresh pork be served rare?

3. Briefly describe the *jus* that is served with the Roast Prime Rib of Beef. How is it prepared? Describe its preparation without turning back to Chapter 10, Stocks and Sauces.

Chapter **13**

BEEF

TEST YOUR KNOWLEDGE

The practice sets provided here have been designed to test your comprehension of the information found in this chapter. It is recommended that you read this chapter completely before attempting these questions.

13A. Terminology

For each primal cut of beef listed, describe the following:

    a.   Percentage of carcass weight
    b.   Bone structure
    c.   Muscle structure
    d.   Cooking processes applied

1. Chuck

    a. _____

    b. _____

    c. _____

    d. _____

2. Brisket and shank

    a. _____

    b. _____

    c. _____

    d. _____

3. Rib

    a. _____

    b. _____

    c. _____

    d. _____

4. Short plate

   a. _____

   b. _____

   c. _____

   d. _____

5. Short loin

   a. _____

   b. _____

   c. _____

   d. _____

6. Sirloin

   a. _____

   b. _____

   c. _____

   d. _____

7. Flank

   a. _____

   b. _____

   c. _____

   d. _____

8. Round

   a. _____

   b. _____

   c. _____

   d. _____

9. Carcass _____

10. Steer _____

11. Domesticated cattle _____

12. Quarters _____

13. Organ meats _____

13B. Primal Cuts of Beef

Identify the primal cuts of beef indicated in the following diagram and write their names in the spaces provided.

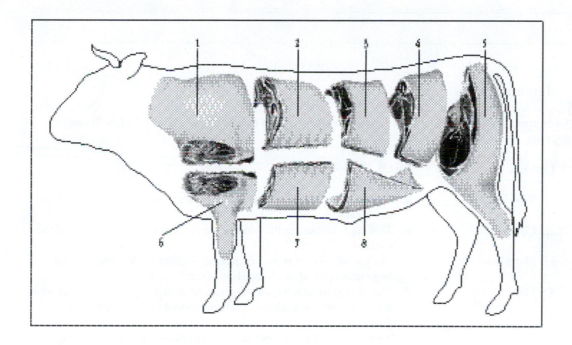

1. _____

2. _____

3. _____

4. _____

5. _____

6. _____

7. _____

8. _____

13C. Cuts from the Round

Name the five (5) subprimal/fabricated cuts from the round and name the most appropriate cooking process or use for each cut.

Subprimal/Fabricated Cut   **Cooking Process/Use**

1. _____   _____

2. _____   _____

3. _____   _____

4. _____   _____

5. _____   _____

13D. Matching I

Match each primal cut in List A with the appropriate description in List B. Each choice in List B can be used only once.

List A

_____ 1. Rib

_____ 2. Chuck

_____ 3. Short loin

_____ 4. Flank

List B

a. Produces the boneless strip loin, which can be roasted whole or cut into steaks.

b. This cut is located in the hindquarter between the short loin and the round.

c. The eye of this cut is well exercised, is quite tender, and contains large quantities of marbling. It is suitable for roasting.

d. The animal constantly uses the muscle in this primal cut, therefore it is tough, contains high levels of connective tissue, and is very flavorful

e. This primal cut produces the hanging tenderloin, which is very tender and can be cooked by any method.

13E. Cuts of Beef and Applied Cooking Methods

Name the cooking method applied to the main ingredient in each of the following beef dishes. Also, identify a subprimal and a primal cut of meat from which the main ingredient is taken.

Name of Dish	Cooking Method	Subprimal/ Fabricated Cut	Primal Cut
1. Pot roast			
2. Tamales/hash			
3. Entrecôtes bordelaise			
4. Hamburgers/meatloaf			
5. Stuffed flank steak			
6. New England boiled dinner			
7. Tournedos Rossini			
8. London broil			
9. Beef Wellington			
10. Roast beef			
11. Beef roulade			
12. Beef fajitas			
13. Beef stew			
14. Chili con carne			
15. Minute steak			

13F. Multiple Choice

For each of the following, choose the one correct response.

1. The outside round and the eye of the round together are called the:

    a. top round.
    b. bottom round.
    c. steamship round.
    d. primal round.

2. A carcass of beef weighs:

    a. between 600 and 950 pounds.
    b. up to 1,000 pounds.
    c. from 500 to more than 800 pounds.
    d. between 400 and 600 pounds.

3. The three fabricated cuts from the tenderloin are:

    a. porterhouse steak, tournedos, and châteaubriand.
    b. butt tenderloin, filet mignon, and tournedos.
    c. châteaubriand, short loin, and loin eye.
    d. tournedos, châteaubriand, and filet mignon.

4. Butterflying is a preparation technique that:

    a. makes the cut of meat thinner.
    b. makes the meat more tender.
    c. improves the flavor of the meat.
    d. improves the appearance of the meat.

5. Pastrami and corned beef are both flavored, preserved meats that come from:

    a. brisket.
    b. chuck.
    c. round.
    d. flank.

6. If the primal chuck accounts for approximately 28 percent of carcass weight, how much would the chuck weigh on a 728-pound carcass?

    a. 524.16 pounds
    b. 333.2 pounds
    c. 203.84 pounds
    d. 178.46 pounds

7. Put the following steaks in order based on the size portion of tenderloin they contain (1 = largest portion, 3 = smallest portion).

    _____ a. T-bone
    _____ b. Porterhouse
    _____ c. Club

13G. Matching II

Match each cooking process in List A with the appropriate cuts of meat in List B. Each cooking process matches only three (3) cuts of meat.

List A	List B
1. Grilling: _____	a. Shank
_____	b. Porterhouse
_____	c. Rib
2. Roasting: _____	d. Top round
_____	e. Strip loin
_____	f. Short ribs
3. Braising: _____	g. Skirt steak
_____	h. Knuckle
_____	i. Bottom round

13H. Chapter Review

For each statement, circle either True or False to indicate the correct answer. If an answer is false, then explain why.

1. The hanging tenderloin is part of the flank.
    True   False _____

2. The meat from the chuck is less flavorful than meat from the tenderloin.
    True   False _____

3. A porterhouse steak is fabricated from the tenderloin.
    True   False _____

4. Prime rib of beef refers to the quality USDA grade.
    True   False _____

5. The subprimal and fabricated cuts from the short loin are the most tender and expensive cuts of beef.
    True   False _____

6. The subprimal and fabricated cuts from the sirloin are not as tender as those from the strip loin.
    True   False _____

7. The short loin can be cut across to produce porterhouse, T-bone, and club steaks.
    True   False _____

8. Pastrami is made from the meat in the short plate.
    True   False _____

9. London broil comes from the flank.
    True   False _____

10. Foreshanks and hindshanks are flavorful cuts of beef that are best ground and used for hamburgers.
    True   False _____

11. In the recipe Beef Bourguignon, 8 pounds of beef chuck are required order to prepare twenty 4-ounce appetizer portions.
    True   False _____

12. To produce a Maillard reaction and achieve good browning on the outside of a steak, a chef needs to use a dry-heat cooking technique with temperatures greater than 300°F.
    True   False _____

13. Shanks are a cut of beef with an added advantage: marrow, which can be added to sauces or spread on toast for improved flavor and texture.
    True   False _____

14. The full flavor of beef is best accompanied by sauces with robust flavors such as pungent pestos or the assertive flavors of chili powder.
    True   False _____

15. When making meatballs, the combination of ground meats used, the ratio of fat to lean meat, and the type of bread crumbs all help determine how flavorful the final product is as well as the tenderness of texture.
    True   False _____

13I. Putting It All Together

Provide a short response for each of the following questions. These questions are designed to help you connect the bigger concepts presented in this chapter and/or text.

1. In reviewing the primal cuts of beef, this chapter discussed the rib. It is common practice when preparing to roast a prime rib to remove the fat cap, season the meat beneath, then return the fat cap to cover the meat. First, in review of Chapter 12, Principles of Meat Cookery, what does the chef have to do to the fat cap in order to keep it in contact with the meat during the roasting process? Second, what is the name of the technique in which you wrap the outside of a piece of meat with fat in order to add moisture and flavor during the cooking process?

2. Based on what you've learned in this chapter and your knowledge of menus and recipe costing from Chapter 3, would it make good financial sense to braise a strip loin? Explain your answer.

Chapter 14

VEAL

TEST YOUR KNOWLEDGE

The practice sets provided here have been designed to test your comprehension of the information found in this chapter. It is recommended that you read this chapter completely before attempting these questions.

14A. Terminology

Fill in each blank space with the correct definition.

1. Foresaddle _____

2. Hindsaddle _____

3. Back _____

4. Veal side _____

5. Sweetbreads _____

6. Organ meats _____

7. Veal scallops _____

8. Émincé _____

14B. Primal Cuts Identification

For each primal cut of veal listed, describe the following:

  a. Percentage of carcass weight
  b. Bone structure
  c. Muscle structure
  d. Cooking processes applied

1. Shoulder

  a. _____

  b. _____

  c. _____

  d. _____

2. Foreshank and breast

   a. _____

   b. _____

   c. _____

   d. _____

3. Rib

   a. _____

   b. _____

   c. _____

   d. _____

4. Loin

   a. _____

   b. _____

   c. _____

   d. _____

5. Leg

   a. _____

   b. _____

   c. _____

   d. _____

14C. Primal Cuts of Veal

Identify the primal cuts of veal indicated in the following diagram and write their names in the spaces provided.

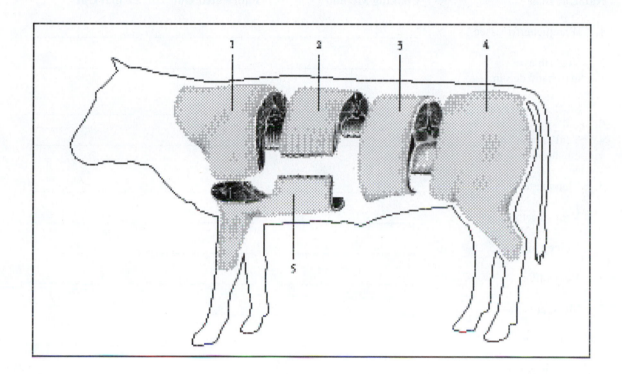

1. _____

2. _____

3. _____

4. _____

5. _____

14D.   Cuts of Veal and Applied Cooking Methods

Name the cooking method applied to the main ingredient in each of the following dishes. Also, identify a subprimal and a primal cut of meat from which the main ingredient is taken.

Name of Dish	Cooking Method	Subprimal/ Fabricated Cut	Primal Cut
1. Blanquette/fricassee			
2. Veal rib eye/ marchand de vin			
3. Stuffed veal breast			
4. Veal chop with mushroom sauce			
5. Blanquette			
6. Veal sweetbreads			
7. Kidney pie			
8. Veal patties			
9. Meatballs			
10. Tenderloin			
11. Veal marsala			
12. Calves' liver			
13. Osso buco			
14. Veal scallopini			

14E. Short Answer

Provide a short response that correctly answers each of the following questions.

1. Briefly describe the eight (8) basic steps to be followed when boning a leg of veal, beginning with:

    a. Remove the shank.

    b. _____

    c. _____

    d. _____

    e. _____

    f. _____

    g. _____

    h. _____

2. Name the six (6) muscles in the leg of veal.

    a. _____

    b. _____

    c. _____

    d. _____

    e. _____

    f. _____

3. Name the three (3) subprimal cuts from the rib and three (3) from the loin, providing a menu example for each cut.

Primal cut	Subprimal/Fabricated Cut	Menu Example
a. Rib	_____	_____
b. Rib	_____	_____
c. Rib	_____	_____
d. Loin	_____	_____
e. Loin	_____	_____
f. Loin	_____	_____

4. Compare and contrast formula-fed veal with free-range veal. Discuss the advantages and disadvantages of using each.

_____

_____

_____

_____

14F. Matching I

Match each primal cut in List A with the appropriate description in List B. Each choice in List B can be used only once.

List A	List B
_____ 1. Leg	a. A cut of veal similar to the chuck in beef
_____ 2. Shoulder	b. A primal cut of veal that is located just below the shoulder and rib section in the front of the carcass
_____ 3. Foreshank	c. The primal cut that produces the short tenderloin and breast
_____ 4. Loin	d. The bones in this cut are still soft, due to the immaturity of the animal
_____ 5. Rib	e. The primal cut that yields the most tender meat
	f. Includes part of the backbone, tail bone, hip bone, aitch bone, round bone, and shank

14G. Matching II

Match each cooking process in List A with the appropriate cuts of meat in List B. Each cooking process matches only two (2) cuts of meat.

List A	List B
1. Sautéing: _____	a. Split veal rack
_____	b. Calves' liver
2. Roasting: _____	c. Veal shank
_____	d. Whole veal loin
3. Braising: _____	e. Veal émincé
_____	f. Veal breast

14H. Chapter Review

For each statement, circle either True or False to indicate the correct answer. If an answer is false, then explain why.

1. Veal scallops are taken from large pieces of veal and are cut on the bias, across the grain of the meat.
   True   False _____

2. Veal flesh begins to change color when the animal consumes iron in its food.
   True   False _____

3. Sweetbreads are pressed to remove the impurities.
   True   False _____

4. Veal émincé is cut with the grain from small pieces of meat.
   True   False _____

5. Veal scallops are pounded in order to make them more tender.
   True   False _____

6. Veal has a milder flavor than beef and is usually paired with light cream sauces or other delicate flavors.
   True   False _____

7. Veal liver has a more delicate flavor than beef liver.
   True   False _____

8. The hindshank and foreshank of veal are prepared and cooked in the same manner.
   True   False _____

9. The feed given to calves during their short life span is formulated to keep their muscles from toughening.
   True   False _____

10. Although free-range veal is a more humane method of producing veal, less of it is raised and therefore it is more expensive.
    True   False _____

11. On a veal carcass weighing 175 pounds, the primal leg would represent 73.5 pounds.
    True   False _____

12. A good use for veal shoulder meat would be to butterfly it for Veal Marsala.
    True   False _____

13. Veal Cordon Bleu is made by rolling ham and Swiss cheese within a veal cutlet, coating it using a standard breading procedure, and then deep-fat frying.
    True   False _____

14. Osso Buco is classically braised in order to further concentrate the flavors of the foreshank.
    True   False _____

15. Stuffed Veal Breast should be cooked to an internal temperature of 165°F/74°C or until tender.
    True   False _____

14I. Putting It All Together

Provide a short response for each of the following questions. These questions are designed to help you connect the bigger concepts presented in this chapter and/or text.

1. Based on what you now know about veal, why are most animals that are slaughtered male rather than female?

2. Based on your newfound knowledge of veal, its age, and its level of activity in its short life, how long do you think a tough cut of veal like the leg or bottom round has to stew or braise compared to the same cut of beef?

Chapter 15

LAMB

TEST YOUR KNOWLEDGE

The practice sets provided here have been designed to test your comprehension of the information found in this chapter. It is recommended that you read the chapter completely before attempting these questions.

15A. Terminology

Fill in each blank space with the correct definition.

1. Sheep _____

2. Mutton _____

3. Domestic lamb _____

4. Rack _____

5. Foresaddle _____

6. Hindsaddle _____

7. Back _____

8. Bracelet _____

9. Spring lamb _____

10. Suckling lamb _____

11. Agneau pre-salé _____

12. Goat _____

15B. Primal Cuts Identification

For each primal cut of lamb listed, describe the following:

    a.   Percentage of carcass weight
    b.   Bone structure
    c.   Muscle structure
    d.   Cooking processes applied

1. Shoulder

    a. _____

    b. _____

    c. _____

    d. _____

2. Breast

    a. _____

    b. _____

    c. _____

    d. _____

3. Rack

    a. _____

    b. _____

    c. _____

    d. _____

4. Loin

    a. _____

    b. _____

    c. _____

    d. _____

5. Leg

    a. _____

    b. _____

    c. _____

    d. _____

15C. Primal Cuts of Lamb

Identify the primal cuts of lamb indicated in the following diagram and write their names in the spaces provided.

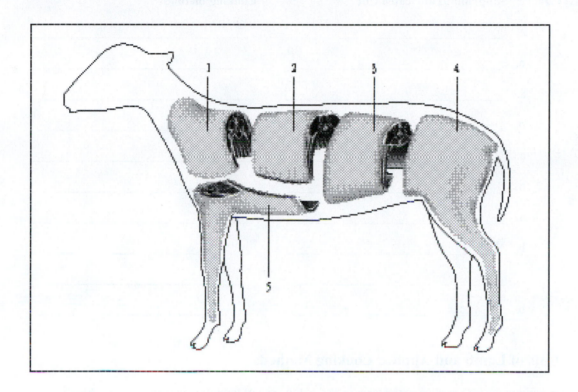

1. _____

2. _____

3. _____

4. _____

5. _____

15D. Subprimal or Fabricated Cuts

For each primal cut named in Section 15C, name two subprimal cuts and an appropriate cooking method for each cut.

Primal Cut	Subprimal/Fabricated Cut	Cooking methods
1.	a. _____	_____
	b. _____	_____
2.	a. _____	_____
	b. _____	_____
3.	a. _____	_____
	b. _____	_____
4.	a. _____	_____
	b. _____	_____
5.	a. _____	_____
	b. _____	_____

15E. Cuts of Lamb and Applied Cooking Methods

Name the cooking method applied to the main ingredient in each of the following lamb dishes. Also, identify a subprimal and a primal cut of meat from which the main ingredient is taken.

Name of Dish	Cooking Method	Subprimal/ Fabricated Cut	Primal Cut
1. Lamb kebabs	_____	_____	_____
2. Lamb curry	_____	_____	_____
3. Noisettes of lamb with roasted garlic sauce	_____	_____	_____
4. Lamb stew	_____	_____	_____
5. Broiled lamb with mustard and hazelnut crust	_____	_____	_____
6. Lamb breast stuffed with mushrooms	_____	_____	_____
7. Rack of lamb	_____	_____	_____
8. Leg of lamb	_____	_____	_____

15F. Short Answer

Provide a short response that correctly answers each of the following questions.

1. Briefly describe the six (6) basic steps to follow when frenching a rack of lamb.

    a. _____

    b. _____

    c. _____

    d. _____

    e. _____

    f. _____

2. Briefly describe the four (4) basic steps to follow when trimming a leg of lamb for roasting/grilling.

    a. _____

    b. _____

    c. _____

    d. _____

3. Briefly describe the eight (8) basic steps to be followed when preparing a loin of lamb for roasting.

    a. _____

    b. _____

    c. _____

    d. _____

    e. _____

    f. _____

    g. _____

    h. _____

15G. Chapter Review

For each statement, circle either True or False to indicate the correct answer. If an answer is false, then explain why.

1. The lamb carcass is classified into two parts: the hindquarter and the forequarter.
    True   False _____

2. Most lamb consumed in America is slaughtered at less than one year old, resulting in tender meat that can be prepared by almost any cooking method.
    True   False _____

3. The primal cuts of both veal and lamb are broken down into bilateral halves.
    True   False _____

4. Because most lamb is consumed so young and tender in the United States, the shanks are usually cooked using dry-heat cooking methods.
    True   False _____

5. The primal leg of lamb is rarely left whole.
    True   False _____

6. The leg of lamb can be broken down to produce steaks.
    True   False _____

7. The chine bone, part of the backbone, runs through the loin of lamb.
    True   False _____

8. The fell is the thin layer of connective tissue on the outside of the loin of lamb.
    True   False _____

9. Denver ribs are ribs that are cut from the breast of lamb.
    True   False _____

10. Frenching is a process that can be performed only on lamb racks or chops.
    True   False _____

11. A conversion factor of 1.25 would yield 20 portions of Irish Lamb Stew.
    True   False _____

12. The tender rib eye comes from the loin of the lamb.
    True   False _____

13. To produce a more economical stew, the chef should use the shank end of the lamb leg in Lamb in Indian Coconut Curry Sauce.
    True   False _____

14. Lamb patties with mint should be cooked to an internal temperature of 160°F/71°C.
    True   False _____

15. The kebab method of cookery, in which small pieces of meat are laced onto a skewer and cooked over an open fire, was believed to have originated in the Middle East and Persia, where fuel was in short supply.
    True   False _____

16. Because lamb is usually slaughtered before it turns one year old, its flavor is mild and therefore it should not be accompanied by strongly flavored accompaniments or sauces.
True   False _____

15H. Putting It All Together

Provide a short response for each of the following questions. These questions are designed to help you connect the bigger concepts presented in this chapter and/or text.

1. What can you surmise about domestic lamb compared to imported lamb? What does the difference mean for a chef planning a menu for his or her restaurant?

2. How does the information in Chapter 3, Menus and Recipes; Chapter 8, Mise en Place; and Chapter 5, Knife Skills, help a chef decide whether to order a whole hotel rack to break down into its component parts as opposed to buying it already dismantled?

Chapter 16

PORK

TEST YOUR KNOWLEDGE

The practice sets provided here have been designed to test your comprehension of the information found in this chapter. It is recommended that you read the chapter completely before attempting these questions.

16A. Terminology

For each primal cut of pork listed, describe the following:

  a.   Percentage of carcass weight
  b.   Bone structure
  c.   Muscle structure
  d.   Cooking processes applied

1.   Boston butt

  a.   _____

  b.   _____

  c.   _____

  d.   _____

2.   Loin

  a.   _____

  b.   _____

  c.   _____

  d.   _____

3.   Fresh ham

  a.   _____

  b.   _____

  c.   _____

  d.   _____

4. Belly

   a. _____

   b. _____

   c. _____

   d. _____

5. Shoulder

   a. _____

   b. _____

   c. _____

   d. _____

6. Hogs _____

7. Heritage or heirloom breed _____

8. Boston butt _____

9. Brining _____

10. Picnic ham _____

11. Canadian bacon _____

12. Fatback _____

16B. Primal Cuts of Pork

Identify the primal cuts of pork indicated in the following diagram and write their names in the spaces provided.

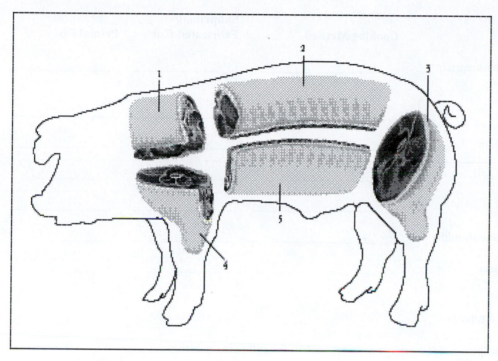

1. _____   2. _____

3. _____   4. _____

5. _____

16C. Subprimal or Fabricated Cuts

For each primal cut listed, name a subprimal cut and an appropriate cooking method. Indicate in the appropriate column(s) whether these cuts are usually smoked or fresh (or both).

Primal Cut	Subprimal/ Fabricated Cut	Cooking Methods	Cured & Smoked	Fresh
ex: Fresh ham	Hock	Any	X	
1. Boston butt	_____	_____	_____	_____
2. Loin	_____	_____	_____	_____
3. Fresh ham	_____	_____	_____	_____
4. Belly	_____	_____	_____	_____
5. Shoulder	_____	_____	_____	_____

117

16D. Cuts of Pork and Applied Cooking Methods

Name the cooking method applied to the main ingredient in each of the following pork dishes. Also, identify a subprimal and a primal cut of meat from which the main ingredient is taken.

Name of Dish	Cooking Method	Subprimal/ Fabricated Cut	Primal Cut
1. Roast pork with apricots and almonds			
2. Choucroute			
3. Pork tenderloin			
4. Pork chops			
5. Spare ribs			
6. Smoked picnic shoulder			
7. Breakfast meat			

16E. Short Answer

Provide a short response that correctly answers each of the following questions.

1. Briefly describe the three (3) basic steps to be followed when boning a pork loin.

    a. _____

    b. _____

    c. _____

2. Name six (6) fabricated cuts that are most often smoked and cured.

    a. _____

    b. _____

    c. _____

    d. _____

    e. _____

    f. _____

16F. Matching

Match each primal cut in List A with the appropriate description in List B. Each choice in List B
can be used only once.

	List A		List B
_____	1. Boston butt	a.	A primal cut that is very fatty with strips of lean meat
_____	2. Shoulder	b.	The primal cut from which the most tender portion of pork is taken
_____	3. Belly	c.	A primal cut that contains large muscles and relatively small amounts of connective tissue; it may be smoked and cured or cooked fresh
_____	4. Loin	d.	A primal cut with a good percentage of fat to lean meat, ideal when a solid piece of pork is required for a recipe
_____	5. Fresh ham	e.	A single, very tender eye muscle that can be braised/roasted/sautéed
		f.	One of the toughest cuts of pork that has a relatively high ratio of bone to lean meat, is relatively inexpensive, and is widely available

16G. Chapter Review

For each statement, circle either True or False to indicate the correct answer. If an answer is false, then
explain why.

1. The Boston butt is located in the hindquarter.
    True   False _____

2. Pork is unique compared to other quadrupeds because the ribs and loin are considered one primal cut.
    True   False _____

3. The term *meat packing* originated in colonial times when pork was packed into barrels for shipment abroad.
    True   False _____

4. The foreshank is also known as the ham hock.
    True   False _____

5. Center-cut pork chops are chops that are split open to form a pocket.
    True   False _____

6. The belly is used to make Canadian bacon.
    True   False _____

7. Fatback is the layer of fat between the skin and the lean muscle of the pork loin.
    True   False _____

8. Hogs are bred to produce short loins.
    True   False _____

9. Picnic ham is made from the hog's hind leg.
    True   False _____

10. The loin is the only primal cut of pork not typically smoked or cured.
    True   False _____

11. All pork comes from hogs slaughtered at a young age, and therefore all cuts are tender enough to be cooked by any method.
    True   False _____

12. Spareribs are cut from the bottom portion of the primal loin.
    True   False _____

13. The fresh ham is the hog's hind leg.
    True   False _____

14. A suckling pig can have consumed only milk and should never have been fed grass or grain.
    True   False _____

16H. Putting It All Together

Provide a short response for each of the following questions. These questions are designed to help you connect the bigger concepts presented in this chapter and/or text.

1. Throughout the last few chapters you've learned about the nutritional value of the various meats. Compare and contrast lamb and pork.

2. Referring to Table 16.1, *Using Common Cuts of Pork*, hypothesize why spareribs are usually cooked by both steaming/boiling and then grilling. When developing your answer, incorporate your knowledge of what makes a cut of meat tough or tender as well as your understanding of regional food traditions.

Chapter 17

POULTRY

TEST YOUR KNOWLEDGE

The practice sets provided here have been designed to test your comprehension of the information found in this chapter. It is recommended that you read the chapter completely before attempting these questions.

17A. Terminology

Fill in each blank space with the correct definition.

1. Duckling _____

2. Guinea _____

3. Squab _____

4. Dinde _____

5. Ratites _____

6. Giblets _____

7. Foie gras _____

8. Suprême/airline breast _____

9. À point _____

10. Trussing _____

11. Presentation side _____

12. Basting _____

13. Dressing _____

14. Poulet de Bresse _____

17B. Short Answer

Provide a short response that correctly answers each of the following questions.

1. List five (5) important guidelines for stuffing poultry.

    a. _____

    b. _____

    c. _____

    d. _____

    e. _____

2. Name one (1) similarity and one (1) major difference between poultry and red meats.

    Similarity: _____

    Difference: _____

3. Poultry is a highly perishable product, and improper storage can lead to food poisoning. Including *exact temperatures and times*, discuss the guidelines for storing poultry products under the following headings.

    Storage and refrigeration: _____

    _____

    Freezing: _____

    _____

    Thawing: _____

    _____

    Reheating: _____

    _____

4. List five (5) differences between the rearing and sale of free-range chicken compared to traditionally reared chicken.

    a. _____

    b. _____

    c. _____

    d. _____

    e. _____

5. What are the six (6) kinds of poultry?

a. _____

b. _____

c. _____

d. _____

e. _____

f. _____

6. For each of the following cooking methods, give a recipe example and accompaniment for the poultry item.

Cooking Method	Recipe Example	Accompaniment
Sautéing		
Pan-frying		
Simmering/poaching		
Braising/stewing		

7. Describe five (5) ways to prevent cross-contamination when handling poultry.

a. _____

b. _____

c. _____

d. _____

e. _____

8. Describe the six (6) steps for portioning poultry into eight pieces.

a. _____

b. _____

c. _____

d. _____

e. _____

f. _____

17C. Matching

Match each term in List A with the appropriate description in List B. Each choice in List B can be used only once.

List A

_____ 1. Hen/stewing

_____ 2. Broiler/fryer

_____ 3. Roaster

_____ 4. Capon

_____ 5. Game hen

List B

a. Young tender meat, smooth skin, breastbone less flexible than a broiler's (3–5 months)

b. Mature female, less tender meat, nonflexible breastbone (over 10 months)

c. Young immature offspring of Cornish chicken, very flavorful (5–6 weeks)

d. Rich, tender dark meat with large amounts of fat, soft windpipe (6 months or less)

e. Young with soft, smooth skin, lean with flexible breastbone (13 weeks)

f. Surgically castrated male, tender meat, smooth skin, high proportion of light to dark meat, relatively high fat content (under 8 months)

17D. Fill in the Blank

Fill in each blank space with the response that correctly completes the statement.

1. The color difference between the legs and the wings of chicken and turkey is due to a higher concentration of the _____ called _____ in the tissue.

2. The internal temperature of fully cooked poultry should be between _____ and _____.

3. The name of the most commonly used duck in foodservice operations is a _____. Its meat is different from chicken in two ways: The flesh is _____ and has large amounts of _____.

4. Chicken is often marinated in a mixture of _____ or _____ , salt, _____ , and _____. A common example of a chicken marinade is _____ sauce.

17E. Multiple Choice

For each of the following, choose the one correct response.

1. Fresh poultry should be refrigerated between:

    a. 30°F–35°F.
    b. 33°F–36°F.
    c. 32°F–34°F.
    d. 30°F–38°F.

2. Which of the following groups does **not** qualify as poultry?

    a. chicken, duck, pigeon
    b. duck, pheasant, goose
    c. pigeon, guinea, chicken
    d. quail, duck, turkey

3. Poultry that is sold in wholesale or retail outlets carries USDA Grade:

    a. A.
    b. B.
    c. C.
    d. A, B, and C.

4. Because of its percentage of bone and fat to meat, a 4-pound duck will serve:

    a. 1 person.
    b. 2 people.
    c. 3 people.
    d. 4 people.

17F. Chapter Review

For each statement, circle either True or False to indicate the correct answer. If an answer is false, then explain why.

1. Poultry fat has a higher melting point than other animal fats.
    True   False _____

2. Duck and goose must be roasted at a higher temperature in order to render as much fat from the skin as possible.
    True   False _____

3. The chicken breast and wings are referred to as white meat, whereas the legs are considered dark meat.
    True   False _____

4. The longer chicken is left in a marinade, the better the flavor.
    True   False _____

5. Dark meat takes less time to cook than light meat.
    True   False _____

6. Poultry should not be frozen below 0°F/–18°C.
   True   False _____

7. The skin color of poultry is partly affected by the amount of sunlight to which it is exposed.
   True   False _____

8. Quality USDA grades do not reflect the tenderness of the poultry.
   True   False _____

9. Older male birds have more flavor than female birds.
   True   False _____

10. When foie gras is overcooked, it becomes tough.
    True   False _____

11. A young pigeon is called a yearling.
    True   False _____

12. *Gizzard* is a term used to describe the chicken's neck.
    True   False _____
13. A capon is a type of pigeon.
    True   False _____

14. Poultry is divided into classes based on the sex of the bird.
    True   False _____

15. Most ratite meat is cut from the back of birds slaughtered between 10 and 13 months.
    True   False _____

16. Ostrich meat is best cooked well done.
    True   False _____

17. Poultry should not be marinated for longer than 2 hours.
    True   False _____

18. After marinating poultry, the marinade should be stored for future use.
    True   False _____

19. For a larger duck breast, chefs prefer to use one from the Peking or Long Island breeds.
    True   False _____

20. Fresh chicken should be stored refrigerated between 32°F and 34°F for up to 4 days.
    True   False _____

21. The poultry class includes any domesticated birds bred for eating.
    True   False _____

22. Although it is classified as poultry, ratite meat is a dark, cherry-red color with a flavor similar to beef but sweeter.
    True   False _____

23. All poultry produced for public consumption in the United States is subject to USDA inspection.
    True   False _____

24. The 1 ounce of clarified butter needed in Chicken Sauté with Onions, Garlic, and Basil is equal to a volume measure of ⅛ cup.
    True   False   _____

25. The conversion factor for 40 portions of Apricot and Bourbon Grilled Chicken is 10.
    True   False   _____

26. A squab's meat is dark, tender, and low in fat, and therefore it would benefit from being barded before cooking.
    True   False   _____

27. Emu and ostrich meat, even though it is classified as poultry, is a dark, cherry-red color and tastes similar to beef.
    True   False   _____

28. Ratite meat, like chicken and most other poultry, should be cooked to an internal temperature of 165°F.
    True   False   _____

17G. Putting It All Together

Provide a short response for each of the following questions. These questions are designed to help you connect the bigger concepts presented in this chapter and/or text.

1. Considering the yield of meat on a duck compared to a chicken, what does a chef have to take into consideration when menu planning and costing recipes for these two proteins?

2. After learning about flavors and flavorings in Chapter 6, what might you use in a marinade for chicken? Make several suggestions for ingredients that might be used for each of the three main ingredients in a marinade and mention how long the meat should be marinated.

Chapter 18

GAME

TEST YOUR KNOWLEDGE

The practice sets provided here have been designed to test your comprehension of the information found in this chapter. It is recommended that you read the chapter completely before attempting these questions.

18A. Terminology

For each of the following game animals, list the following:

   a.   Source of animal
   b.   Composition of flesh
   c.   Recommended cooking methods

1.   Antelope

   a. _____

   b. _____

   c. _____

2.   Bison

   a. _____

   b. _____

   c. _____

3.   Venison

   a. _____

   b. _____

   c. _____

4.   Rabbit

   a. _____

   b. _____

   c. _____

5. Wild boar

   a. _____

   b. _____

   c. _____

6. Partridge

   a. _____

   b. _____

   c. _____

7. Pheasant

   a. _____

   b. _____

   c. _____

8. Quail

   a. _____

   b. _____

   c. _____

9. Furred game _____

10 Feathered or winged game _____

11. Domestic game _____

12. Hanging _____

18B. Short Answer

Provide a short response that correctly answers each of the following questions.

1. List three (3) uses for tougher cuts of game.

    a. _____

    b. _____

    c. _____

2. Explain the process and purpose of hanging wild game.

    Process: _____

    _____

    _____

    Purpose: _____

    _____

3. Describe the origins and composition of beefalo.

    _____

    _____

    _____

4. Describe the guidelines for refrigeration and freezing of game.

    Refrigeration: _____

    _____

    Freezing: _____

    _____

18C. Multiple Choice

For each of the following, choose the one correct response.

1. Which of the following **cannot** be categorized as furred game?

   a. antelope
   b. pheasant
   c. bison
   d. rabbit

2. Because of the lean nature of game birds, they are barded and cooked:

   a. medium.
   b. rare.
   c. medium rare.
   d. well done.

3. Which of the following is **not** a member of the deer family?

   a. elk
   b. bison
   c. mule deer
   d. moose

4. Feathered game include the following:

   a. pheasant, quail, woodcock
   b. partridge, pheasant, pigeon
   c. turkey, lark, squab
   d. guinea, goose, duck

5. Quail weighs approximately:

   a. 10–12 ounces.
   b. 1–2 pounds.
   c. 4–5 pounds.
   d. 4–8 ounces.

6. The most popular game bird is:

   a. quail.
   b. partridge.
   c. pheasant.
   d. woodcock.

7. If the recipe for Chili-Rubbed Venison with Caramelized Beer Sauce was converted to yield 15 portions, how much venison leg cut into 5-ounce servings would be needed?

   a. 4.69 pounds
   b. 5.25 pounds
   c. 5.33 ounces
   d. 3.46 pounds

18D. Chapter Review

For each statement, circle either True or False to indicate the correct answer. If an answer is false, then explain why.

1. Most farmed deer is not slaughtered or processed in the slaughterhouse.
   True   False _____

2. Wild antelope, venison, and rabbit are not subject to inspection under federal law.
   True   False _____

3. A mature boar (3–4 years old) has a better flavor than a baby boar.
   True   False _____

4. Wild game birds can be purchased by request from most butchers.
   True   False _____

5. Wild boar is closely related to the domestic pig.
   True   False _____

6. Game is higher in fat and vitamins than most other meats.
   True   False _____

7. Venison is very moist because of the marbling throughout the tissue.
   True   False _____

8. Large game animals are usually sold in primal portions.
   True   False _____

9. Furred game meat has a finer grain than other meats.
   True   False _____

10. The aroma, texture, and flavor of game is affected by the lifestyle of the animal.
    True   False _____

11. Antelope, deer, and rabbit are the game most widely available to food service operations.
    True   False _____

12. The flesh of game is generally moist and tender.
    True   False _____

13. During the hanging process, carbohydrates convert into lactic acid, which tenderizes the flesh.
    True   False _____

14. Commercially raised game should always be marinated.
    True   False _____

15. Only a few species of furred game are widely available to food service operations.
    True   False _____

16. Beefalo steaks should always be cooked rare or medium rare.
    True   False _____

17. Farm-raised pheasant usually comes dressed and seldom weighs more than 2¼ pounds.
    True   False _____

18. Mellow tropical fruits such as coconut, banana, and papaya balance the stronger flavors of furred game well.

    True   False _____

19. Because of the small size of quail, a portion size for an entrée is usually one whole bird.

    True   False _____

20. Beefalo is considered the meat of the future because it is a newly discovered, distant relative to bison that was only recently discovered in remote areas of the United States.

    True   False _____

18E. Putting It All Together

Provide a short response for each of the following questions. These questions are designed to help you connect the bigger concepts presented in this chapter and/or text.

1. This chapter provides some information on bison, saying that its meat is juicy and flavorful and may be prepared in the same manner as lean beef. From the knowledge you gained from Chapter 13, Beef, suggest some ways that you might prepare bison.

2. Think about all the four-legged animals that the text has reviewed, including beef, pork, lamb, and even game. Although names of cuts may vary among the different animals, what area of the animal's body tends to be most tender?

3. The past several chapters in this text have given information about all different types of meats from land animals, explaining how to season them. This chapter does not say a lot about how to season game with various herbs and spices, but based on the fact that most of them have dark meat and based on what you know about other strongly flavored meats examined in other chapters, what might be your guess of what flavors might go well with game?

Chapter 19

FISH AND SHELLFISH

TEST YOUR KNOWLEDGE

The practice sets provided here have been designed to test your comprehension of the information found in this chapter. It is recommended that you read the chapter completely before attempting these questions.

19A. Terminology

Fill in each blank space with the correct definition.

1. En papillote _____

2. Cephalopods _____

3. Mollusks _____

4. Anadromous _____

5. Aquafarmed _____

6. Bivalves _____

7. Pan-dressed _____

8. Univalves _____

9. Round fish _____

10. Whole or round _____

11. Crustaceans _____

12. Butterflied _____

13. Steak _____

14. Submersion poaching _____

15. Drawn _____

16. Cuisson _____

17. Fillet _____

18. Shallow poaching _____

19. Tranche _____

20. Flatfish _____

21. Wheel or center cut _____

22. Freshwater fish _____

23. Tomalley _____

24. Pin bones _____

25. Devein _____

26. Debeard _____

19B. Multiple Choice

For each of the following, choose the one correct response.

1. To maintain optimum freshness, at what temperature should fish and shellfish be stored?

   a. 41°F
   b. 30°F–34°F
   c. 41°F–45°F
   d. 38°F–40°F

2. How are fish graded in the United States?

   a. USDA Prime, Choice, Select, or Utility
   b. type 1, type 2, type 3
   c. Premium, Commercial Grade, Cutter/Canner
   d. USDC A, B, or C

3. Clams, mussels, and oysters should be stored:

   a. at 36°F.
   b. on ice and in refrigeration.
   c. in boxes or net bags.
   d. at 20 percent humidity.

4. Univalves and bivalves are both examples of:

   a. mollusks.
   b. cephalopods.
   c. clams.
   d. crustaceans.

5. The "universal" meaning of *prawn* refers to:

   a. shrimp sautéed in garlic and butter.
   b. all shrimp, freshwater or marine varieties.
   c. shrimp from the Gulf of Mexico.
   d. freshwater varieties of shrimp only.

6. In terms of the market forms of fish, dressed fish have the following characteristics:

   a. The viscera are removed.
   b. The viscera, gills, fins, and scales are removed.
   c. The fish is as caught, intact.
   d. The viscera, fins, and gills are removed, the fish is scaled, and the tail is trimmed.

7. The most important commercial variety of salmon is:

   a. Atlantic salmon.
   b. Pacific salmon.
   c. Chinook salmon.
   d. king salmon.

8. Which type of sole **cannot** be caught off the coastline of the United States?

   a. lemon sole
   b. English sole
   c. Petrale sole
   d. Dover sole

9. In what way do mackerel, wahoo, herring, sardines, and salmon have similar characteristics?

   a. The color of their flesh is the same.
   b. They all migrate.
   c. Their flesh is moderately to highly oily.
   d. Their geographic availability is the same.

10. All clams are categorized as:

    a. cephalopods.
    b. crustaceans.
    c. univalves.
    d. bivalves.

11. What is the best-selling fish in America?

    a. Atlantic salmon
    b. lemon sole
    c. cod
    d. ahi tuna

12. When cooking fish fillets with the skin on, what can be done to prevent the fillet from curling?

    a. Cook the fillet at a high temperature for a short time.
    b. Cook the fillet at a low temperature for a longer time.
    c. Score the skin of the fish before cooking.
    d. Flatten the fillet by weighing it down with a semiheavy object during cooking.

13. Which is the fastest method of freezing fish, therefore increasing the likelihood of the freshest thawed product (with the best possible quality)?

    a. glazed
    b. frozen
    c. fresh-frozen
    d. flash-frozen

14. Assuming that fresh sides of salmon naturally have a shelf life of 7 days, how much will the shelf life be decreased by if stored in the refrigerator at 40°F/4°C?

    a. one-quarter
    b. one-third
    c. one-half
    d. two-thirds

19C. Market Forms of Fish

Identify the market forms indicated in the following diagram and write their names in the spaces provided.

1. _____

2. _____

3. _____

4. _____

5. _____

6. _____

7. _____

19D. Short Answer

Provide a short response that correctly answers each of the following questions.

1. Give two (2) reasons why fish fillets and steaks are the best market forms to bake.

    a. _____

    b. _____

2. List the four (4) guidelines for determining the doneness of fish and shellfish.

    a. _____

    b. _____

    c. _____

    d. _____

3. List four (4) cooking methods that would be appropriate for preparing a tranche of salmon.

   a. _____

   b. _____

   c. _____

   d. _____

4. List two (2) oily fish and two (2) lean fish that grill well.

   Oily   **Lean**

   a. _____   c. _____

   b. _____   d. _____

5. Name four (4) types of shellfish good for sautéing.

   a. _____   c. _____

   b. _____   d. _____

6. List three (3) dishes that exemplify why shellfish are good for baking.

   a. _____

   b. _____

   c. _____

7. Explain two (2) reasons why combination cooking methods are not traditionally used to prepare fish and shellfish.

   a. _____

   b. _____

8. List four (4) of the seven (7) quality points used to determine the freshness of fish.

   a. _____   c. _____

   b. _____   d. _____

19E. Chapter Review

For each statement, circle either True or False to indicate the correct answer. If an answer is false, then explain why.

1. All fish are eligible for grading.
    True   False _____

2. Fish and shellfish inspections are mandatory.
    True   False _____

3. A lobster is an example of a crustacean.
    True   False _____

4. Fatty fish are especially good for baking.
    True   False _____

5. The natural supply of seafood in our oceans is dwindling, and if we do not adopt alternative practices, some species may become extinct.
    True   False _____

6. The only difference between Maine lobsters and spiny lobsters is the geographic location where they're caught.
    True   False _____

7. Atlantic hard-shell clams are also known as geoducks.
    True   False _____

8. Fillet of halibut is a good fish to pan-fry.
    True   False _____

9. Cooking fish or shellfish en papillote is an example of baking.
    True   False _____

10. Shellfish has as much cholesterol as lamb.
    True   False _____

11. Salmon gets its pink-red flesh color from the crustaceans it eats.
    True   False _____

12. Halibut and sole are examples of flatfish.
    True   False _____

13. The best market form in which to purchase monkfish in is steaks.
    True   False _____

14. Surimi has equal nutritional value to the real fish and shellfish it replaces.
    True   False _____

15. Crustaceans are the same as shellfish.
    True   False _____

16. The FDA permits the practice of marketing many types of flounder as sole.
    True   False _____

17. When preparing a tilapia fillet to shallow poach, the chef should sprinkle it well with seasonings before submerging it in the cooking medium.
    True   False _____

18. Cod, sea bream, trout, scallops, and shrimp are all popular items to sauté.
    True   False _____

19. Pollock is also known as Boston bluefish and has pink flesh when raw that turns white when cooked.
    True   False _____

20. To improve flavor, all fish should be brushed with butter or oil before broiling or grilling.
    True   False _____

21. Fish should be cooked to an internal temperature of 145°F for 15 seconds.
    True   False _____

22. Salmon, pollock, trout, and haddock are all examples of round fish.
    True   False _____

19F. Putting It All Together

Provide a short response for each of the following questions. These questions are designed to help you connect the bigger concepts presented in this chapter and/or text.

1. Aside from the fact that most fish and shellfish are low in calories, fat, and sodium and are high in protein and vitamins A, B, D, omega-3 fatty acids and many minerals, what else contributes to their healthfulness? Refer Chapters 12 and 19 when crafting your response regarding the preparation options for fish and shellfish.

2. Based on your knowledge of professionalism, food safety, menus, recipes and knife skills, what are some things a chef has to consider when determining what market forms of fish or shellfish to purchase?

Chapter 20

EGGS AND BREAKFAST

TEST YOUR KNOWLEDGE

The practice sets provided here have been designed to test your comprehension of the information found in this chapter. It is recommended that you read the chapter completely before attempting these questions.

20A. Terminology

Fill in each blank space with the correct definition.

1. Soft boiled _____

2. Chalazae chords _____

3. Shell _____

4. Pasteurization _____

5. Sunny side up _____

6. Yolk _____

7. Hard boiled _____

8. Egg white _____

9. Over easy _____

10. Basted eggs _____

11. Over hard _____

12. Over medium _____

13. Spread _____

14. Shirred eggs _____

15. Continental-style breakfast _____

16. Griddlecakes _____

17. Belgian waffles _____

18. Decoction _____

19. Tisanes _____

20. Blintzes _____

20B. Multiple Choice

For each of the following, choose the correct response(s).

1. At what temperature does an egg yolk solidify (coagulate) when cooking?

    a. 135°F–143°F
    b. 120°F–132°F
    c. 160°F–171°F
    d. 149°F–158°F

2. What would be a good use for grade B eggs?

    a. as a compound in facial creams and other cosmetic products
    b. for baking, scrambling, or the production of bulk egg products
    c. grade B eggs are not recommended for use in food service operations
    d. for frying, poaching, or cooking in the shell

3. What should a chef do to help the egg whites cling together when poaching an egg?

    a. Add salt to the water.
    b. Add a small amount of white vinegar or other acid to the water.
    c. Add the egg to the cooking liquid before it has a chance to simmer.
    d. Use only Grade A eggs.

4. In-shell cooking of eggs uses what method of cookery?

    a. frying
    b. steaming
    c. boiling
    d. simmering

5. Which **four** of the following are criteria for grading eggs?

    a. certification of farmer
    b. albumen
    c. spread
    d. shell
    e. breed of bird
    f. yolk

6. What is the maximum amount of time an egg dish can be left at room temperature (including preparation and service time) before it becomes potentially hazardous to consume?

    a. 20 minutes
    b. 40 minutes
    c. 1 hour
    d. 2 hours or more

7. Shirred eggs and quiche are both prepared by using a dry-heat cooking method. Which method do they have in common?

   a. baking
   b. roasting
   c. frying
   d. sautéing

8. Which of the following is **false** regarding brunches?

   a. They are composed of a combination of breakfast and lunch items.
   b. They are an eat-on-the-go meal experience.
   c. They may be accompanied by alcoholic beverages.
   d. They are a social, leisurely meal.

9. Which of the following statements is **false** regarding frittatas?

   a. They are omelets containing a generous amount of ingredients and are folded in half when served.
   b. They are of Spanish-Italian origin.
   c. They are started on the stovetop, then placed in the oven or under a salamander or broiler to finish cooking.
   d. They are different sizes, depending on the size of the pan used to prepare them.

10. Cartons of fresh, uncooked (refrigerated) eggs in the shell are safe to use in cooking:

    a. until the expiration date stamped on the package.
    b. until 3 weeks beyond the packing date stamped on the package.
    c. until 4 to 5 weeks beyond the packing date stamped on the package.
    d. up to 3 months after they are laid by the chicken.

11. Egg yolks do not contain as much cholesterol as once feared. According to the American Heart Association, how many eggs per week can a person consume and still maintain a balanced diet?

    a. up to 2
    b. up to 4
    c. up to 6
    d. up to 10

12. The average weight of the yolk of a shelled large egg is:

    a. 0.4 oz.
    b. 0.6 oz.
    c. 0.8 oz.
    d. 1 oz.

13. The internal temperature of a cheese blintz served on a brunch buffet should be:

    a. 145°F.
    b. 155°F.
    c. 165°F.
    d. 175°F.

14. The average weight of the white of a large, shelled egg is:

    a. ¼ oz.
    b. ½ oz.
    c. ¾ oz.
    d. 1 oz.

15. Free-range chickens are allowed to roam freely, outside cages, and only eggs that are produced by such chickens can be called free range. In order to market their eggs this way, what must farmers do?

    a. Apply to the USDA.
    b. Apply to the USDA and send pictures proving that their chickens are raised this way.
    c. Apply to the USDA and pass an inspection of their facility.
    d. There are no requirements for being able to market their eggs as free range.

20C. Egg Identification

Label the parts of the egg indicated on the following diagram.

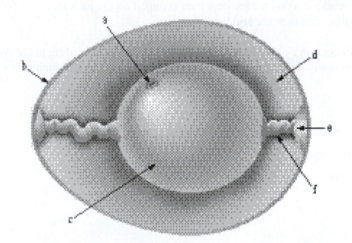

a. _____

b. _____

c. _____

d. _____

e. _____

f. _____

146

20D. Coffees and Teas

Fill in each blank space with the response that correctly completes the statement.

1. Coffee can be judged on four characteristics:

   a. _____ refers to the feeling of heaviness or thickness that coffee provides on the palate.

   b. _____ often indicates the taste of coffee.

   c. _____ refers to the tartness of the coffee, lending a snap, life, or thinness.

   d. _____ is the most ambiguous as well as the most important characteristic, having to do with taste.

2. _____ is a commercial coffee bean from which the finest coffees are produced.

3. _____ is a bean that does not produce as flavorful a coffee but is becoming more significant commercially because the trees are heartier and more fertile than their predecessors.

4. The best results for brewing a good cup of coffee are nearly always achieved by using _____ level tablespoons of ground coffee per ¾ cup (_____ ounces) of water.

5. A cup of _____ is often either the very first or the very last item consumed by a customer.

6. Whether iced or hot, _____ is often consumed throughout the meal.

7. _____ , _____ and _____ are the three basic types of tea.

20E. Chapter Review

For each statement, circle either True or False to indicate the correct answer. If an answer is false, then explain why.

1. Egg whites solidify (coagulate) when cooked at temperatures between 144°F and 149°F.
   True   False _____

2. Shell color has an effect on the grade of the egg but not on flavor or nutrition.
   True   False _____

3. A French-style omelet is prepared by filling the egg mixture with a warm, savory mixture of ingredients while the eggs cook in the pan.
   True   False _____

4. The temperature of the cooking surface on which pancakes are made should be 225°F.
   True   False _____

5. To ensure maximum volume when preparing whipped egg whites, the whites should be thoroughly chilled before whipping.
   True   False _____

6. Eggs should be stored at temperatures below 30°F and at a relative humidity of 70 to 80 percent.
    True   False _____

7. Egg substitutes can replace whole eggs in all cooking applications.
    True   False _____

8. Egg whites contain cholesterol.
    True   False _____

9. Pancakes are ready to be flipped when the first side is golden brown or when bubbles appear on the pancakes' surface.
    True   False _____

10. Eggs used for pan-frying should be a high grade and very fresh because the yolk holds its shape better and the white spreads less.
    True   False _____

11. Waffles and pancakes are examples of quick breads.
    True   False _____

12. Eggs can absorb strong aromas while in storage.
    True   False _____

13. A custard is made by poaching a mixture of eggs, cream or milk, and seasonings.
    True   False _____

14. Meat is seldom the main part of the meal at breakfast but rather an accompaniment.
    True   False _____

15. If properly refrigerated, a carton of fresh, uncooked eggs will keep for at least 4 to 5 weeks beyond the pack date found on the carton.
    True   False _____

16. Waffle irons should be washed after each use to maintain a sanitary cooking surface.
    True   False _____

17. Eggs are considered a potentially hazardous food product.
    True   False _____

18. When making an egg white omelet, one should use the same amount of heat and cooking temperature used when making a traditional omelet.
    True   False _____

19. Crêpes are the same as the thick, fluffy pancakes we make and serve at American breakfasts.
    True   False _____

20. When preparing mise en place for breakfast service, a chef must be sure that cracked eggs and pancake, waffle, or crêpe batters are stored in small batches on ice on the service line in order to maintain internal temperatures of 40°F or lower before cooking.
    True   False _____

21. Green tea is yellow-green in color and partially fermented to release its characteristics.
    True   False _____

22. Caffè latte is made by mixing one-fourth espresso with three-fourths steamed milk without foam.
    True   False _____

23. Whole coffee beans will stay fresh for a few weeks at room temperature, whereas ground coffee will stay fresh for only 3 or 4 days.
    True   False _____

24. Decoction is the oldest method of making coffee but is now used only when preparing extremely strong Turkish coffee.
    True   False _____

25. Serving flavored coffees is a relatively new practice started by the Americans.
    True   False _____

26. Tisanes have a long history in the United States, dating back to the American Revolution, and contain no real tea but rather a mixture that may contain herbs, dried flowers, seeds, or roots.
    True   False _____

27. The tea bag was invented quite by accident when an American merchant sent samples of his teas sewn into small bags made of light material to customers. The customers, without instruction, placed the bags in a cup and poured hot water over them, creating an instant cup of tea that required no straining or mixing.
    True   False _____

28. You have a recipe that requires three whole large eggs, but you have only pasteurized egg product in the refrigerator. Based on how much each whole large egg weighs on average, you should substitute 3 ounces of pasteurized egg product in the recipe.
    True   False _____

29. A soufflé is a sweet, light, fluffy custard-based dish that is baked in the oven in a water bath.
    True   False _____

30. Chai tea is black tea that has been sweetened and flavored with cinnamon, cardamom, vanilla, or other spices and is served hot or cold with milk.
    True   False _____

31. Southern sweet tea is not merely iced tea that has had sugar added to it; it is likened to a tea-flavored soft drink to which lemon can be added if desired.
    True   False _____

20F. Putting It All Together

Provide a short response for each of the following questions. These questions are designed to help you connect the bigger concepts presented in this chapter and/or text.

1. What things can a person do to make sure s/he is **not** consuming too many eggs in one week because of the level of cholesterol they contain?

2. What food safety precautions should a chef consider when handling eggs for breakfast service?

150

Chapter 21

VEGETABLES

TEST YOUR KNOWLEDGE

The practice sets provided here have been designed to test your comprehension of the information found in this chapter. It is recommended that you read the chapter completely before attempting these questions.

21A. Terminology

Fill in each blank space with the correct definition.

1. Parboiling _____

2. Vegetable _____

3. Beurre noisette _____

4. Cellulose _____

5. Blanching _____

6. Refreshing or shocking _____

7. Vegetarian _____

8. Fruitarian _____

9. Demi-vegetarian _____

10. Lacto-ovo-vegetarian or ovo-lacto-vegetarian _____

11. Lacto-vegetarian _____

12. Vegan _____

13. Tofu _____

14. Seitan _____

15. Tempeh _____

16. Textured soy protein _____

17. Brassica _____

18. Scoville heat units _____

19. Pigments _____

    a. Chlorophyll _____

    b. Flavonoids _____

    c. Carotenoids _____

21B. Multiple Choice

For each of the following, choose the one correct response.

1. A braised vegetable dish differs from a stewed vegetable dish in that it:

    a. contains an acid product.
    b. is usually prepared with only one vegetable.
    c. has a longer cooking time.
    d. is served with a reduction of the cooking liquid.

2. Grades for all vegetables include the following:

    a. U.S. No. 1, U.S. No. 2, U.S. No. 3
    b. U.S. Grade A, U.S. Grade B, U.S. Grade C
    c. U.S. Extra Fancy, U.S. Fancy, U.S. Extra No. 1, U.S. No. 1
    d. USDA Recommended, USDA Approved

3. According to the definition of *savory*, vegetables are savory because they:

    a. are an herbaceous plant that can be partially or wholly eaten.
    b. have less sugar than fruit.
    c. have little or no woody tissue.
    d. are usually eaten cooked, not raw.

4. Which of the following is **false** about sautéing vegetables?

    a. The finished product should be firm to the bite, be brightly colored, and show little moisture loss.
    b. All preparation of ingredients should be done in advance because the cooking process proceeds rapidly.
    c. Seasonings should be added to the pan when warming the oil or fat so their flavors have time to develop during this quick cooking process.
    d. A wide variety of vegetables can be sautéed.

5. Which of the following is a disadvantage when grilling vegetables?

    a. The high heat of the cooking process kills much of the nutritional content.
    b. The types of vegetables to be grilled must be carefully selected based on their cooking times.
    c. Vegetables often need to be brushed or marinated with a little oil or fat before cooking.
    d. Smaller vegetables should be skewered to make handling easier.

6. Which of the following vegetables is **not** suitable for roasting or baking?

    a. eggplant
    b. potatoes
    c. spinach
    d. peppers

7. Fresh vegetables are sold in what quantities?

    a. cases or flats
    b. degree of processing
    c. weight or count
    d. specifications

8. To preserve nutrients, color, and texture, what would be the best process to follow?

    a. Cut the vegetables into uniform shapes before cooking.
    b. Cook the vegetables whole, then peel and cut.
    c. Add acid to the cooking liquid.
    d. Cook the vegetables as little as possible.

9. What is true about pan-steaming vegetables?

    a. Overcooking is less likely to happen.
    b. The cooking apparatus must be covered to retain heat.
    c. More nutrients are lost than in other techniques.
    d. Only vegetables with a firm texture may be pan-steamed.

10. Which of the following is **true** about microwave cooking?

    a. It substitutes well for all cooking techniques except broiling and grilling.
    b. It is best used as a substitute for traditional steaming.
    c. It is dangerous to use in large-scale food service operations.
    d. Its cooking process, agitating water molecules within food, depletes nutrients.

11. Which of the following is a characteristic of fresh soy beans?

    a. purple
    b. expensive
    c. categorized as a fruit
    d. a potentially hazardous food product

12. Which is **false** regarding organic foods?

    a. The USDA regulates production and labeling of organic foods.
    b. Organic foods may contain pesticides, fungicides, and/or herbicides.
    c. Foods labeled "100% organic" must contain only organic ingredients.
    d. Organic foods contain few if any intentional additives and are free of incidental additives.

13. Creating a "vegetable sauna" by cooking the vegetables slowly in a little oil over low heat in a covered pot (to gently extract flavor) uses which cooking technique?

    a. sautéing
    b. grilling
    c. poaching
    d. sweating

14. Which of the following finely chopped ingredients is **not** included in a duxelle?

   a. duck liver (foie gras)
   b. mushrooms
   c. butter
   d. shallots

21C. Product Identification

Match each vegetable in List A with the appropriate description in List B. Each choice in List B can be used only once.

List A	List B
_____ 1. Artichokes	a. A winter squash variety especially popular in October
_____ 2. Swiss chard	b. A type of beet used only for its greens
_____ 3. Okra	c. A firm orange taproot that is eaten raw or cooked
_____ 4. Bok choy	d. Tubers that grow near oak or beech tree roots
_____ 5. Pumpkin	e. A member of the *Capsicum* family commonly used in Asian, Indian, Mexican, and Latin American cuisines
_____ 6. Tomatillos	f. From Arab and African cuisines, a pod often used for thickening
_____ 7. Leeks	g. A sweet, onion-flavored vegetable with flat, wide leaves
_____ 8. Truffles	h. A white-stemmed variety of southern Chinese cabbage
_____ 9. Corn	i. The immature flowers of a thistle plant; often canned or marinated
_____ 10. Cucumbers	j. Husk tomatoes with a crisp, tart flesh
_____ 11. Carrots	k. The immature stalks of bulb onions
_____ 12. Hot peppers	l. A squash that comes in two varieties: pickled and sliced
_____ 13. Bean curd	m. A plant seed that is really a grain or type of grass; grows on a cob
_____ 14. Olive	n. A cheeselike soybean product with high nutritional value, low cost, and high flavor adaptability
_____ 15. Broccoli rabe	o. The fruit of a tree native to the Mediterranean area that is inedibly bitter and must be washed, soaked, and cured or pickled before eating
	p. A leafy green with small broccoli-like florets and a peppery, bitter flavor

21D. Chapter Review

For each statement, circle either True or False to indicate the correct answer. If an answer is false, then explain why.

1. Although frozen vegetables are often colorful, their texture may be softer than fresh vegetables.
   True   False _____

2. Puréed vegetables are usually prepared by first sautéing, steaming, or boiling.
   True   False _____

3. Winter squash is commonly braised or stewed because of its dense texture.
   True   False _____

4. Food is irradiated by exposing it to gamma rays to sterilize it, slow ripening, or prevent sprouting.
   True   False _____

5. Eggplants, peppers, and tomatoes are considered fruit-vegetables.
   True   False _____

6. The larger the size of the chile pepper, generally the milder its flavor.
   True   False _____

7. Dried beans and peas are examples of legumes.
   True   False _____

8. The grading of vegetables is not required by the USDA.
   True   False _____

9. Potatoes, onions, shallots, and garlic are best stored between 34°F and 40°F.
   True   False _____

10. An acid added to the cooking liquid causes a vegetable to resist softening and therefore require a longer cooking time.
    True   False _____

11. Flavonoids are found mainly in beets, cauliflower, and winter squash.
    True   False _____

12. Timing a vegetable as it cooks is the best way to determine doneness.
    True   False _____

13. The ripening of vegetables proceeds more rapidly in the presence of carbon dioxide gas.
    True   False _____

14. If the only goal is to help vegetables retain color when cooked, then an alkali is a good ingredient to add to the cooking liquid.
    True   False _____

15. The FDA classifies food irradiation as a preservative.
    True   False _____

16. Slicing eggplant and sprinkling it with salt is necessary when preparing to roast the vegetable.
    True   False _____

17. A chipotle chile pepper is made by drying a jalapeño.
    True   False _____

18. The excess liquid used to can vegetables causes the contents of the can to lose nutrients and the texture to soften.
    True   False _____

19. In South America and the southern United States, collard greens are most commonly prepared by slowly simmering until very tender.
    True   False _____

20. Cooking destroys much of the sweetness and special flavor of Walla-Walla, Vidalia, and Maui onions.
    True   False _____

21. Pickling uses air and gentle heat to remove moisture from foods so that bacteria can no longer cause spoilage.
    True   False _____

22. Seven 3-ounce servings of Braised Celery with Basil would require approximately 12 fresh basil leaves cut chiffonade.
    True   False _____

23. Tofu is a potentially hazardous food product.
    True   False _____

24. Vegetables are valuable in our daily diets because of the carbohydrates, fiber, vitamins, and minerals they provide.
    True   False _____

25. Vegetables are braised or stewed for the primary purpose of tenderizing.
    True   False _____

26. When soaking dried beans, allow 2 cups of cold, unseasoned liquid for each cup of dried beans.
    True   False _____

27. Pea shoots are the delicate tendrils of the plant that form before it produces pea pods, and they are often used in Chinese cuisine, stir-fried like spinach or other leafy greens.
    True   False _____

28. Today the preservation techniques of vegetables are often limited to pickling, freezing, and canning in order to maintain vegetables in a state as close to fresh as possible.
    True   False _____

21E. Putting It All Together

Provide a short response for each of the following questions. These questions are designed to help you connect the bigger concepts presented in this chapter and/or text.

1. Create some healthy rules for incorporating a variety of vegetables into your daily diet. You may refer to Chapter 23, Healthy Cooking, for additional ideas.

2. This chapter talks about applying various cooking methods to vegetables and discusses the colors of the vegetables and what might happen to those colors when they're cooked under certain conditions. Relate the information on color presented in this chapter to the information on color presented in Chapter 6, Flavors and Flavorings. What are the similarities and differences of the messages?

Chapter 22

POTATOES, GRAINS AND PASTA

TEST YOUR KNOWLEDGE

The practice sets provided here have been designed to test your comprehension of the information found in this chapter. It is recommended that you read the chapter completely before attempting these questions.

22A. Terminology

Fill in each blank space with the correct definition.

1. Extruded _____

2. Foglia _____

3. Tossing method _____

4. Rice

    a. Converted rice _____

    b. Instant/quick-cooking rice _____

    c. Short-grain rice _____

    d. Medium-grain rice _____

    e. Long-grain rice _____

    f. Brown rice _____

    g. Arborio rice _____

    h. Wild rice _____

5. Potatoes

    a. New potatoes _____
    b. Mealy potatoes _____

    c. Waxy potatoes _____

6. Hulling _____

7. Endosperm _____

8. Berry _____

9. Durum wheat _____

10. Germ _____

11. Dumpling

    a. Filled _____

        1. Tortellini _____

        2. Ravioli _____

    b. Plain/drop dumpling _____

    c. Gnocchi _____

12. Still-frying method _____

13. Groat _____

14. Hull _____

15. Cracking _____

16. Masa harina _____

17. Pearling _____

18. Grinding _____

19. Bran _____

20. Oats

    a. Steel-cut _____
    b. Rolled _____

21. Posole _____

22B. Short Answer

Provide a short response that correctly answers each of the following questions.

1. Why shouldn't a baked potato be cooked by wrapping in foil or microwaving?

    a. _____

    b. _____

2. Name three (3) dishes that are traditionally made with short-grain rice.

    a. _____

    b. _____

    c. _____

3. Why is it so important to use ample water when cooking pasta?

_____

4. The finest commercial pastas are made with pure semolina flour. Why?

   _____

5. Duchesse potatoes are considered the mother to many classical potato dishes. List four (4) different classical dishes prepared with duchesse potatoes, briefly describing the ingredients.

   a. _____

   b. _____

   c. _____

   d. _____

6. Identify the three (3) main shapes of Italian pasta.

   a. _____ b. _____ c. _____

7. What are the three (3) basic cooking methods for cooking grains?

   a. _____ b. _____ c. _____

8. Give three (3) reasons for soaking most dried Asian noodles in hot water before cooking.

   a. _____

   b. _____

   c. _____

22C. Multiple Choice

For each of the following, choose the one correct response..

1. Which of the following classical potato preparations includes duchesse potatoes as part of the ingredients?

   a. Anna
   b. Berny
   c. Rösti
   d. Boulangère

2. Which of the following grains **cannot** be used to make risotto?

   a. barley
   b. oats
   c. buckwheat
   d. Arborio rice

3. Why **doesn't** American-grown rice need to be rinsed before cooking?

   a. All of the starch will be washed away.
   b. The rice will become soggy before cooking.
   c. Rinsing will result in a sticky rice.
   d. Such rice is generally clean and free of insects.

4. When boiling pasta, "ample water" is defined by the following measurements:

   a. 1 quart of water to 1 pound of pasta
   b. 2 quarts of water to 1 pound of pasta
   c. a 15:1 ratio of water to pasta
   d. 1 gallon of water to 1 pound of pasta

5. Which of the following is **false** about converted rice?

   a. It tastes the same as regular milled white rice.
   b. It retains more nutrients than regular milled white rice.
   c. It has been pearled in order to remove the surface starch.
   d. It cooks more slowly than regular milled white rice.

6. Why is long-grain rice more versatile and popular than other types of rice?

   a. It has a higher nutritional content than short- or medium-grain rice.
   b. It remains firm and separate when cooked properly.
   c. It is far more affordable for a larger variety of food service operations.
   d. It is easier and faster to cook than other types of rice.

7. Which type of potato would be good for making potatoes Berny?

   a. mealy potatoes
   b. waxy potatoes
   c. new potatoes
   d. sweet potatoes

8. Which statement is **false** about the nutritional content of grains?

   a. They contain all of the essential amino acids.
   b. They are high in fat.
   c. They are a good source of dietary fiber.
   d. They are a good source of vitamins and minerals.

9. Which of the following flours is used to make Asian noodles?

   a. potato
   b. bean
   c. corn
   d. oat

10. Duchesse potatoes that are shaped, breaded, and fried result in:

   a. croquettes.
   b. dauphine potatoes.
   c. marquis potatoes.
   d. lorette potatoes.

11. What is the difference between cooking fresh pasta and dry, factory-produced pasta?

   a. Fresh pasta takes significantly less time to cook.
   b. Dried pasta should be cooked to order.
   c. Dried pasta takes significantly less time to cook.
   d. Fresh pasta contains a much different list of ingredients.

12. How hot should the fat be for blanching potatoes for French fries?

   a. 250°F–300°F
   b. 275°F–325°F
   c. 300°F–350°F
   d. 350°F–375°F

13. Which grain contains all nine essential amino acids and therefore is considered a complete protein?

   a. brown rice
   b. barley
   c. millet
   d. quinoa

14. How are rösti potatoes, a classic potato dish, made?

   a. Mashed potatoes are bound with egg, breaded, and fried.
   b. Raw potatoes are sliced thin, layered in a casserole, topped with stock, and baked.
   c. Potatoes are boiled until al dente, grated, and fried in a large pancake with lard and bacon, then cut into wedge shapes and served.
   d. Raw potatoes are grated and mixed with eggs and seasoning, fried in pancake shapes, and served as mini potato pancakes.

22D. Chapter Review

For each statement, circle either True or False to indicate the correct answer. If an answer is false, then explain why.

1. Grains cooked by the risotto or pilaf method are first coated with hot fat.
   True   False _____

2. Medium-grain rice is best when freshly made and piping hot.
   True   False _____

3. The only grain eaten fresh as a vegetable is corn.
   True   False _____

4. Making a dough with semolina flour makes it softer, more supple, and easier to work with.
   True   False _____

5. Asian noodle dough can be used to make dumplings.
   True   False _____

6. *Yam* is an industry term for sweet potato.
   True   False _____

7. Potatoes should be stored between 40°F and 50°F.
   True   False _____

8. The best applications for mealy potatoes are sautéing and pan-frying.
    True   False _____

9. A ravioli is a dumpling.
    True   False _____

10. Fresh pasta is best when cooked to order.
    True   False _____

11. Top-quality russet potatoes are recommended for deep-frying.
    True   False _____

12. Three basic cooking methods are used to prepare grains: simmering, risotto, and pilaf.
    True   False _____

13. The standard ratio for cooking rice is 1 part liquid to 1 part rice.
    True   False _____

14. Pasta is widely used in the cuisines of Asia, North America, and Europe.
    True   False _____

15. Generally cracked wheat and bulgur can be substituted for one another in recipes.
    True   False _____

16. Buckwheat is neither wheat nor grain.
    True   False _____

17. The high pH and high protein content of rice make it a potentially hazardous food product.
    True   False _____

18. One cup of dry quinoa will yield approximately 1 cup of cooked quinoa.
    True   False _____

19. Dumplings are always stuffed.
    True   False _____

20. *Al dente* means firm but tender.
    True   False _____

21. Potato and grain dishes are potentially hazardous foods and should be heated to 145°F and then held
    for service at 135°F.
    True   False _____

22. Pasta and risotto dishes are usually served as a separate course in Italy, preceding the main dish and
    following the appetizer.
    True   False _____

23. Unlike Italian pasta, Asian noodle dough is nearly always cut into ribbons.
    True   False _____

22E. Putting It All Together

Provide a short response for each of the following questions. These questions are designed to help you connect the bigger concepts presented in this chapter and/or text.

1. This chapter and Chapter 21, Vegetables, emphasize that vegetables, potatoes, pastas, and grains are potentially hazardous foods. Explain again the characteristics of potentially hazardous foods and why there seems to be such a heavy warning in these two particular chapters.

2. Building on your answer to the previous question, explain why wrapping a baked potato in aluminum foil during the baking and holding process during service can be so dangerous, even if the proper holding temperature is maintained.

Chapter 23

HEALTHY COOKING

TEST YOUR KNOWLEDGE

The practice sets provided here have been designed to test your comprehension of the information found in this chapter. It is recommended that you read this chapter completely before attempting these questions.

23A. Terminology

Fill in each blank space with the correct definition.

1. Nutrition _____

2. Essential nutrients

    a. Macronutrients _____

    b. Micronutrients _____

3. Calorie _____

4. Dietary fiber _____

5. Carbohydrates _____

6. Lipids _____

7. Trans fats _____

8. Proteins _____

9. Metabolism _____

10. Fat soluble _____

11. Water soluble _____

12. Minerals _____

13. Water _____

14. Phytochemicals _____

15. Cholesterol _____

16. Additives _____

17. Ingredient alternatives _____

18. Ingredient substitutes _____

19. Allergens _____

20. Celiac disease _____

21. Lactose _____

22. Registered dietitian _____

23. Vegetarianism

    a. Vegan _____

    b. Ovo-vegetarian _____

    c. Lacto-ovo vegetarian _____

24. Keeping kosher (and vegetarianism) _____

25. Halal (and vegetarianism) _____

26. Soybean-based ingredients _____

27. Analogous foods _____

23B. Short Answer

Provide a short response that correctly answers each of the following questions.

1. List five (5) things a food service worker can do to meet the diverse nutritional needs of consumers.

    a. _____

    b. _____

    c. _____

    d. _____

    e. _____

2. Chefs should be receptive to patron requests that attempt to control calorie and fat intake, such as:

    a. _____

    b. _____

    c. _____

    d. _____

3. When modifying a recipe, the chef should first identify the ingredient(s) or cooking method(s) that may need to be changed. Once that is done, what three (3) principles should the chef follow to make the dish healthier?

a. _____

b. _____

c. _____

4. List four (4) reasons why one might choose a vegetarian lifestyle.

a. _____

b. _____

c. _____

d. _____

5. List five (5) guidelines for chefs to follow in planning and preparing to add vegetarian dishes to a restaurant menu.

a. _____

b. _____

c. _____

d. _____

e. _____

6. What are some common questions a server and/or chef should ask a guest when a vegetarian meal has been requested and a vegetarian option does not exist on the menu?

_____

_____

_____

7. What are four (4) ingredient options chefs can add to a vegetarian meal in order to increase the complexity of the dish while also adding vital protein?

a. _____

b. _____

c. _____

d. _____

23C. Roles of Nutrients in Health

Match each nutrient in List A with the role it plays in the body in List B. Each choice in List B can be used only once.

List A	List B
_____ 1. Lipids	a. An important source of energy for the body
_____ 2. Fiber	b. Help generate energy from foods we eat
_____ 3. Cholesterol	c. The body produces all it needs; none is needed in the diet
_____ 4. Proteins	d. Necessary for transporting nutrients and wastes
_____ 5. Vitamins and minerals	e. Provide calories, help carry fat-soluble vitamins, and give food a pleasant mouth feel
_____ 6. Carbohydrates	f. Necessary for manufacturing, maintaining, and repairing body tissue and regulating body processes
_____ 7. Water	g. Keeps digestive tract running smoothly
	h. Helps moderate heart rate

23D. Essential Nutrients

For each of the following, choose the one correct response.

1. Saturated fats are usually solid at room temperature and are found in which of the following food sources?

    a. fruits, vegetables, grains
    b. canola and olive oils
    c. corn, cottonseed, sunflower, and safflower oils
    d. milk, eggs, meats, and other foods from animal sources

2. According to the Food Guide Pyramid, for how long each day should a person participate in moderate physical activity, as a baseline for maintaining a healthy weight and lifestyle?

    a. 20 minutes
    b. 30 minutes
    c. 60 minutes
    d. 90 minutes

3. Which of the following statements is **false** about complex carbohydrates?

    a. They occur naturally in sugars in fruit, vegetables, and milk.
    b. Fiber is a complex carbohydrate that cannot be digested.
    c. Complex carbohydrates are digested into glucose.
    d. Starch is a complex carbohydrate.

4. Which of the following is **false** about vitamins?

    a. They are vital dietary substances needed to regulate metabolism.
    b. They are can be divided into two categories: fat soluble and water soluble.
    c. They are necessary for manufacturing, maintaining, and repairing body tissue.
    d. They are noncaloric and needed in small amounts.

5. Which of the following statements is **false**?

   a. One gram of pure fat supplies 9 kcal of energy.
   b. One gram of pure protein supplies 4 kcal of energy.
   c. One gram of pure vitamins supplies 0 kcal of energy.
   d. One gram of pure carbohydrates supplies 2 kcal of energy.

6. Which of the following is **not** considered a food that contains simple carbohydrates?

   a. fruit
   b. milk
   c. oats
   d. vegetables

7. Which essential nutrient forms a gel-type substance in the digestive tract and helps reduce serum cholesterol by removing it from the body?

   a. soluble fiber
   b. lipids
   c. simple carbohydrates
   d. protein

8. Which statement is **false** about hydrogenation?

   a. Hydrogenization results in the formation of *trans* fats.
   b. *Trans* fats contain cholesterol.
   c. *Trans* fats are considered risk factors for heart disease and possibly other diseases like cancer.
   d. Margarine is a product that has been hydrogenized.

9. Which of the following organizations is responsible for providing recommendations for planning a diet and lifestyle to enhance health?

   a. USDA
   b. NRA
   c. FDA
   d. ACS

10. Which of the following artificial sweeteners has no calories, tastes 200–700 times as sweet as table sugar, and at one time was linked to causing cancer in laboratory animals, although further testing suggested that it is safe enough for human consumption?

   a. aspartame
   b. Sunnette or Sweet One
   c. stevia
   d. saccharin

23E. Parts of a Food Label

Identify the six areas of importance on the following food label. Briefly explain the significance of each.

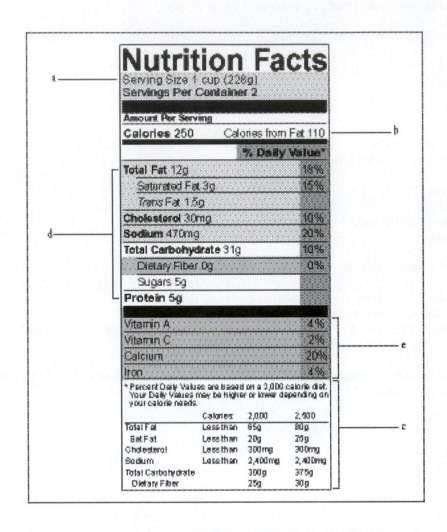

Nutrition Facts
Serving Size 1 cup (228g)
Servings Per Container 2

Amount Per Serving

Calories 250   Calories from Fat 110

% Daily Value*

Total Fat 12g	18%
Saturated Fat 3g	15%
Trans Fat 1.5g	
Cholesterol 30mg	10%
Sodium 470mg	20%
Total Carbohydrate 31g	10%
Dietary Fiber 0g	0%
Sugars 5g	
Protein 5g	

Vitamin A	4%
Vitamin C	2%
Calcium	20%
Iron	4%

* Percent Daily Values are based on a 2,000 calorie diet. Your Daily Values may be higher or lower depending on your calorie needs.

	Calories	2,000	2,500
Total Fat	Less than	65g	80g
Sat Fat	Less than	20g	25g
Cholesterol	Less than	300mg	300mg
Sodium	Less than	2,400mg	2,400mg
Total Carbohydrate		300g	375g
Dietary Fiber		25g	30g

Part of Label	Significance
a. _____	_____
b. _____	_____
c. _____	_____
d. _____	_____
e. _____	_____

23F. Chapter Review

For each statement, circle either True or False to indicate the correct answer. If an answer is false, then explain why.

1. Peas, most nuts and seeds, and oats are the only plant-based foods that are equivalent to animal proteins.
    True   False _____

2. Once opened, soy milk that is sold in aseptic packaging (can be stored at room temperature before opening) is good for 1 year as long as it is refrigerated.
    True   False _____

3. Restaurateurs are required to supply nutrition information to customers who request it only if they have made a nutrition claim about a menu item, such as "low fat."
    True   False _____

4. The same quantity of soy milk can be substituted for dairy milk in all recipes.
    True   False _____

5. Tossed salads are a good source of quality protein.
    True   False _____

6. The body cannot digest fiber, so it passes through the body almost completely unchanged.
    True   False _____

7. Eggs are consumed by ovo-vegetarians as well as vegans.
    True   False _____

8. RDI stands for Recommended Dietary Intake.
    True   False _____

9. Food processing and preparation can reduce a food's mineral content.
    True   False _____

10. Carbohydrates, proteins, and fats can be categorized as energy nutrients.
    True   False _____

11. A chef's moral and primary responsibility as a food service professional is to prepare and serve food that meets or exceeds the guidelines set forth by the Food Guide Pyramid.
    True   False _____

12. Cholesterol can be found in foods from both plant and animal sources.
    True   False _____

13. Canola, olive, cottonseed, and corn oil are examples of oils that are a combination of three kinds of fat.
    True   False _____

14. Only 9 of the 20 amino acids are essential.
    True   False _____

15. Any artificial sweetener can be substituted for sugar when preparing baked goods.
    True   False _____

16. The six categories of essential nutrients are carbohydrates, lipids, proteins, vitamins, minerals, and water.
    True   False   _____

17. Insoluble and soluble fibers are considered simple carbohydrates.
    True   False   _____

18. Proteins can be found in chicken, beef, and salmon as well as beans, rice, and pasta.
    True   False   _____

19. A portion of roasted beef tenderloin cooked to a medium doneness will likely contain more vitamins than a portion of beef stew because of the different ways they are cooked.
    True   False   _____

20. People are told to lower their cholesterol because they consume too much of it in food and it has a negative effect on bodily functions.
    True   False   _____

21. One thing that all essential nutrients have in common is that they all contribute calories to the body.
    True   False   _____

22. Compared to years past, vegetarianism is gaining acceptability in the United States for more reasons than just religious or philosophical beliefs.
    True   False   _____

23. Butter is an example of a hydrogenated fat.
    True   False   _____

24. Tempeh should be cooked before eating just to temper its pronounced flavor.
    True   False   _____

25. Of all the vegan protein ingredients, tofu is the only one that has a texture similar to meat.
    True   False   _____

26. Some Jews and Christians believe that God originally intended humans to be vegetarians, even though consumption of meat is allowed.
    True   False   _____

23G. Putting It All Together

Provide a short response for each of the following questions. These questions are designed to help you connect the bigger concepts presented in this chapter and/or text.

1. Considering what you learned about high amounts of fat and cholesterol in the diet in this chapter, explain why including veal in place of other more mature beef cuts would be advantageous to achieving your goals of healthy cooking.

2. Some see the bland flavor of tofu as a negative quality, and therefore they shy away from cooking with it. Based on what you learned in this chapter as well as in Chapter 6, Flavors and Flavorings, what are the advantages of starting with a bland flavor profile? In what ways could you flavor the tofu to fit with almost any dish you're preparing?

3. How can your knowledge of meat and meat cookery be used to understand protein substitutions for vegan dishes, such as tofu, texturized soy protein, grains, or beans?

Chapter 24

SALADS AND SALAD DRESSINGS

TEST YOUR KNOWLEDGE

The practice sets provided here have been designed to test your comprehension of the information found in this chapter. It is recommended that you read the chapter completely before attempting these questions.

24A. Terminology

Fill in each blank space with the correct definition.

1. Dressing _____

2. Bound salads _____

3. Mesclun _____

4. Base _____

5. Basic French dressing _____

6. Vegetable salads _____

7. Emulsified sauce _____

8. Green salads _____

9. Garnish _____

10. Composed salad _____

11. Body _____

12. Tossed salad _____

13. Fruit salad _____

14. Microgreens _____

15. Butterhead lettuce _____

16. Salad spinner _____

17. Head lettuce _____

18. Enzymatic browning _____

19. Chicory _____

20. Core _____

24B. Multiple Choice

For each of the following, choose the one correct response.

1. What is the best type of oil to use when making mayonnaise?

    a. nut oil
    b. vegetable oil
    c. seed oil
    d. olive oil

2. What are the **two** forms in which lettuce grows?

    a. bunch and leaf
    b. leaf and head
    c. head and stalks
    d. stalks and bunch

3. At what temperature should lettuces and salad greens should be stored in protective containers?

    a. 30°F–32°F
    b. 32°F–34°F
    c. 34°F–38°F
    d. 40°F–50°F

4. What type of emulsion is a basic vinaigrette?

    a. permanent
    b. semipermanent
    c. temporary
    d. semitemporary

5. Approximately how much oil can one egg yolk emulsify?

    a. 2 ounces
    b. 4 ounces
    c. 1 cup
    d. 7 ounces

6. What part does the green serve as in a composed salad?

    a. base
    b. body
    c. garnish
    d. dressing

7. What kind of salad would Tomato and Asparagus Salad with Fresh Mozzarella, a chapter recipe, be?

    a. fruit salad
    b. composed salad
    c. vegetable salad
    d. bound salad

8. Traditional potato salad is considered a:

   a. green salad.
   b. composed salad.
   c. vegetable salad.
   d. bound salad.

9. Which of the following greens would **not** have complementary flavors to mâche in a salad?

   a. Boston lettuce
   b. radicchio
   c. bibb lettuce
   d. iceberg lettuce

10. Radicchio, escarole, frisée, Belgian endive, and dandelion are all examples of:

    a. lettuce.
    b. sprouts.
    c. fresh herbs.
    d. bitter greens.

11. From a food safety standpoint, extra care should be taken when preparing salads because:

    a. certain ingredients are expensive and should not be wasted.
    b. salads are usually foods that will not be cooked before service.
    c. salad ingredients have mild flavors that may easily become tainted by strong odors.
    d. they wilt quickly and easily.

12. If a temporary emulsion separates during service, the chef should:

    a. rewhisk it immediately before use.
    b. whisk in one egg yolk for every 7 ounces of oil used in the recipe.
    c. whisk in one-third more oil.
    d. whisk in 2 tablespoons Dijon mustard.

24C. Short Answer

Provide a short response that correctly answers each of the following questions.

1. What are three (3) things that the chef should avoid overusing when making a nutritionally balanced salad?

   a. _____

   b. _____

   c. _____

2. Give two (2) reasons why greens should be stored separately from tomatoes and apples.

   a. _____

   b. _____

3. List five (5) of the ingredients that may be included in mayonnaise-based dressings.

a. _____   d. _____

b. _____   e. _____

c. _____

4. Briefly describe the eight (8) basic steps to be followed when making mayonnaise.

a. _____

b. _____

c. _____

d. _____

e. _____

f. _____

g. _____

h. _____

5. List four (4) possible ingredients for a fruit salad dressing that may complement the mild, sweet flavors.

a. _____   c. _____

b. _____   d. _____

24D. Chapter Review

For each statement, circle either True or False to indicate the correct answer. If an answer is false, then explain why.

1. The balance of vinegar, oil, lecithin, and whipping is crucial to achieve a proper emulsion.
   True   False _____

2. Chicory, Belgian endive, sorrel, and spinach are all examples of salad greens that can be eaten raw or cooked.
   True   False _____

3. Romaine or cos lettuce benefits from hand-tearing to break it into smaller pieces, whereas butterhead and baby lettuces can be cut with a knife.
   True   False _____

4. The first step to washing lettuce in a sink is to sanitize the sink.
   True   False _____

5. Tossed salads should be dressed at the last possible moment before service to prevent overmarination from the dressing.
   True   False _____

6. Generally softer-leaved varieties of lettuces such as iceberg and red leaf tend to perish more quickly in storage than crisper-leaved varieties.
   True   False _____

7. The best rule of thumb to follow when matching dressings to salad greens is, "The milder the flavor of the salad green, the milder the flavor of the dressing."
   True   False _____

8. All greens should be washed *after* they've been torn or cut.
   True   False _____

9. The standard ratio of oil to vinegar in a temporary emulsion is three to one; however this ratio may vary when using strongly flavored oils, thus decreasing the proportion of oil to vinegar to one part oil to one part vinegar.
   True   False _____

10. Once washed, salad greens should be dried well to maintain a crisp texture and to ensure that oil-based dressings will adhere to the leaves.
    True   False _____

11. An advantage of using an emulsified vinaigrette dressing instead of a mayonnaise-based dressing is that it has the basic flavor of a vinaigrette without being as heavy as mayonnaise.
    True   False _____

12. Nasturtiums, miniature roses, and zinnias are all examples of edible flowers grown to enhance food presentations.
    True   False _____

13. Although salads are generally believed to be healthful foods, they can easily become laden with fat and calories based on the choice of dressings and toppings/garnishes.
    True   False _____

14. If the conversion factor of 9.17 were used to produce Salad Niçoise, then 48 portions would result.
    True   False _____

15. The original Caesar salad was prepared tableside by servers, who first coddled the eggs (simmered them in water for a minute, lightly cooking them) before making the dressing.
    True   False _____

16. Raw egg yolks are safe to use when making homemade mayonnaise.
    True   False _____

17. A vinaigrette can serve as a dressing, a light sauce, or a marinade.
    True   False _____

18. Baking pieces of bread to make croutons is the best cooking technique to use when making a base for a canapé.
    True   False _____

24E. Putting It All Together

Provide a short response for each of the following questions. These questions are designed to help you connect the bigger concepts presented in this chapter and/or text.

1. What obligation does a chef have to offer vegetarian and/or low-fat salad options on the menu?

2. A common misconception about salads is that they are always a healthful, balanced way to eat. Look at the nutritional analysis for Salad Niçoise and discuss what you find.

Chapter 25

FRUITS

TEST YOUR KNOWLEDGE

The practice sets provided here have been designed to test your comprehension of the information found in this chapter. It is recommended that you read the chapter completely before attempting these questions.

25A. Terminology

Fill in each blank space with the correct definition.

1. Ripened _____

2. Acidulation _____

3. Preserve _____

4. Pectin _____

5. Marmalade _____

6. Papain _____

7. Gel _____

8. Jam _____

9. Jelly _____

10. Heirloom varieties _____

11. Hybrids _____

12. Respiration rate _____

13. Zest _____

14. Pith _____

15. Ethylene gas _____

16. Astringency _____

17. IQF _____

18. Juice extractor _____

19. Fritter _____

25B. Short Answer

Provide a short response that correctly answers each of the following questions.

1. List the four (4) fruits that emit ethylene gas.

   a. _____   c. _____

   b. _____   d. _____

2. What does a banana that has been damaged by being stored at too cold a temperature look like?

   _____

3. Fruits vary in their vitamin and mineral content. In each column, identify the fruits that are plentiful in that nutrient.

Vitamin C	Vitamin A	Potassium
_____	_____	_____
_____	_____	_____
_____	_____	_____

4. List four (4) uses for lower grades of fruit.

   a. _____   c. _____

   b. _____   d. _____

5. List five (5) methods of fruit preservation.

   a. _____   d. _____

   b. _____   e. _____

   c. _____

6. Name four (4) fruits that benefit from acidulation.

   a. _____   c. _____

   b. _____   d. _____

7. Name five (5) fruits that maintain their texture when sautéed.

   a. _____   d. _____

   b. _____   e. _____

   c. _____

25C. Fill in the Blank

Fill in each blank space with the response that correctly completes the statement.

1. _____ is the moist-heat cooking method most commonly used for preparing pears.

2. In classical dishes, the term *à la Normande* refers to the use of _____.

3. Three examples of fruits or vegetables in the gourd family are _____ , _____ , and _____.

4. _____ are the single largest fruit crop in the world.

5. When deep-frying fruits, the best results are achieved by first dipping the fruit slices in _____ before submerging them in the hot fat.

25D. Product Identification

Match each fruit in List A with the appropriate description in List B. Each choice in List B can be used only once.

List A	List B
_____ 1. Tangerines	a. A tart firm berry grown on low vines in bogs
_____ 2. Grapes	b. Also known as mandarins
_____ 3. Quince	c. Related to the prickly pear; is the size of eggplant but tastes like kiwi or melon
_____ 4. Lemons	d. Too astringent to eat raw, but great when sweetened with sugar
_____ 5. Sour cherries	e. The single largest fruit crop in the world
_____ 6. Dates	f. Deep golden-yellow color and a full floral aroma when ripe
_____ 7. Rhubarb	g. Appear to be dried, but are actually fresh fruits cultivated since ancient times
_____ 8. Plantains	h. Unpleasant to eat raw, but great for flavoring savory foods and sweets
_____ 9. Star fruits	i. Light to dark red and so acidic they are rarely eaten uncooked
_____ 10. Pomegranates	j. Larger than but not as sweet as bananas; often cooked as a starchy vegetable
_____ 11. Cranberries	k. A vegetable that is prepared as a fruit, using lots of sugar to offset its tart flavor
_____ 12. Nectarines	l. A sour Japanese citrus fruit
_____ 13. Dragon fruit	m. A peach variety with smooth skin
_____ 14. Yuzu	n. Its concentrated juice is made into grenadine syrup
_____ 15. Montmorency cherries	o. Tart flavor, red fruit, usually cooked

25E. Chapter Review

For each statement, circle either True or False to indicate the correct answer. If an answer is false, then explain why.

1. Carryover cooking occurs with fruit.
   True   False _____

2. The two primary methods of juicing are pressure and blending.
   True   False _____

3. Sulfur dioxide is added to dried fruits to maintain their flavor during storage.
   True   False _____

4. Freezing is the best method of preserving the fresh appearance of fruit.
   True   False _____

5. The highest grade of fruit is U.S. No 1.
   True   False _____

6. Pineapples don't ripen after picking.
   True   False _____

7. Irradiation maintains fruit's flavor and texture while slowing the ripening process.
   True   False _____

8. Papayas are also known as carambola.
   True   False _____

9. Tropical fruit flavors complement rich or spicy meat, fish, and poultry dishes.
   True   False _____

10. Papayas are ripe when a greater proportion of the skin is yellow rather than green.
    True   False _____

11. Red Delicious apples are good for making pies.
    True   False _____

12. Stone fruits such as mangoes are commonly dried or made into liqueurs and brandies.
    True   False _____

13. Nutritionally speaking, fruits are low in protein and fat, high in fiber, and a good source of energy.
    True   False _____

14. Meat tenderizers often contain enzymes similar to those found naturally in the seeds of kiwis, papayas, and passion fruit.
    True   False _____

15. Fresh fruits are sold by weight or count.
    True   False _____

16. Although canning makes fruit's texture soft, it has little or no effect on vitamins A, B, C, and D.
    True   False _____

17. Fruits laid in a pan and sprinkled with a strudel topping and then baked are called cobblers.
    True   False _____

18. Raspberries, blueberries, and strawberries are often picked before they are fully ripe in order to extend shipping time.
    True   False _____

19. A fruit should be refrigerated in order to retard ripening once it has been harvested.
    True   False _____

20. Peaches with the stone removed are excellent as a "container" to be stuffed and baked.
    True   False _____

21. Continuing to plant heirloom varieties is important in order to maintain a food supply with genetic diversity.
    True   False _____

22. Dried fruits retain 16 to 26 percent residual moisture, which makes them susceptible to becoming moldy in humid weather if exposed to air.
    True   False _____

23. Chefs need not worry about washing organically grown fruits before preparation because they're grown all naturally, without pesticides.
    True   False _____

25F.   Putting It All Together

Provide a short response for each of the following questions. These questions are designed to help you connect the bigger concepts presented in this chapter and/or text.

1.   Citrus juices are often added to marinades and add great flavor, but how can they help preserve food or at least slow bacterial growth?

2.   In most cases, what is the most nutritiously beneficial way to consume fruits? Why?

3.   What is the big deal about heirloom varieties of fruit, and will chefs eventually get back to using more readily available produce?

Chapter 26

SANDWICHES

TEST YOUR KNOWLEDGE

The practice sets provided here have been designed to test your comprehension of the information in this chapter. It is recommended that you read the chapter completely before attempting these questions.

26A. Terminology

Fill in each blank space with the correct definition.

1. Hot closed sandwich _____

2. Hot open-faced sandwich _____

3. Cold closed sandwich _____

4. Cold open-faced sandwich _____

5. Club _____

6. Panini _____

7. Tea sandwich _____

8. Gyro _____

9. BLT _____

10. French dip _____

26B. Short Answer

Provide a short response that correctly answers each of the following questions.

1. The cardinal rule of food handling is, "Keep hot foods _____ and keep cold foods _____."

2. Most sandwich fillings contain ingredients high in the micronutrient _____ , and therefore they are especially prone to causing food-borne illness if not handled properly and stored at appropriate temperatures.

3. Although we tend to blame the dirty cutting board or slicer, the deadliest source of cross-contamination in the kitchen is human _____ because nothing is moved from one place to the next without them.

4. The three principal sandwich spreads are vegetable _____ , _____ , and _____ .

5. Tuna salad (as a filling for a sandwich) is an example of a _____ salad.

6. Pizza is an example of a(n) _____-_____ hot sandwich.

7. Name and describe the three (3) steps for sandwich preparation.

   a. _____

   b. _____

   c. _____

8. Explain what kind of grilled sandwiches have become particularly popular in recent years.

   _____

   _____

26C. Multiple Choice

For each of the following, choose the one correct response.

1. The purpose of a sandwich spread is to add:

   a. flavor.
   b. color.
   c. texture.
   d. mouth feel.

2. Which of the following is **not** a sandwich filling?

   a. cheese
   b. shellfish
   c. vegetable purée
   d. eggs

3. A Monte Cristo sandwich is an example of which of the following types of sandwiches?

   a. wrap
   b. hot open-faced
   c. multidecker
   d. deep-fried

4. Which of the following is an example of a hot open-faced sandwich?

   a. pizza
   b. quesadillas
   c. tacos
   d. tea sandwiches

5. Which of the following is **not** an important consideration when choosing bread for a sandwich?

   a. Dense breads are easier to slice.
   b. The bread should be fresh and flavorful.
   c. Overly crusty breads are harder to eat.
   d. Texture should withstand moisture from fillings and spreads.

26D. Matching

Match each regional American sandwich name in List A with the appropriate description in List B. Each choice in List B may be used only once.

	List A		List B
_____	1. Hoagie	a.	Sandwich soaked in gravy
_____	2. Grinder	b.	New England sandwich that is a workout for the jaw
_____	3. Po' boy	c.	Name given to a huge sandwich by a food journalist
_____	4. Hero	d.	Sandwich made in a plancha
_____	5. Muffuletta	e.	Sandwich from Philadelphia
		f.	Round sandwich whose bread is coated with a garlicky green-olive spread

26E. Chapter Review

For each statement, circle either True or False to indicate the correct answer. If an answer is false, then explain why.

1. Vegetable purées provide a barrier to prevent the bread from getting soggy.
   True   False _____

2. A club sandwich is an example of a multidecker sandwich.
   True   False _____

3. Chicken salad is an example of a spread.
   True   False _____

4. Tea sandwiches are a small version of a cold closed sandwich.
   True   False _____

5. Sandwich ingredients should be covered to prevent dehydration.
   True   False _____

6. Hamburgers are usually served closed so that the burger stays warm.
   True   False _____

7. An example of a cold open-faced sandwich is a bagel with lox and cream cheese.
   True   False _____

8. A gyro is made by placing a ground beef patty with grilled onion and cheese between two slices of buttered rye bread.
   True   False _____

9. Ingredients for sandwiches should always be stored at room temperature.
   True   False _____

10. A Reuben contains sliced roast beef, Swiss cheese, sauerkraut, and mustard or Thousand Island dressing on rye bread.
    True   False _____

11. Because sandwiches are often served cold (ready to eat) and/or contain potentially hazardous foods, the chef should wear gloves during the final plating process to prevent cross-contamination.
True   False _____

26F. Putting It All Together

Provide a short response for each of the following questions. These questions are designed to help you connect the bigger concepts presented in this chapter and/or text.

1.   What modifications can a chef perform to make a sandwich more nutritionally sound? When answering, consider recommended portion sizes and nutritional values of various ingredients commonly used in sandwiches.

2.   What should chefs packing sandwiches "to go" for guests be aware of regarding food safety?

Chapter 27

CHARCUTERIE

TEST YOUR KNOWLEDGE

The practice sets provided here have been designed to test your comprehension of the information found in this chapter. It is recommended that you read this chapter completely before attempting these questions.

27A. Terminology

Fill in each blank space with the correct definition.

1. Forcemeat _____

2. Dominant meat _____

3. Canadian bacon _____

4. Collagen casings _____

5. Pâté spice _____

6. Liver terrines _____

7. Smoker _____

8. Country-style forcemeats _____

9. Prosciutto _____

10. Cold smoking _____

11. Fat _____

12. Vegetable terrines _____

13. Panada _____

14. Mousse _____

15. Common bacon _____

16. Foie gras terrines _____

17. Hot smoking _____

18. Chopped chicken liver _____

19. Mousseline forcemeats _____

20. Curing salt _____

21. Dried or hard sausages _____

22. Boneless or formed hams _____

23. Westphalian ham _____

24. Fresh sausages _____

25. Basic forcemeats _____

26. Smoked and cooked sausages _____

27. Pâté _____

28. Country ham _____

29. Natural casings _____

30. Terrines _____

31. Pâtés en croûte _____

32. Fresh ham _____

33. Pancetta _____

34. Galantine _____

35. Brawns or aspic terrines _____

36. Rillette _____

37. Confit _____

38. Ballotine _____

39. Aspic _____

40. Emulsification _____

27B. Short Answer

Provide a short response that correctly answers each of the following questions.

1. Name three (3) kinds of forcemeat that can be used to make a pâté en croûte.

   a. _____

   b. _____

   c. _____

2. What steps can be taken if a forcemeat won't emulsify while preparing it in a warm kitchen?

   _____

   _____

3. Compare and contrast a galantine and a ballotine.

   Galantine   **Ballotine**

   a. _____   _____

   b. _____   _____

   c. _____   _____

   d. _____   _____

   e. _____   _____

   f. _____   _____

4. What are three (3) steps one can take to ensure proper emulsification of a forcemeat?

   a. _____

   b. _____

   c. _____

5. List five (5) reasons to use an aspic jelly.

   a. _____

   b. _____

   c. _____

   d. _____

   e. _____

27C. Multiple Choice

For each of the following, choose the one correct response.

1. When making a forcemeat, ingredients as well as equipment should be kept at what temperature throughout preparation?

   a. below 41°F
   b. as cold as possible
   c. room temperature, but not to exceed 60°F
   d. 43°F–45°F

2. Which of the following is **false** about salt curing?

   a. It inhibits bacterial growth.
   b. It dehydrates the food.
   c. It is quick and easy.
   d. It can take the place of cooking.

3. Meat-based galantines, terrines, and pâtés en croûte should be cooked to an internal temperature of:

   a. 145°F.
   b. 125°F.
   c. 150°F.
   d. 160°F.

4. When meats are cold smoked, what process is usually performed before the smoking?

   a. salt curing and brining
   b. trimming
   c. barding
   d. marinating

5. What gives ham, bacon, and other smoked meats their pink color?

   a. Red Dye #7 is added during the curing process.
   b. The meat is cooked to medium-rare.
   c. Smoking, when done slowly, maintains the natural color of meats.
   d. Nitrites are added to the cure.

6. Which of the following statements is **false** about a panada?

   a. It aids in emulsification.
   b. It adds significant flavor.
   c. It should not make up more than 20 percent of the forcemeat.
   d. It is a binder.

7. A chef preparing a batch of Pâté Spice has determined that she needs a total of 26.85 ounces. The conversion factor would be:

   a. 3.0.
   b. 2.86.
   c. 3.5.
   d. 3.37.

8. Which of the following would **not** be an appropriate garnish for a forcemeat?

    a. whole, shelled, and toasted pistachios
    b. ground pork
    c. brunoise carrot
    d. bâtonnet of tongue

9. A classically prepared aspic would include all of the following **except**:

    a. a strongly flavored meat stock.
    b. fortification with gelatin.
    c. clarification.
    d. an acid ingredient to balance flavor.

10. A chef wants to produce 3.75 pounds of Dough for Pâté, a recipe chapter. Based on the following information, what would be the ingredient cost?

    A.P. flour: $0.30 per pound   Shortening: $0.78 per pound
    Salt: $0.05 per ounce   Eggs: $1.00 per dozen

    a. flour: $0.60; shortening: $0.68; salt: $0.03; egg: $0.16
    b. flour: $0.30; shortening: $0.34; salt: $0.01; egg: $0.08
    c. flour: $0.45; shortening: $0.34; salt: $0.02; egg: $0.16
    d. flour: $0.75; shortening: $0.88; salt: $0.03; egg: $0.20

27D. Matching

Match each term in List A with the appropriate definition in List B. Each choice in List B can be used only once.

List A

_____ 1. Mousse
_____ 2. Country-style forcemeat
_____ 3. Brawn
_____ 4. Forcemeat

_____ 5. Mousseline forcemeat

_____ 6. Pâté en croûte

_____ 7. Galantine

_____ 8. Quenelle

_____ 9. Terrine

List B

a. Pâté cooked in pastry dough
b. A cooked, light, airy, delicately flavored forcemeat
c. A poached dumpling of mousseline forcemeat
d. Meat, fish, or poultry, bound, seasoned, with or without garnishes
e. A terrine made from highly simmered gelatinous cuts of meat, wine, and flavoring
f. A purée of fully cooked meats, poultry, game, fish, shellfish, or vegetables, lightened with cream and bound with aspic
g. A whole poultry item boned, stuffed, and reshaped, poached and served cold
h. A deboned, stuffed poultry leg, poached or braised and usually served hot
i. A hearty, highly seasoned, coarse-textured forcemeat
j. A coarse forcemeat cooked in an earthenware mold

27E. Chapter Review

For each statement, circle either True or False to indicate the correct answer. If an answer is false, then explain why.

1. It is possible to make a vegetable mousseline forcemeat.
    True   False _____

2. The best type of mold to use to make a pâté en croûte is a metal loaf pan.
    True   False _____

3. Sausages are forcemeat stuffed into casings.
    True   False _____

4. Béchamel sauce is used as a primary binding agent in most styles of forcemeats.
    True   False _____

5. Pork bellies are usually made into bacon.
    True   False _____

6. When marinating forcemeat ingredients before grinding, the trend today is to marinate them for longer periods to kill bacteria.
    True   False _____

7. Galantines are always served cold.
    True   False _____

8. Any type of forcemeat can be used to make a terrine.
    True   False _____

9. A fresh ham is made from the hog's shoulder.
    True   False _____

10. If testing a forcemeat's texture shows that it is too firm, a little egg white should be added to fix the problem.
    True   False _____

11. A mousseline forcemeat can be served hot or cold.
    True   False _____

12. Only hams made in rural areas can be called country hams; all others must be called country-style hams.
    True   False _____

13. Chopped chicken liver has a longer shelf life than a rillette.
    True   False _____

14. Brining and pickling are the same procedure.
    True   False _____

15. The stock used to make sauce chaud-froid often determines the color and flavor of the sauce.
    True   False _____

16. Forcemeats, both raw and cooked, are considered potentially hazardous food products.
    True   False _____

17. A vegetable mousse should be cooked to a minimum internal temperature of 145°F.
    True   False _____

18. Using the traditional ratio for types of meat used in a forcemeat, the mixture should contain 2.6 pounds of venison and 1.3 pounds of pork.
    True   False _____

19. Smithfield and prosciutto hams are not actually cooked before consumption.
    True   False _____

20. Jamón Serrano is a salt-cured and air-dried (unsmoked) mountain ham from Spain.
    True   False _____

21. Pork products are the only meats that were classically cured.
    True   False _____

27F. Putting It All Together

Provide a short response for each of the following questions. These questions are designed to help you connect the bigger concepts presented in this chapter and/or text.

1. Take a look at the list of ingredients in the chapter recipe for basic forcemeat: meat, eggs, seasonings, and so on. Looking at the whole list while thinking back to Chapter 13, Beef, what other common recipe contains similar ingredients but perhaps in different quantities?

2. Review the paragraph in this chapter that discusses panadas. What other recipes/preparations other than forcemeats can you think of that use a panada to enhance smoothness of the final product?

Chapter 28

HORS D'OEUVRE AND CANAPÉS

TEST YOUR KNOWLEDGE

The practice sets provided here have been designed to test your comprehension of the information found in this chapter. It is recommended that you read the chapter completely before attempting these questions.

28A. Terminology

Fill in each blank space with the correct definition.

1. Brochettes _____

2. Canapé

    a. Base _____

    b. Spread _____

    c. Garnish _____

3. Barquette _____

4. Tartlet _____

5. Profiterole _____

6. Crudité _____

7. Sushi _____

8. Sashimi _____

9. Rumaki _____

10. Wonton skins _____

11. Bruschetta _____

12. Nori _____

28B. Short Answer

For questions 1–8, describe the following attributes of each type of caviar:

    a. Price
    b. Source
    c. Consistency

1. Beluga caviar

    a. _____

    b. _____

    c. _____

2. Osetra caviar

    a. _____

    b. _____

    c. _____

3. Sevruga caviar

    a. _____

    b. _____

    c. _____

4. Pressed caviar

    a. _____

    b. _____

    c. _____

5. American sturgeon caviar

    a. _____

    b. _____

    c. _____

6. Golden whitefish caviar

    a. _____

    b. _____

    c. _____

7. Lumpfish caviar

   a. _____

   b. _____

   c. _____

8. Salmon caviar

   a. _____

   b. _____

   c. _____

9. List the three (3) main ingredients found in sushi.

   a. _____

   b. _____

   c. _____

10. List the four (4) guidelines for preparing hors d'oeuvre.

   a. _____

   b. _____

   c. _____

   d. _____

11. List six (6) canapé spreads and an appropriate garnish for each.

   a. _____

   b. _____

   c. _____

   d. _____

   e. _____

   f. _____

12. Name and describe four (4) seasonings used in making sushi rice.

    a. _____

    b. _____

    c. _____

    d. _____

13. Briefly describe the six (6) guidelines for preparing appetizers.

    a. _____

    b. _____

    c. _____

    d. _____

    e. _____

    f. _____

14. List the three (3) guidelines for preparing canapé spreads.

    a. _____

    b. _____

    c. _____

15. Describe the three (3) factors that indicate the freshness of caviar.

    a. _____

    b. _____

    c. _____

28C. Multiple Choice

For each of the following, choose the one correct response.

1. At what temperature is caviar best stored?

   a. 34°F
   b. 30°F
   c. 35°F
   d. 32°F

2. Caviar connoisseurs prefer to serve the delicacy in containers made of:

   a. glass.
   b. china.
   c. metal.
   d. plastic.

3. Which of the following fish is **not** used to make sushi?

   a. ahi tuna
   b. flounder
   c. sea bass
   d. salmon

4. Rice wine is also known as:

   a. wasabi.
   b. mirin.
   c. shoyu.
   d. nori.

5. When making brochettes as appetizers, all of the following should be considered **except**:

   a. the skewer should be 4 to 8 inches long.
   b. the brochettes should be served with a dipping sauce.
   c. the main ingredients should be carefully cut into consistent sizes and shapes.
   d. enough skewer should be left exposed so diners can pick up the brochettes easily.

28D. Fill in the Blank

Fill in each blank space with the response that correctly completes the statement.

1. Small skewers holding a combination of meat, poultry, game, fish, or vegetables are called
   _____.

2. Wontons can be steamed but are more often fried in one of two ways: _____-
   _____ or _____-_____.

3. The recommended number of hors d'oeuvre served before a meal is _____ to
   _____ pieces per person at an hour-long cocktail reception. However, if they are being
   served alone with no meal following, then _____ to _____ pieces per person
   per hour will probably be needed.

4. The key to good sushi is the freshness of the fish, which should be no more than _____ day(s) out of the water.

5. _____, made from a mixture of ground beef, veal, pork, or poultry (as well as seasonings and a panada) and covered with a sauce, are a popular hot hors d'oeuvre, particularly on a buffet.

6. _____ _____ is a recipe found in this chapter that is a good example of an hors d'oeuvre served en brochette.

28E. Matching

Match each sushi ingredient in List A with the appropriate description in List B. Each choice in List B can be used only once.

	List A		List B
_____	1. Nori	a.	Japanese soy sauce, which is lighter and more delicate than the Chinese variety
_____	2. Wasabi	b.	Fresh ginger pickled in vinegar
_____	3. Shoyu	c.	A strong aromatic root, purchased as a green powder; it is sometimes called horseradish but is no relation
_____	4. Zushi	d.	A dried seaweed used to add flavor and to contain the rolled rice and other ingredients
		e.	Sushi rice that has been mixed with vinegar, sugar, and seasonings

28F. Chapter Review

For each statement, circle either True or False to indicate the correct answer. If an answer is false, then explain why.

1. An appetizer is usually served before lunch.
    True   False _____

2. Frozen caviar should be used only as a garnish.
    True   False _____

3. Most refrigerators are warmer than 32°F, and therefore caviar should be stored on ice.
    True   False _____

4. Caviar should be served in a stainless steel bowl because such a container keeps it cooler.
    True   False _____

5. The primary purpose of spreading the canapé base with butter is to add flavor.
    True   False _____

6. Canapés are best stored overnight in the refrigerator before service.
    True   False _____

7. The best-quality caviar is always the most expensive.
    True   False _____

8. If properly handled, fresh caviar will last up to 2 weeks before opening.
   True   False _____

9. Sushi is prepared by adding rice wine and other seasonings to long-grain rice.
   True   False _____

10. Fruits de Mer en Bouchée is a convenient hot hors d'oeuvre to serve because it has a long holding time.
    True   False _____

11. Rumaki is a hot hors d'oeuvre that uses the barding method.
    True   False _____

12. Phyllo dough is a French puff pastry that rises into a thick, yet light crust to surround whatever filling is inside the hors d'oeuvre.
    True   False _____

13. Regardless of how or when hors d'oeuvre are served, attractive preparation and display are vital guidelines to follow.
    True   False _____

14. Hot hors d'oeuvre can be displayed on trays or platters, providing they are replaced frequently to ensure they stay hot.
    True   False _____

15. Hors d'oeuvre are typically presented on platters in preparation for either passing by service staff or placement on a buffet.
    True   False _____

28G. Putting It All Together

Provide a short response for each of the following questions. These questions are designed to help you connect the bigger concepts presented in this chapter and/or text.

1. What food safety precautions does the chef need to take when preparing and serving large quantities of hot hors d'oeuvre such as stuffed, fried wontons and rumaki for a cocktail party that will last 2 hours?

2. A chef is preparing a brunch buffet that will be open for a total of 4 hours on Sunday morning. She is considering including a display of sushi (previously prepared) on the buffet. What precautions should she take?

Chapter 29

PRINCIPLES OF THE BAKESHOP

TEST YOUR KNOWLEDGE

The practice sets provided here have been designed to test your comprehension of the information found in this chapter. It is recommended that you read this chapter completely before attempting these questions.

29A. Terminology

Fill in each blank space with the correct definition.

1. Conching _____

2. Tapioca _____

3. All-purpose flour _____

4. Dough _____

5. Gluten _____

6. Hygroscopic _____

7. Cooked syrups _____

8. Chocolate liquor _____

9. Bleached flour _____

10. Granulated sugar _____

11. Nib _____

12. Molasses _____

13. Sugar syrup _____

14. Emulsions _____

15. Vanillin _____

16. Cocoa powder _____

17. Fermentation _____

18. Extracts _____

19. Turbinado sugar _____

20. Gelatinization _____

21. Gianduja _____

22. Sucrose _____

23. Refined/table sugar _____

24. Raw sugar _____

25. Bloom (related to gelatin) _____

26. Simple syrup _____

27. Interferents _____

28. Mixing methods _____

29. Chocolate mass _____

30. Gelatin _____

31. Starch retrogradation _____

32. Batter _____

33. Cocoa butter _____

34. Couverture _____

35. Friable _____

36. Weak (or soft) flour _____

37. Strong (or hard) flour _____

38. Composite flour _____

39. Wheat germ _____

40. Vital wheat gluten _____

41. Sugarcane _____

42. Rye flour _____

43. Cornstarch _____

44. Arrowroot _____

45. Fat bloom _____

46. Sugar bloom _____

47. Formula _____

29B. Matching

Match each term in List A with the appropriate description in List B. Each choice in List B can be used only once.

List A

_____ 1. Blending
_____ 2. Cutting
_____ 3. Sifting
_____ 4. Whipping
_____ 5. Folding
_____ 6. Creaming
_____ 7. Beating
_____ 8. Kneading
_____ 9. Stirring

List B

a. Using a spoon or electric mixer with paddle attachment
b. Using a whisk or electric mixer with whip attachment
c. Using a rubber spatula
d. Using a spoon, rubber spatula, whisk, or electric mixer with paddle attachment
e. Using an electric mixer with paddle attachment on medium speed
f. Using a rotary or drum sifter or mesh strainer
g. Using a whisk, spoon, or rubber spatula
h. Using a flat cake spatula or metal spatula
i. Using pastry cutters, fingers, or an electric mixer with paddle attachment
j. Using hands or an electric mixer with dough hook attachment

29C. Multiple Choice

For each of the following, choose the correct response(s).

1. All fats are considered shortenings in baking because they tenderize the product and:

    a. leaven it.
    b. strengthen the gluten strands.
    c. give good color.
    d. shorten the gluten strands.

2. Composite flours are:

    a. made from corn, soybeans, and rice.
    b. categorized as nonwheat flours.
    c. naturally high in protein.
    d. made with the bran intact.

3. Sanding sugar is primarily used for:

    a. a granulated sugar substitute.
    b. making light, tender cakes.
    c. decorating cookies and pastries.
    d. making icings and glazes for decorating.

4. The most frequently used and therefore the most important ingredient in the bakeshop is:

    a. granulated sugar.
    b. wheat flour.
    c. shortening.
    d. yeast.

5. Whole-wheat flour, which includes the bran and germ, is also called:

   a. wheat germ.
   b. composite flour.
   c. whole flour.
   d. graham flour.

6. Which of the following is **false** about the role of sugar and sweeteners in the bakeshop?

   a. They act as a crisping agent.
   b. They act as a preservative.
   c. They tenderize products.
   d. They act as a creaming agent.

7. Which of the following factors in a dough or batter cause the rise, which determines the baked good's final texture?

   a. temperature, sugar, yeast
   b. protein, gluten, strands
   c. glutenin, gliadin, water
   d. carbon dioxide, air, steam

8. 160°F is the temperature at which gluten, dairy, and egg proteins:

   a. brown.
   b. soften.
   c. crystallize.
   d. solidify.

9. Which statement is **false** about cooked sugars?

   a. As sugars caramelize, their sweetening power decreases.
   b. As water evaporates, the temperature of the sugar rises.
   c. As sugars caramelize, their sweetening power increases.
   d. The sugar's temperature indicates its concentration.

10. A change in a baked good's texture and starch granule structure results in:

    a. staling.
    b. browning.
    c. leavening.
    d. gluten development.

11. _____ is the brown powder left after the _____ is (are) removed.

    a. Unsweetened chocolate; sugar
    b. Cocoa powder; sugar
    c. Milk chocolate; dairy solids
    d. Cocoa powder; cocoa butter

12. Which of the following are grades of sugar?

    a. U.S. Grade No. 1, No. 2, No. 3, No. 4
    b. there are no government standards regulating grade labels
    c. U.S. Grade Extra Fancy, Fancy, Good, Standard
    d. U.S. Superior Grade, Standard Grade, Good Grade

13. The purpose of a hydrometer is to:

    a.   measure specific gravity and degrees of concentration.
    b.   show the temperature of sugar syrups.
    c.   determine doneness.
    d.   measure the amounts of sugar needed in sugar syrups.

14. Which of the following statements regarding measuring ingredients is **false**?

    a.   Most foods do not weigh their volume.
    b.   Baking formulas usually use weight as the primary means of measure.
    c.   Spring scales are most commonly used for measuring in the bakeshop.
    d.   Precise, accurate measurement of ingredients is vital in the bakeshop.

15. Which **two** of the following products do **not** contain chocolate products?

    a.   white chocolate truffles with Grand Marnier
    b.   Nestlé's Toll House cookies with semisweet chocolate chips
    c.   a Hershey's milk chocolate bar with almonds
    d.   a chocolate-flavored solid chocolate Easter bunny

29D. Short Answer

Provide a short response that correctly answers each of the following questions.

1.   List six (6) important steps to follow when melting chocolate.

    a. _____

    b. _____

    c. _____

    d. _____

    e. _____

    f. _____

2.   List four (4) differences between unsweetened (baking) and bittersweet/semisweet chocolate.

Unsweetened	**Bittersweet/Semisweet**
a. _____	_____
b. _____	_____
c. _____	_____
d. _____	_____

3. Name three (3) characteristics achieved by tempering chocolate.

a. _____

b. _____

c. _____

4. List five (5) types of equipment used specifically in the bakeshop.

a. _____   d. _____

b. _____   e. _____

c. _____

5. What two (2) things can prevent the development of gluten in a recipe, thus making it less elastic?

a. _____

b. _____

29E. Chapter Review

For each statement, circle either True or False to indicate the correct answer. If an answer is false, then explain why.

1. Self-rising flour is bread flour with salt and baking powder added to it.
   True   False _____

2. Glutenin and gliadin contain the gluten necessary to create a quality dough or batter.
   True   False _____

3. Chocolate as we know it today did not exist in Europe until Columbus brought the first cacao beans back to Spain from the New World.
   True   False _____

4. Unsweetened chocolate is pure hardened cocoa butter.
   True   False _____

5. Most white chocolate products are not made from cocoa beans because they substitute vegetable oils for cocoa butter.
   True   False _____

6. Chocolate will melt just below body temperature.
   True   False _____

7. Gluten provides structure in dough by enabling the gases from fermentation to be retained.
   True   False _____

8. Flour derived from the portion of the endosperm closest to the germ is coarser.
   True   False _____

9. Whole-wheat flours have a shorter shelf life because their higher fat content causes them to go rancid.
   True   False _____

10. Unopened bags of flour can be stored anywhere as long as the location is relatively cool and free of moisture.
    True   False _____

11. Beets and sugarcane are the two main sources of sugar.
    True   False _____

12. Unsalted butter is usually preferred to salted butter in baking strictly because the salt may interfere with the product formula.
    True   False _____

13. The concept of carryover baking is similar to carryover cooking.
    True   False _____

14. A batter generally contains more fat, sugar, and liquid than dough.
    True   False _____

15. Fats are like other bakeshop ingredients in that they will combine completely with liquids.
    True   False _____

16. Shortenings are versatile and therefore oils may be substituted for solid shortening, regardless of what the recipe suggests.
    True   False _____

17. Granulated and sheet gelatin may be used interchangeably in a formula, provided that the same weight of both ingredients is used.
    True   False _____

18. If vanilla beans develop a white coating while in storage, they have become contaminated with mold and should not be used.
    True   False _____

19. Milk chocolate chips may be substituted for semisweet chocolate chips when making chocolate chip cookies.
    True   False _____

20. All countries use similar refining processes for chocolate, and therefore there is little difference in the resulting texture.
    True   False _____

21. The real definition of a nut is the edible, single-seed kernel of a fruit surrounded by a hard shell.
    True   False _____

22. There are several types of bakeshop ovens to choose from, including convection, conventional, and steam injected.
    True   False _____

29F. Putting It All Together

Provide a short response for each of the following questions. These questions are designed to help you connect the bigger concepts presented in this chapter and/or text.

1. Most everyone is familiar with the dense, chewy texture of a bagel. Without looking up a recipe, use your newfound knowledge regarding flour and gluten and your experiences eating bagels to determine what kind of flour is used in many bagel formulas.

2. A guest comes into your restaurant and informs your pastry chef that she is allergic to wheat. Your pastry chef really wants to make an impression on the guest by providing her with a wheat-free dessert option. Based on your knowledge of composite flours and your understanding of allergies from Chapter 23, Healthy Cooking, is your pastry chef correct in assuming that she can simply make an ingredient substitute by replacing the all-purpose flour in her chocolate chip cookie recipe with composite flour?

Chapter 30

QUICK BREADS

TEST YOUR KNOWLEDGE

The practice sets provided here have been designed to test your comprehension of the information found in this chapter. It is recommended that you read the chapter completely before attempting these questions.

30A. Terminology

Fill in each blank space with the correct definition.

1. Streusel _____

2. Biscuit method _____

3. Single-acting baking powder _____

4. Creaming method _____

5. Tunneling _____

6. Muffin method _____

7. Double-acting baking powder _____

8. Sodium bicarbonate _____

9. Acid _____

10. Base _____

11. Baking ammonia _____

30B. Short Answer

Provide a short response that correctly answers each of the following questions.

1. Suggest a reason why muffins might have a soapy or bitter taste.

    _____

2. Why might a recipe call for both baking soda and baking powder?

    _____

    _____

3. What situation might call for the use of double-acting baking powder?

    _____

4. What does the higher fat content in the creaming method do to the gluten in the mixture and therefore to the texture of the final product?

_____

_____

5. Explain why the fat is softened in recipes using the creaming method.

_____

_____

6. Suggest a reason for elongated holes running through the center of baked muffins.

_____

7. What is the basic difference between a scone and a biscuit?

_____

_____

8. List three (3) products that result from using the biscuit method of mixing.

    a. _____

    b. _____

    c. _____

30C. Chapter Review

For each statement, circle either True or False to indicate the correct answer. If an answer is false, then explain why.

1. Bread flour is used to make biscuits.
    True   False _____

2. The creaming method is comparable to the mixing method.
    True   False _____

3. Honey, molasses, fresh fruit, and buttermilk are all examples of acids that may be used with baking soda.
    True   False _____

4. Baking powder requires an acid ingredient in the formula in order to create the chemical reaction.
    True   False _____

5. Some quick breads use yeast as the leavening agent.
    True   False _____

6. Too much kneading toughens biscuits.
    True   False _____

7. Fats used in the muffin method should be in a solid form.
    True   False   _____

8. The reason for a flat top on a loaf of banana bread is probably that the leavening agent was not sufficiently strong.
    True   False   _____

9. When carbon dioxide is trapped within a batter or dough, it expands when heated, causing the product to rise.
    True   False   _____

10. Batters and dough made with single-acting baking powder do not need to be baked immediately, as long as the product is refrigerated immediately.
    True   False   _____

11. In order for baking soda to leaven it, a batter or dough must be baked.
    True   False   _____

12. Shortcakes are made using the muffin method.
    True   False   _____

13. The biscuit method of mixing results in flaky, tender products particularly because of the way the chilled solid fat is cut into the other ingredients.
    True   False   _____

14. A muffin batter has a different composition from a quick-bread batter and therefore must be baked in a different way.
    True   False   _____

15. Liquid fat and the general mixing procedure used in the muffin mixing method generally results in a cakelike baked product.
    True   False   _____

16. *Makeup* refers to the method by which the ingredients are combined to make the batter of the quick bread.
    True   False   _____

30D. Putting It All Together

Provide a short response for each of the following questions. These questions are designed to help you connect the bigger concepts presented in this chapter and/or text.

1. Turn to the recipe for Blueberry Muffins and study it. At the end of the recipe, the author makes some recommendations for substituting ingredients that flavor the muffin. Why do you think the Pecan Spice Muffins call for only 4 ounces of pecans while the Blueberry Muffins call for 5 ounces of blueberries?

2. Think back to the last time you had a dessert with streusel topping and how crumbly it was. Now look at the recipe for Streusel Topping; study the ingredients and make an educated guess about why it has that texture, based on observing either the ingredients listed or the ratio in which they are used in the recipe.

Chapter 31

YEAST BREADS

TEST YOUR KNOWLEDGE

The practice sets provided here have been designed to test your comprehension of the information found in this chapter. It is recommended that you read the chapter completely before attempting these questions.

31A. Terminology

Fill in each blank space with the correct definition.

1. Fermentation _____

2. Punch down _____

3. Straight dough method _____

4. Oven spring _____

5. Slashing or docking _____

6. Fresh yeast _____

7. Wash _____

8. Sponge method _____

9. Proof box _____

10. Rolled-in doughs _____

11. Rounding _____

12. Proofing _____

13. Quick-rise dry yeast _____

14. Absorb (in relation to scaling) _____

15. Bulk fermentation _____

16. Couche _____

17. Banneton _____

18. Brotform _____

19. Scoring _____

20. Leavening _____

21. Baker's yeast _____

22. Sourdough _____

23. Natural starter _____

24. Sponge _____

25. Fresh yeast _____

31B. Multiple Choice

For each of the following, choose the one correct response.

1. Which is an example of a rich dough?

   a. biscuits
   b. Italian bread
   c. challah bread
   d. muffins

2. Quick-rise dry yeast uses water at what temperature in order to activate the fermentation process?

   a. 138°F
   b. 95°F
   c. 100°F–110°F
   d. 125°F–130°F

3. When yeast is combined with carbohydrates, the result is alcohol and:

   a. oxygen.
   b. gas.
   c. carbon dioxide.
   d. water.

4. What is the disadvantage of using butter in rolled-in doughs?

   a. It has a high moisture content.
   b. It cracks and breaks.
   c. It adds too much salt to the dough.
   d. It needs to be clarified before using.

5. Yeast products should be cooled to approximately what temperature?

   a. 32°F–34°F
   b. 60°F–70°F
   c. 45°F–50°F
   d. 80°F–90°F

6. Which of the following is **not** important when considering the amount of flour used in a yeast bread?

   a. the percentage of salt in the formula
   b. flour storage conditions
   c. the humidity level
   d. accuracy in measuring other ingredients

7. Commercial baking yeast was **not** made available in stores until:

    a. 1654.
    b. 1857.
    c. 1910.
    d. 1868.

8. There are primarily two market forms of bakers' yeast:

    a. compressed yeast and active dry yeast.
    b. brewer's yeast and compressed yeast.
    c. quick-rise dry yeast and instant yeast.
    d. fresh yeast and compressed yeast.

9. What is the primary chemical function of rounding?

    a. smooth the dough into round balls
    b. stretch the gluten into a smooth coating
    c. help retain the gases from fermentation
    d. proof the dough

10. At what point in the production sequence is the dough punched down?

    a. after initial fermentation
    b. after proofing
    c. during proofing
    d. after initial mixing of dough

31C. Short Answer

Provide a short response that correctly answers each of the following questions.

1. Explain the two (2) steps involved in the sponge method.

    a. _____

    b. _____

2. Why is the organism in active dry yeast considered dormant?

    _____

3. List four (4) factors in determining doneness of a baked yeast-leavened product.

    a. _____

    b. _____

    c. _____

    d. _____

4. List three (3) examples of a rolled-in dough product.

    a. _____   b. _____   c. _____

5. How is the quantity of dry yeast determined when it is being substituted for compressed yeast?

   _____

6. Describe the method for producing dough using the straight dough method.

   _____

7. Briefly list the ten (10) sequential stages of yeast bread production.

   a. _____   f. _____

   b. _____   g. _____

   c. _____   h. _____

   d. _____   i. _____

   e. _____   j. _____

8. Visually examining bread is one way to determine doneness, but for the less experienced, taking an internal temperature is more accurate. Using an instant-read thermometer, provide the internal temperatures that each type of bread should reach before it is cooked throughout.

   a. Lean bread dough: _____

   b. Rich bread dough: _____

31D. Chapter Review

For each statement, circle either True or False to indicate the correct answer. If an answer is false, then explain why.

1. Punching down occurs before the proofing process.
   True   False _____

2. Salt's primary role in bread making is seasoning.
   True   False _____

3. Italian bread is an example of a product made using the straight dough method.
   True   False _____

4. Washes can be applied before or after proofing occurs.
   True   False _____

5. Underproofing may result in a sour taste, poor volume, and a paler color after baking.
   True   False _____

6. Rich doughs are baked without steam.
   True   False _____

7. When properly stored, compressed yeast has a shelf life of 2 to 3 weeks.
   True   False _____

8. Active dry yeast has a moisture content of approximately 10 percent.
    True   False   _____

9. Instant yeast can be substituted measure for measure for regular dry yeast.
    True   False   _____

10. Starters are used primarily for flavor in bread making.
    True   False   _____

11. There is very little difference between the flavors of dry and compressed yeasts.
    True   False   _____

12. Overkneading is a common problem in bread making.
    True   False   _____

13. Yeast is very sensitive to temperature and moisture and prefers temperatures between 60°F and 90°F.
    True   False   _____

14. To prepare compressed yeast for using in a formula, soften it in twice its weight of warm water at 100°F before adding it to bread dough.
    True   False   _____

15. Yeast is a living organism, and instant dry yeast will be destroyed at temperatures above 138°F.
    True   False   _____

16. Other yeasts used in baking, aside from instant dry yeast, are destroyed at temperatures above 138°F.
    True   False   _____

17. Underproofed or overproofed loaves can be fixed by putting them into the oven, where the yeast will automatically reach its maximum volume and leavening when it comes in contact with the heat.
    True   False   _____

18. The fermentation process happens in only a few hours. If a baker wants to slow down that process and extend it over 8 to 10 hours (or more) so the flavors of the bread become more complex, such as in artisan-style breads, he or she can put the dough into a piece of equipment called a retarder.
    True   False   _____

19. The doneness of bread during the baking process can be determined only by taking the internal temperature.
    True   False   _____

20. Both small-scale and industrial producers can produce artisan breads.
    True   False   _____

21. Croissants are known around the world as a famous baked good that was invented by the French, and to this day they are the one menu item people imagine being served in every Parisian sidewalk café.
    True   False   _____

31E. Putting It All Together

Provide a short response for each of the following questions. These questions are designed to help you connect the bigger concepts presented in this chapter and/or text.

1. Can someone who is allergic to wheat still eat bread? Answer the question based on your knowledge of various types of flours.

2. In everyday terms, explain how a bread dough rises, using your knowledge of yeast, flour, sugar, and liquid.

Chapter 32

PIES, PASTRIES AND COOKIES

TEST YOUR KNOWLEDGE

The practice sets provided here have been designed to test your comprehension of the information found in this chapter. It is recommended that you read the chapter completely before attempting these questions.

32A. Terminology

Fill in each blank space with the correct definition.

1. Pie dough

    a. Flaky dough (pâte brisée) _____

    b. Mealy dough _____

2. Sweet dough (pâte sucrée) _____

3. Crumb crusts _____

4. Fillings

    a. Cream filling _____

    b. Custard filling _____

    c. Chiffon _____

    d. Fruit fillings _____

        1. Cooked fruit _____

        2. Cooked juice _____

        3. Baked _____

5. Éclair paste (pâte à choux)

    a. Éclairs _____

    b. Cream puffs _____

    c. Beignets _____

    d. Paris-Brest _____

    e. Churros _____

    f. Crullers _____

6. Meringue

    a. Common _____

    b. Soft _____

    c. Hard _____

    d. Swiss meringue _____

    e. Italian meringue _____

7. Puff pastry (pâte feuilletée)

    a. Détrempe _____

    b. Bouchées _____

    c. Vol-au-vents _____

    d. Feuilletées _____

8. Cookies

    a. Icebox cookies _____

    b. Rolled/cut-out cookies _____

    c. Wafer cookies (stencil batter) _____

    d. Bar cookies _____

    e. Drop cookies _____

    f. Pressed cookies _____

32B. Short Answer

Provide a short response that correctly answers each of the following questions.

1. List three (3) types of fillings that are used to fill prebaked pie crusts.

    a. _____   b. _____   c. _____

2. List four (4) types of fillings that are appropriate for filling a crumb crust.

    a. _____   c. _____

    b. _____   d. _____

3. What two (2) types of fillings are cooked by baking them **in** a crust?

    a. _____   b. _____

4. List three (3) reasons for using a flaky dough to prepare pies.

    a. _____   c. _____

    b. _____

5. Why is a sweet dough, or pâte sucrée, better for making tarts?

_____

6. When is it appropriate to use a mealy crust?

_____

7. Why is hand mixing best when making small to moderate quantities of flaky dough?

_____

_____

8. What makes pâte à choux unique among doughs?

_____

_____

9. What determines whether a meringue is hard or soft?

_____

10. List four (4) uses for puff pastry.

a. _____   c. _____

b. _____   d. _____

11. List three (3) factors that have an effect on a cookie's texture.

a. _____

b. _____

c. _____

32C. Multiple Choice

For each of the following, choose the one correct response.

1.   What is the most common method for preparing cookie doughs?

   a.   beating
   b.   whipping
   c.   blending
   d.   creaming

2.   Which is **not** a use for pâte à choux?

   a.   profiteroles
   b.   palmiers
   c.   éclairs
   d.   Paris-Brest

3.   What do all meringues have in common?

   a.   the ratio of egg whites to sugar
   b.   whipped egg whites and sugar
   c.   the flavoring ingredient used
   d.   the method of preparation

4.   Lacy pecan cookies are a cookie variety classified as:

   a.   a pressed cookie.
   b.   an icebox cookie.
   c.   a wafer cookie.
   d.   a drop cookie.

5.   Egg whites will whip better if:

   a.   a small amount of salt is added before whipping.
   b.   they are well chilled before whipping.
   c.   a portion of the sugar is added before whipping.
   d.   they are brought to room temperature before whipping.

6.   In which of the following pie preparations is cornstarch recommended as a thickener?

   a.   when the filling is combined with large amounts of sugar
   b.   when the pie will be frozen after baking
   c.   when a custard or fruit-filled pie is being prepared
   d.   when the pie contains large quantities of an acid, such as key lime juice

32D. Chapter Review

For each statement, circle either True or False to indicate the correct answer. If an answer is false, then explain why.

1. A baked meringue containing ground nuts is called a dacquoise.
    True   False _____

2. Cherries and apples are appropriate fruits to use for a cooked juice filling.
    True   False _____

3. A cream filling is basically a flavored pastry cream.
    True   False _____

4. Pumpkin pie is a good example of a custard filling.
    True   False _____

5. The ratio for making a crumb crust is one part sugar, four parts crumbs, and two parts melted butter.
    True   False _____

6. Either rice or beans can be used for blind baking.
    True   False _____

7. Any dough can be used to make a tart shell as long as it tastes good and has a good appearance.
    True   False _____

8. Cookies can be stored for up to 1 week, usually in an airtight container at room temperature, and different kinds of cookies—both soft and hard—can be stored in the same container.
    True   False _____

9. Italian and Swiss meringues work equally well in buttercreams.
    True   False _____

10. A cooked juice filling should be combined with a raw crust and then baked.
    True   False _____

11. Baked fruit pies must be refrigerated to retard bacterial growth.
    True   False _____

12. The type of fat used in a flaky or mealy dough affects both the flavor and the flakiness.
    True   False _____

13. An American gâteau is a pastry item made with puff pastry, éclair paste, short dough, or sweet dough.
    True   False _____

14. Flour works as a good thickener in baked fruit pies in which the fruits are not excessively juicy.
    True   False _____

32E. Putting It All Together

Provide a short response for each of the following questions. These questions are designed to help you connect the bigger concepts presented in this chapter and/or text.

1. Based on your knowledge of fats and flour, what might happen to a blind-baked pie shell if stored at room temperature (wrapped) for more than 2 to 3 days?

2. What food safety issue may exist for cream-filled and custard pies, and what does that issue indicate about the shelf life?

Chapter 33

CAKES AND FROSTINGS

TEST YOUR KNOWLEDGE

The practice sets provided here have been designed to test your comprehension of the information found in this chapter. It is recommended that you read this chapter completely before attempting these questions.

33A. Terminology

Fill in each blank space with the correct definition.

1.   Creamed-fat cakes

    a.   Butter cakes/creaming method cakes _____

    b.   High-ratio cakes _____

2.   Whipped-egg cakes

    a.   Genoise _____

    b.   Spongecake _____

    c.   Angel food cake _____

    d.   Chiffon cake _____

3.   Frosting or icing

    a.   Foam (or boiled) _____

    b.   Fondant _____

        1.   Prepared _____

        2.   Rolled _____

    c.   Fudge _____

    d.   Glaze (flat or water frosting) _____

    e.   Royal (or decorator's) icing _____

    f.   Ganache _____

    g.   Buttercream _____

        1.   Simple (or American-style) buttercream _____

        2.   Italian (or meringue) buttercream _____

        3.   French (or mousseline) buttercream _____

4.   Glucose _____

5.   Side masking _____

6. Stencils _____

7. Baker's comb _____

8. Crumb coat _____

33B. Basic Cake Mixes

Describe the **basic** steps for the preparation of each of the following cakes and give a menu example of each type. Exact quantities of ingredients are not necessary for this exercise.

ex: **Chiffon Cake**

a. *Whip egg whites with a little sugar until stiff.*
b. *Add liquid ingredients, including oil, to sifted dry ingredients.*
c. *Fold in egg whites.*
d. *Bake in ungreased pan.*

Menu example: *Lemon Chiffon Cake*

1. **Butter Cake**

_____

_____

_____

_____

_____

_____

Menu example: _____

2. **Genoise Cake**

_____

_____

_____

_____

_____

_____

Menu example: _____

3. **Spongecake**

_____

_____

_____

_____

_____

Menu example: _____

4. **Angel Food Cake**

_____

_____

_____

_____

_____

Menu example: _____

33C. Matching I—Ingredients

Match each ingredient category in List A with the appropriate ingredients in List B. Each choice in List B can be used only once.

List A

_____ 1. Flavoring
_____ 2. Toughener
_____ 3. Leavener
_____ 4. Tenderizer
_____ 5. Drier
_____ 6. Moistener

List B

a. Flour, milk, eggs
b. Flour, butter, water
c. Sugar, fats, yolks
d. Flour, starches, milk solids
e. Baking powder, baking soda
f. Cocoa, chocolate, spices, sour cream
f. Water, milk, juice, eggs

33D. Matching II—Frostings

Match each frosting in List A with the appropriate ingredients in List B. Each choice in List B can be used only once.

List A	List B
_____ 1. Ganache	a. Sugar, fat, egg yolks or whites
_____ 2. Fudge	b. Uncooked confectioner's sugar and egg whites
_____ 3. Royal icing	c. Meringue made with hot sugar syrup
_____ 4. Glaze	d. Blend of melted chocolate and cream
_____ 5. Buttercream	e. Confectioner's sugar with liquid
_____ 6. Fondant	f. Cooked mixture of sugar, butter, and water/milk; applied warm
	g. Cooked mixture of sugar and water, applied warm

33E. Cake Mix Categories

Cake mixes fall into two categories: creamed fat or whipped egg. For each of the following, identify a creamed-fat mix with the letter A and a whipped-egg mix with the letter B.

A = Creamed Fat
B = Whipped Egg

_____ 1.	Chiffon cake		_____ 6.	Yellow cake
_____ 2.	Continental brownies		_____ 7.	Carrot cake
_____ 3.	Devil's food cake		_____ 8.	Gâteau Benoit
_____ 4.	Chocolate spongecake		_____ 9.	Vanilla raspberry layer cake
_____ 5.	Sacher torte		_____ 10.	Sour cream coffee cake

33F. Short Answer—Frostings

Describe the **basic** steps for the preparation of each of the following frostings. Exact quantities of ingredients are not important for this exercise.

1. **Simple Buttercream**

_____

_____

_____

_____

_____

2. **Italian Buttercream**

_____

_____

_____

_____

_____

3. **French Buttercream**

_____

_____

_____

_____

_____

33G. Fill in the Blank

Fill in each blank space with the response that correctly completes the statement.

1. At higher altitudes, baking ingredients and temperatures need to be adjusted; the amount of leavening should be _____ and the eggs in the mixture should be under _____. Temperatures should also be increased by _____ °F at altitudes over 3500 feet.

2. The three tests for determining a cake's doneness are _____ , _____ , and _____.

3. Most cakes are baked at temperatures between _____ °F and _____ °F.

4. Royal icing is also known as _____ icing.

5. Pan coating consists of equal parts _____ , _____ , and _____.

6. When mixing any cake batter, the goals are to combine the ingredients uniformly, incorporate _____ , and develop _____.

33H. Chapter Review

For each statement, circle either True or False to indicate the correct answer. If an answer is false, then explain why.

1. The best way to cool a cake is to leave it in an area where there is a cool breeze.
    True   False _____

2. Frostings are not usually frozen.
    True   False _____

3. As a general guide for setting oven temperatures for cakes, the greater the surface area, the higher the temperature.
    True   False _____

4. For best results when baking cakes, pans should be filled one-half to three-fourths full with batter.
    True   False _____

5. Angel food cake is ideal for frosting.
    True   False _____

6. Solid shortening is better than butter for coating pans because it does not contain any water.
    True   False _____

7. Packaged mixes are inferior in quality to cakes made from scratch.
    True   False _____

8. The fat used in high-ratio cake mixes can be either butter or shortening.
    True   False _____

9. When a baker tests the doneness of a cake by touch, it should spring back quickly without feeling soggy or leaving an indentation.
    True   False _____

10. Compotes, buttercream, foam, fudge, and ganache are all examples of icings.
    True   False _____

11. Angel food cake is the best cake to use if a low-fat or fat-free dessert is desired.
    True   False _____

33I. Putting It All Together

Provide a short response for each of the following questions. These questions are designed to help you connect the bigger concepts presented in this chapter and/or text.

1. When making cakes, what aspects of food safety should chefs consider?

2. How should a food service establishment determine whether to bake and decorate its own cakes and desserts or outsource production?

Chapter 34

CUSTARDS, CREAMS, FROZEN DESSERTS AND DESSERT SAUCES

TEST YOUR KNOWLEDGE

The practice sets provided here have been designed to test your comprehension of the information found in this chapter. It is recommended that you read the chapter completely before attempting these questions.

34A. Terminology

Fill in each blank space with the correct definition.

1. Custard

   a. Stirred custard _____

      1. Vanilla custard sauce _____

         a. Pudding _____

      2. Pastry cream _____

         a. Mousseline _____

         b. Crème Chiboust _____

      3. Lemon curd _____

      4. Sabayon _____

   b. Baked custard _____

      1. Flan _____

      2. Crème caramel _____

      3. Crème brûlée _____

      4. Cheesecake _____

      5. Bread pudding _____

   c. Soufflés

      1. Baked _____

      2. Frozen _____

2. Creams

   a. Crème Chantilly _____

   b. Charlotte russe/royale _____

   c. Chiffon _____

   d. Mousse _____

   e. Semifreddi _____

3. Frozen desserts

    a. Ice cream _____

    b. Gelato _____

    c. Overrun _____

    d. Churned _____

    e. Sorbet _____

    f. Sherbet _____

4. Dessert sauces

    a. Fruit purées or coulis _____

    b. Chocolate syrup _____

5. Assembling desserts

    a. Base _____

    b. Filling _____

    c. Garnish _____

34B. Short Answer

Provide a short response that correctly answers each of the following questions.

1. Eggs are a high-protein food and can easily become contaminated. List and describe six (6) sanitary guidelines for handling eggs.

    a. _____

    b. _____

    c. _____

    d. _____

    e. _____

    f. _____

2. Describe the basic steps and essential ingredients for the preparation of vanilla custard sauce.

_____

_____

_____

_____

_____

_____

3. Briefly describe the eight (8) sequential steps in the procedure for making ice cream.

   a. _____

   b. _____

   c. _____

   d. _____

   e. _____

   f. _____

   g. _____

   h. _____

4. Describe the four (4) sequential steps in the procedure for making baked soufflés.

   a. _____

   b. _____

   c. _____

   d. _____

5. Describe the four (4) sequential steps in the procedure for making a sabayon.

   a. _____

   b. _____

   c. _____

   d. _____

6. Describe the three (3) sequential steps in the procedure for making a mousse.

   a. _____

   b. _____

   c. _____

7. Briefly describe the nine (9) guidelines for assembling desserts.

a. _____

b. _____

c. _____

d. _____

e. _____

f. _____

g. _____

h. _____

i. _____

8. Because ice cream is a potentially hazardous food product as well as being ready to eat, list three (3) precautions one can take to maintain a safe product for consumption.

a. _____

b. _____

c. _____

34C. Fill in the Blank

Fill in each blank space with the response that correctly completes the statement.

1. _____ is the Italian name for sabayon.

2. Pastry cream can be lightened by folding in whipped cream to produce a _____ or by adding Italian _____ to produce a crème Chiboust.

3. Some creams such as Bavarians and _____ are thickened with gelatin, but others such as mousses and _____ _____ are not and therefore are softer and lighter.

4. When preparing a soufflé, the custard base and egg whites should be at room temperature because egg whites will _____ and the two mixtures are _____.

34D. Chapter Review

For each statement, circle either True or False to indicate the correct answer. If an answer is false, then explain why.

1. Once a coulis has been cooked, it becomes a compote.
    True   False _____

2. A frozen soufflé is not really a soufflé in the true sense.
    True   False _____

3. Crème anglaise is typically flavored with vanilla but may be flavored in a variety of ways.
    True   False _____

4. The purpose of serving a dessert with a sauce is to add moisture, texture, and flavor and to enhance the presentation.
    True   False _____

5. A coulis is a fruit purée made from either fresh or individually quick-frozen (IQF) fruits.
    True   False _____

6. Quiche is an example of a baked custard.
    True   False _____

7. The chef has made a fresh sorbet and has allowed ample time for it to freeze thoroughly, yet it is still soft and syrupy. The problem is likely that he used too many egg whites.
    True   False _____

8. Once a vanilla custard sauce is curdled, it should be discarded.
    True   False _____

9. A sherbet differs from a sorbet in that a sorbet contains milk or egg yolk for added creaminess.
    True   False _____

10. A fudge sauce is a variation of a ganache.
    True   False _____

11. Chefs should be trained in using a propane torch before using it to brown sugar or other dessert preparations.
    True   False _____

12. Crème brûlée was invented in France in the 17th century.
    True   False _____

34E. Putting It All Together

Provide a short response for each of the following questions. These questions are designed to help you connect the bigger concepts presented in this chapter and/or text.

1. In the section on soufflés, the formula provided for Chocolate Soufflés asks the chef to fold the whipped egg whites into the other ingredients. Describe the differences in the processes of mixing and folding.

2. In Table 34.1 the reader is told to add nothing or gelatin for a thickening agent when making a mousse. What characteristic does gelatin add to the formula that would help the chef decide whether to use it?

3. Quality ice creams, sherbets, and sorbets are all available from retailers. What factors might one consider when deciding to purchase these as convenience products versus making them in-house?

Chapter 35

PLATE PRESENTATION

TEST YOUR KNOWLEDGE

The practice sets provided here have been designed to test your comprehension of the information found in this chapter. It is recommended that you read the chapter completely before attempting these questions.

35A. Terminology

Fill in each blank space with the correct definition.

1. Service _____

2. Composition _____

3. Presentation _____

4. Garnishing _____

5. Painting sauces _____

6. Eye appeal _____

7. Small-plate dining _____

35B. Fill in the Blank

Fill in each blank space with the response that correctly completes the statement.

1. _____ is a thin cookielike dough delicately piped and baked for use in making decorations and garnishes.

2. Proper cooking procedures can enhance the texture, _____ , and _____ of many cooked foods.

3. Once the color or pattern is chosen for a plate, the next important element to consider is _____ , keeping in mind the amount of food being presented.

4. The _____ point is often the highest point on the plate.

5. Plate drawing is most typically done with _____ -temperature sauces.

35C. Short Answer

Provide a short response that correctly answers each of the following questions.

1. List two (2) ways of presenting polenta.

    a. _____

    b. _____

2. List five (5) things that a sauce should add to a plate presentation.

    a. _____   d. _____

    b. _____   e. _____

    c. _____

3. List two (2) things that a hippen masse garnish might do for a presentation.

    a. _____

    b. _____

4. List three (3) reasons for carefully cutting foods in preparation or presentation.

    a. _____

    b. _____

    c. _____

5. List three (3) guidelines for arranging foods on a plate.

    a. _____

    b. _____

    c. _____

6. List three (3) reasons for molding foods.

    a. _____

    b. _____

    c. _____

35D. Chapter Review

For each statement, circle either True or False to indicate the correct answer. If an answer is false, then explain why.

1. A rice pilaf is a good example of a dish that would mold well for an attractive presentation.
   True   False _____

2. The garnish should always be the focal point of the plate.
   True   False _____

3. Small plates are usually consumed at the beginning of the meal, before the entrée.
   True   False _____

4. Generally speaking, foods with similar textures look boring together.
   True   False _____

5. As long as the flavors complement the foods on the plate, finely chopped herbs or even nuts can be used to add a finishing touch to a plate.
   True   False _____

6. A piping bag would be a good choice of equipment for performing sauce drawings.
   True   False _____

7. The primary consideration with sauce drawing is that the colors of the sauces used contrast each other.
   True   False _____

8. Properly preparing the main food product on a plate is the most important way to make the presentation look attractive.
   True   False _____

9. Small-plate dining gives customers a taste for an eclectic meal similarly to the way ethnic counterparts such as Spanish tapas, Chinese dim sum, and Middle Eastern mezze provide satisfaction.
   True   False _____

10. Plate dusting is a garnishing technique most associated with culinary preparations.
    True   False _____

11. Presenting food on a plate that is proportionately too large may make the food portion look too sparse, thereby creating poor value perception.
    True   False _____

12. The most important factor to consider when decorating a plate presentation with simple or elaborate details is cost.
    True   False _____

13. Because each small plate needs to create as much impact as a large plate, it is especially important for the chef to pay close attention to presentation details related to balancing the colors, flavors, textures, and temperatures of the food.
    True   False _____

14. Small plates should be more complicated in presentation than traditional menus in order to give the customer "more bang for the buck."
    True   False _____

35E. Putting It All Together

Provide a short response for each of the following questions. These questions are designed to help you connect the bigger concepts presented in this chapter and/or text.

1. This chapter discusses using two large spoons to form purées or mousses into a quenelle shape. What things does a chef have to ensure so that this plan is carried out effectively when the time comes to actually plate the food?

2. Considering the time/temperature control principles discussed in Chapter 2, Food Safety and Sanitation, and the need to serve foods at the appropriate temperature, what rules does a chef need to follow when planning food presentations?

Chapter 36

BUFFET PRESENTATION

TEST YOUR KNOWLEDGE

The practice sets provided here have been designed to test your comprehension of the information found in this chapter. It is recommended that you read the chapter completely before attempting these questions.

36A. Terminology

Fill in each blank space with the correct definition.

1. Theme _____

2. Buffet

   a. Single-sided _____
   b. Double-sided _____

3. Chafing dish _____

4. Grosse piece _____

5. Risers _____

6. Butler service _____

7. Layout _____

8. Stations _____

36B. Short Answer

Provide a short response that correctly answers each of the following questions.

1. Describe the four (4) guidelines for avoiding repetition of foods on a buffet.

   a. _____

   b. _____

   c. _____

   d. _____

2. Explain why each of the following aspects of presentation is important when preparing a buffet.

    a. Height: _____

    _____

    b. Pattern: _____

    _____

    c. Color: _____

    _____

    d. Texture: _____

    _____

    e. Negative space: _____

    _____

3. Describe three (3) styles of buffet setup designed to promote efficient service of large groups.

    a. _____

    b. _____

    c. _____

4. Describe four (4) guidelines for presenting hot foods on a buffet.

    a. _____

    b. _____

    c. _____

    d. _____

36C. Multiple Choice

For each of the following, choose the one correct response.

1. On a buffet, hot foods are served in/on:

    a. platters.
    b. bowls.
    c. chafing dishes.
    d. mirrors.

2. Which of the following best describes the logical flow for a buffet table?

    a. appetizers, entrées, plates, vegetable
    b. plates, soups, entrées, desserts
    c. plates, entrées, vegetable, appetizers
    d. desserts, vegetable, entrées, appetizers

3. Which of the following items are appropriate to use as a centerpiece on a buffet table?

    a. flowers
    b. ice carvings
    c. whole turkey
    d. all of the above

4. Having waiters stationed behind the buffet table is called:

    a. waiter service.
    b. buffet service.
    c. butler service.
    d. restaurant service.

5. All of the following are measures that can be taken to prevent food safety issues on a buffet **except**:

    a. Provide clean serving utensils regularly.
    b. Don't add new food to old food in a serving dish.
    c. Reheat food in the chafing dish.
    d. Provide an ample supply of clean plates.

36D. Chapter Review

For each statement, circle either True or False to indicate the correct answer. If an answer is false, then explain why.

1. More guests help themselves to little portions of every item on a buffet rather than gorging themselves on one or two items.
    True   False _____

2. Cost is **not** a factor when preparing buffet menus.
    True   False _____

3. When designing a buffet, the food tables should be located as far from the kitchen as possible for ease of service.
    True   False _____

4. The start of the buffet should be located near the entrance to the room.
   True   False _____

5. A buffet table with 10 items should be approximately 10 feet long.
   True   False _____

6. Dishes containing sauces should be positioned at the back of the table.
   True   False _____

7. Dead space on the buffet should never be filled in with decorations or props.
   True   False _____

8. Guests will generally take larger portions of foods at the beginning of the buffet than at the end.
   True   False _____

9. Spaghetti is an appropriate food to serve on a hot buffet.
   True   False _____

10. Dishes of food on the buffet should be replenished when they are two-thirds empty.
    True   False _____

11. The word *buffet* is used to describe the event as well as the table on which the food is served.
    True   False _____

12. A chef should not plan one portion of each food item on the buffet for each guest.
    True   False _____

13. To ensure proper portion control, a chef or server should be stationed behind every item on a buffet table.
    True   False _____

14. Stations offer the buffet designer greater flexibility and also help minimize the line of guests that forms at a single buffet table.
    True   False _____

36E. Putting It All Together

Provide a short response for each of the following questions. These questions are designed to help you connect the bigger concepts presented in this chapter and/or text.

1. Referring to the sidebar in this chapter titled "The Buffet: An Ancient Extravaganza," hypothesize (researching if necessary) how food safety practices have likely evolved over time with the development of the buffet. Compare and contrast how the Italian *banchetto* may have differed during the Renaissance period compared to an American buffet in a fine hotel today.

2. Name a minimum of three controls that food service establishment management can use once the buffet is set up to control cross-contamination of the food during service.

Answer Key

A Note to Chef Instructors

The fifth edition of the *Study Guide to accompany On Cooking* has been modified in order to maximize the benefits to all involved. The study guide was always intended to be first and foremost a way for students to practice with each chapter's concepts before the final test on the chapter.

- For instructors, the efficiency has been improved by allowing you to assign the study guide as homework, minus the answer key, in order to maximize the attention each student gives it.
- For students, the effectiveness lies in enabling them to complete each chapter in the study guide as it is covered during class.

In order to maximize both the efficiency and effectiveness of the study guide, the chef instructor should use the following guidelines: On the first day of class, or when students first receive their study guide, ask them to turn to this page.

1. Have students remove the pages of the study guide, using the perforations along the side of the page.
2. Ask students to come to the front of the room and place their pages of the study guide in piles labeled Chapter 1, Chapter 2, Chapter 3, and so on. The study guide's answer key has been organized in such a way that each chapter's contents are on their own page exclusively, in most cases one page per chapter.
3. Once all students have separated and piled their answer keys for each chapter, enter them into a filing system where you can store them.
4. Each time your class completes a chapter of subject matter (*and before the chapter test*), distribute the answer key for the chapter to each student. This will enable them to refer to the answer key as they're studying, confirming the accuracy with which they responded to each question when they had originally completed the study guide as a homework assignment.

The *Study Guide* has always been intended as a tool that enables your students to practice and better understand the content of each chapter. The more practice students have with new subjects before they are formally tested, through the exercises provided in this study guide, the better chances they will have to master the information and apply it in the kitchen. In this way the study guide helps both students and chef instructors be successful.

CHAPTER 1 ANSWER KEY

1A. Terminology
Answers will not be provided in answer key. All answers can be found in text.

1B. Fill in the Blank
1. back of the house
2. French
3. front of the house
4. Russian
5. front waiter
6. American
7. backwaiter or busperson
8. chef de vin
9. the Internet

1C. Short Answer
1. a. Cooks could prepare many items simultaneously, especially those needing constant and delicate attention.
    b. Cooks could more comfortably and safely approach the heat source and control its temperatures.
    c. Cooks could efficiently prepare and hold a multitude of smaller amounts of items requiring different cooking methods or ingredients for later use or service.
2. Canned foods, freeze-drying, refrigerators, vacuum-packing, freezers, radiation
3. a. Absorbs facial perspiration
    b. Disguise stains
    c. Double-breasted design hides dirt and protects from scalds and burns
    d. Protects the uniform and insulates the body
4. a. Personal performance and behavior
    b. Good grooming practices
    c. Clean, pressed uniform

1D. Defining Professionalism
1. Judgment
2. Dedication
3. Taste
4. Pride
5. Skill
6. Knowledge

1E. Noteworthy Chefs
1. h   5. a
2. g   6. e
3. c   7. f
4. d

1F. Matching
1. a   5. g   9. h
2. i   6. l   10. k
3. e   7. b   11. d
4. c   8. f   12. m

1G. Chapter Review

1. True
2. False   (p. 11) Today most food service operations use a simplified version of Escoffier's brigade.
3. False   (p. 10) Most new concerns that affect the food service industry are brought on by the demands of the customer. Such concerns may eventually encourage government interaction to ensure public well-being.
4. False   (p. 9) Advances in the transportation industry began to positively influence the food service industry during the early 1800s.
5. True
6. True
7. True
8. True
9. False   (p. 9) Many of the preserving techniques used before the 19th century destroyed or distorted the appearance and flavor of the foods. Therefore, when new preserving techniques were developed, they were favored because of their minimal effect on appearance and flavor.
10. True
11. False   (p. 14) Dining in a linear fashion does not allow for a full, simultaneous satisfaction of the categories of tastes, which, from a Western perspective, generally do not include spicy.
12. False   (p. 6) The book is an astounding collection of more than 5000 classic cuisine recipes and garnishes, and Escoffier emphasizes mastery of techniques, thorough understanding of cooking principles, and appreciation of ingredients—attributes he considered the building blocks professional chefs should use to create great dishes.
13. True

1H. Putting It All Together

1. Answers may vary, but here are some major ideas to consider: Understanding the history of how the culinary profession evolved enables us to appreciate the significance of our industry today. Examples may include but are not limited to the challenges early chefs faced, creating a profession from nothing (and realizing that such a practice can take hundreds of years), changing the way the public thinks about food for more than sustenance but rather enjoyment, preparing foods in a way people had literally never experienced before, developing early sanitation and safety practices, inventing recipes, designing the professional persona of the chef through uniform design and modeling professional and appropriate behaviors, determining what positions are needed in a classical kitchen, developing a training system (albeit not necessarily a uniform one) for various positions in a professional kitchen, creating an organizational system for a classical kitchen that clearly delineates the responsibilities of all employees, defining and perfecting various cooking techniques and methods that are still used today, creating various cooking styles based on cultural influences and regional variations, and constantly redefining cuisine—taking it beyond cultural boundaries and evolving as our economy has become globalized.

2. Lenôtre, whose impact on the chef profession is more recent than that of others mentioned in this chapter, made tremendous advances in baking and pastry arts. The development of baking and pastry arts as we know them today began much later than the culinary arts, and so he built on techniques developed earlier by such greats as Antonin Carême, but in the *nouvelle cuisine* style. In addition, unlike Carême, who was chef to a French diplomat, and Escoffier, who developed his culinary skills in the kitchens of the finest hotels in Europe, Lenôtre was more like Fernand Point in that he owned his own establishment. Like most great chefs, he built on the techniques and recipes that were developed before him, but Lenôtre took it several steps further. He opened not only one establishment, but numerous bakeries, and not all in the same town—let alone the same country.

    In addition, Lenôtre realized with the growth in his business the need to be able to train many employees in consistent methods of food preparation so that he could ensure that the quality of product was the same, no matter which establishment his customers frequented. This private school for his own chefs was eventually opened up (for a fee) to competitors' chefs who also needed training. Like his predecessors, he advanced the evolution of baking and pastry arts relative to the period of time in which he was living, developing a new mixing technique and perfecting Bavarians, charlottes, fruit mousses, cakes, and tortes. He also applied modern technologies of his day, mastering the technique of freezing as a preserving method. Some gastronomes say he single-handedly saved the classical pastry profession in the 20th century from being taken over by mass-production bakeries. The era in which he lived likely had a significant impact on his success and the impact he had on the food service profession based on the items summarized here; he was innovative and professional, benefiting from the information created in our industry by chefs who came before so that his impact became so much more monumental.

3. Developments in the production of new food ingredients for use in the modern food industry have all occurred because of the demands of the day; some have been more controversial than others. Although many chefs disdain commercial produce that has been raised with the use of chemical fertilizers and pesticides, such practices have enabled farmers to better meet the food demands of a growing world population. Likewise, animal husbandry has helped produce animals that yield a better quality and proportion of meat, increasing the yield for the farmer and therefore the chef. Aquaculture developments have made certain fish species more available in a time of overfishing and increased pollution of our rivers, lakes, streams, and oceans. Although some chefs challenge the resulting flavor and quality of farmed fish, the development of the process has resulted in a more readily available food supply, often with equal or greater raw product quality, and many times fresher and safer to consume from a food safety standpoint.

   Although these are just a few examples of how one can justify such developments, they illustrate an important challenge to the modern chef that is in line with the authors' emphasis on the idea that chefs must continue to expand their knowledge far past their culinary school education. Chefs must continually research current trends and availability of food ingredients and, based on their own values and the demands of their customers, choose those that are in alignment with both philosophies.

CHAPTER 2 ANSWER KEY

2A. Terminology
Answers will not be provided in answer key. All answers can be found in text.

2B. Multiple Choice

1.	d	3.	b	5.	c
2.	d	4.	d	6.	d

2C. Chapter Review

1. True
2. False   (p. 30) A licensed pest control operator should be contacted immediately. Such professionals will go beyond simply locating the source of infestation; they will also prescribe a plan of action to prevent ongoing occurrences in the future.
3. False   (p. 19) Toxins cannot be smelled, seen, or tasted.
4. False   (p. 23) Semisolid foods should be placed in containers that are less than 2 inches deep because increasing the surface area decreases the cooling time.
5. True
6. True
7. True
8. False   (p. 27) Just as hands should be washed regularly during food production to prevent cross-contamination, so too should gloves be changed regularly. Wearing gloves does not eliminate the need to wash hands regularly.
9. False   (p. 24) Hepatitis A is a virus.
10. True
11. False   (p. 23) A low water activity level only halts bacterial growth; it does not kill the microorganisms.
12. True
13. True
14. False   (p. 27) The two-tasting-spoon method involves using the first spoon to remove a sampling of the food from the pan in which it was made or stored. Pour that food into the second spoon before tasting it. The cook can repeat the process if necessary, depending on how many tastings are needed to make final adjustments to the food product, preventing the soiled spoon from going back into the food being prepared.
15. True
16. True

2D. HACCP Overview

1. a: 1;   b: 6;   c: 3;   d: 2;   e: 4;   f: 7;   g: 5;   h: 8
2. b
3. b
4. b, c

2E. Food-Borne Diseases Review

1. Botulism
    - O: *Clostridium botulinum*
    - F: Toxin, cells, spores
    - S: Cooked foods held for an extended time at warm temperatures with limited oxygen: rice, potatoes, smoked fish, canned vegetables
    - P: Keep internal temperature of cooked foods above 140°F or below 41°F; reheat leftovers thoroughly; discard swollen cans

2. Hepatitis A

    O: Virus

    S: Enters food supply through shellfish harvested from polluted waters; it is also carried by humans, often without knowledge of infection

    P: Confirm source of shellfish; practice good personal hygiene; avoid cross-contamination

3. Strep

    O: *Streptococcus*

    F: Cells

    S: Infected food workers

    P: Do not allow employees to work if ill; protect foods from customers' coughs and sneezes

4. Perfringens or CP

    O: *Clostridium perfringens*

    F: Cells, toxin

    S: Reheated meats, sauces, stews, casseroles

    P: Keep cooked foods at an internal temperature of 140°F or higher; reheat leftovers to an internal temperature of 165°F or higher

5. Norwalk virus

    O: Virus

    S: Spread almost entirely by poor personal hygiene of food service employees; it is found in human feces, contaminated water, and vegetables fertilized with manure

    P: Can be destroyed by high cooking temperatures but not by sanitizing solutions or freezing

6. Salmonella

    O: *Salmonella*

    F: Cells

    S: Poultry, eggs, milk, meats, fecal contamination

    P: Thoroughly cook all meat, poultry, fish, and eggs; avoid cross-contamination with raw foods; maintain good personal hygiene

7. *E. coli* or 0157

    O: *Escherichia coli* 0157:H7

    F: Cells, toxin

    S: Any food, especially raw milk, raw vegetables, raw or rare beef; humans

    P: Thoroughly cook or reheat items

8. Trichinosis

    O: Parasitic worms

    S: Eating undercooked game or pork infected with trichina larvae

    P: Cook foods to a minimum internal temperature of 137°F for 10 seconds

9. Anisakiasis

    O: Parasitic roundworms

    S: The organs of fish, especially bottom feeders or those taken from contaminated waters; raw or undercooked fish are often implicated

    P: Thoroughly clean fish immediately after they are caught so that the parasites do not have the opportunity to spread; thoroughly cook to a minimum internal temperature of 140°F

10. Listeriosis

    O: *Listeria monocytogenes*

    F: Cells

    S: Milk products, humans

    P: Avoid raw milk and cheese made from unpasteurized milk

11. Staphylococcus

    O: *Staphylococcus aureus*

    F: Toxin

    S: Starchy foods, cold meats, bakery items, custards, milk products, humans with infected wounds or sores

    P: Wash hands and utensils before use; exclude unhealthy food handlers; avoid having foods at room temperature

2F. Matching

1. c	4. f	7. j	10. g
2. a	5. d	8. k	11. c
3. a	6. a	9. c	12. l

CHAPTER 3 ANSWER KEY

3A. Terminology
Answers will not be provided in answer key. All answers can be found in text.

3B. Units of Measure

1. 16 oz.
2. 28.35 g
3. 435.6 g = 0.4536 kg
4. 1000 g
5. 0.035 oz.
6. 35 oz. = 2.187 lb./2 lb.
7. 16 tbsp. = 8 fl. oz.
8. 1 qt. = 32 fl. oz.
9. ½ gal. = 4 pt.
10. 32 tbsp. = 16 fl. oz.
11. 8 tbsp. = 24 tsp.
12. 1 pt. = ½ qt.
13. ¼ c. = 4 tbsp. = 12 tsp.
14. 128 fl. oz. = 4 qt. = 16 c.
15. 3 pt. = 0.38 gal.

3C. Conversion Factors

1. 2.5
2. 0.7
3. 0.58
4. 2.5
5. 0.25
6. 0.75
7. a: 0.6;   b: 120
8. 10

3D. Conversion Problems

1. Larger quantities may require the use of a electric mixer rather than hand mixing. Also, the mixing time may need to be modified accordingly.
2. The difference in surface area between using a saucepan versus a tilting skillet impacts evaporation. Thickness of the liquid should be modified accordingly.
3. Some recipes may have errors. Read recipes carefully and draw on professional knowledge to compensate for such errors.
4. Cooking time of individual items should not vary according to volume. Cooking time will be affected by the evaporation rate due to equipment changes. Rely on professional knowledge to compensate for such changes.

3E. Recipe Conversion

	Conversion Factor I: 0.88	Yield I: 28 portions, 6 oz. each 168 oz.	Conversion Factor II: 1.31	Yield II: 84 portions 3 oz. each 252 oz.
Butter		3.08 oz.		4.59 oz.
Onion		10.56 oz.		15.72 oz.
Celery		2.2 oz.		3.28 oz.
Broccoli		42.24 oz. = 2.64 lb.		62.88 oz. = 3.93 lb.
Chicken velouté		128 fl. oz. = 3.52 qt.		5.24 qt.
Chicken stock		64 fl. oz. = 1.76 qt.		2.62 qt.
Heavy cream		21.12 fl. oz.		31.44 fl. oz.
Broccoli florets		7.04 oz.		10.48 oz.

3F. Unit Costs

1. $0.53
2. $0.25
3. $3.25
4. $0.15
5. $0.04
6. $0.58
7. $1.97
8. $4.02

3G. Cost per Portion

1. $4.50
2. $4.13
3. $0.25
4. $0.75
5. a. $2.25
   b. $1.13

6. a. $4.07
   b. 140 oz.
   c. 28
   d. $1.27
7. a. $0.64
   b. 112
8. $2.16

3H. Controlling Food Cost

1. The menu should be designed based on customer desires, space, equipment, ingredient availability, cost of goods sold, employee skills, and competition. Include all personnel when planning the menu.
2. Correct purchasing techniques help control cost. Purchase specifications and periodic quotes help ensure value for money.
3. The person signing for the goods should be the person who actually checked them. Freshness, quality, and quantity should always be checked.
4. Proper storage is crucial to prevent spoilage, pilferage, and waste. Use the FIFO method.
5. Maintaining ongoing inventory records sheets simplifies the ordering process and ensures proper stock rotation.
6. Standardized portions are a key factor in controlling food cost. Once an acceptable portion size has been determined, the staff must adhere to it.
7. An accurate sales history helps prevent overproduction, but the chef must also be able to use leftovers to lower food cost.
8. Front-of-the-house personnel must be trained to avoid loss of sales caused by giving out free meals or spilling foods during the serving process.

3I. Chapter Review

1. True
2. False (p. 40) Portion or balance scales are commonly used in commercial kitchens to determine weights of ingredients, the most accurate form of measurement.
3. True
4. True
5. False (p. 38) For a meal served in the European tradition, the salad would be presented as a palate cleanser after the main dish and before the dessert.
6. True
7. False (p. 47) Figuring the portion cost of everything on the plate is just one of many things that may be considered to determine the selling price.
8. False (p. 48) The minimum selling price should be $8.00.
9. True
10. True

3J. Putting It All Together

1. Tasting menus are a new and unique gastronomic journey for guests when a chef carefully produces a special menu around an ingredient in season or a special occasion. The result is usually one of heightened sensory satisfaction and can help strengthen the bond of customer loyalty because the experience is new and different. The more connected the guest becomes to an establishment in varied ways, through its service and food quality, the more committed that guest is for the long run—an important goal for any successful establishment.

   From the chef's perspective, a tasting menu is an opportunity to create a special gastronomic experience that stretches beyond the establishment's menu, regardless of its format. The result may bring in additional business, or it may simply be an added value for regular guests to enjoy. Creating a tasting menu may also be another opportunity to collaborate with food suppliers, other chefs, beverage distributors, and the sommelier/bartender to prepare a balanced menu that builds in experience and complexity from the first course to the last. It gives the chef an additional challenge and can help keep his or her creative juices flowing, thus increasing job satisfaction.

2. When an establishment invests time in creating standardized recipes, the resulting formulas are usually used to develop the ordering list for purveyors. In addition, the chef usually uses the formulas to accurately determine overall food cost even before the actual sale is made. As a result, if the chef does not follow accurate measuring techniques as per the standardized recipe, it will be nearly impossible for him or her to determine accurate ordering quantities for the ingredients needed; the restaurant could also run short of ingredients needed for other menu items. Finally, taking away the predictability of food usage could also lead to an increased cost for producing a particular menu item.

   If a recipe has been standardized to create consistency in preparation from cook to cook as well as maintaining a consistent food cost in the establishment, then deviating from the predetermined portion guidelines could cause the restaurant to run out of the prepped item prematurely.

   From the guests' perspective, inaccurate measurement could lead to varying perceived value. A huge portion may make the guest feel that he or she got a great value, but only days later, when ordering the menu item again, the guest may feel cheated if the portion served is unusually small.

3. If a chef cannot accurately convert recipes, the result could be an increase in production cost because he or she is not following the predetermined measures; waste of food caused by producing more portions than needed; not having enough of the menu item needed (a particular problem if serving a large party on a fixed menu); or simply lack of quality in the final menu item. To illustrate the final example, this is especially a problem in baking, where if the quantity of an ingredient such as shortening is inaccurately calculated, the finished product does not have the same quality and sensory appeal as the intended result. Accurately converting recipes and carefully employing proper measuring techniques should result in a menu item whose final quality is identical to the original recipe, whether it is produced for 4 people or 400.

CHAPTER 4 ANSWER KEY

4A. Terminology

Answers will not be provided in answer key. All answers can be found in text.

4B. Equipment Identification

Name of item:	Major use:
1. Zester	Removing zest from citrus fruits
2. Straight spatula	Applying frosting to cakes
3. Grill spatula	Lifting hot food items from pan or grill
4. Meat mallet	Flattening or tenderizing meat
5. Chef's fork	Serving meats
6. French or chef's knife	All-purpose chopping
7. Rigid boning knife	Separating meat from bone
8. Paring knife	Detailed cutting of curved surfaces, namely vegetables
9. Flexible slicer	Slicing meats and fish
10. Butcher knife/scimitar	Fabricating raw meat
11. Steel	Honing blade between sharpenings
12. Stockpot with spigot	Making large quantities of soup or stock
13. Rondeau/brazier	Stove top cooking for large amounts of food
14. Sautoir	Stove top cooking for small amounts of food
15. Sauteuse	Stove top sautéing
16. Wok	Stir-frying and sautéing
17. Full hotel pan	Holding food during service; baking, roasting, poaching
18. Drum sieve	Sifting flour or straining
19. China cap	Straining liquids
20. Skimmer	Skimming stocks
21. Spider	Removing particles from hot fat
22. Food mill	Puréeing and straining foods
23. Mandoline	Slicing small quantities of vegetables
24. Heavy-duty blender	Preparing smooth drinks and purées; chopping ice
25. Stack oven	Baking
26. Tilt skillet	A large cooking utensil that can be used as a stockpot, brazier, frying pan, griddle, or steam table
27. Steam kettle	Making stocks, soups, custards, or stocks
28. Deep-fat fryer	Deep-frying foods
29. Insulated carrier	Keeping food hot during transportation

4C. Short Answer

1. Easily cleaned; nontoxic food surfaces; smooth food surfaces; smooth and sealed internal surfaces; nontoxic coating surfaces; waste easily removed
2. a. Is it necessary for production?
   b. Will it do the job in the space available?
   c. Is it the most economical for the establishment?
   d. Is it easy to clean and repair?
3. a. Carbon steel
   b. Stainless steel
   c. High-carbon stainless steel
4. a. Foods are vacuum sealed in pouches (in a chamber vacuum machine).
   b. Pouches are cooked very slowly in a water bath ranging from 125ºF to 195ºF (51ºC to 90ºC), using a thermal circulator or immersion circulator.
   c. Foods are precisely cooked but not overcooked.
   d. The technique concentrates flavors and extends the shelf life of foods.

5. a. Fill a glass with shaved ice, then add water.
   b. Place thermometer in the slush and wait until the temperature reading stabilizes. Following the manufacturer's directions, adjust the thermometer's calibration nut until the temperature reads 32°F.
   c. Check the calibration by returning the thermometer to the slush.
   d. Repeat the procedure by substituting boiling water for the slush and calibrate the thermometer to 212°F.

4D. Matching

1. i
2. h
3. a
4. e
5. g
6. d
7. c
8. f
9. j
10. k

4E. Fill in the Blank

1. utility
2. tang
3. griddle
4. buffalo chopper
5. Wooden
6. scimitar
7. Japanese
8. digital or infrared

4F. Chapter Review

1. False (p. 60) Stem-type thermometers should be calibrated after dropping.
2. False (p. 73) Ventilation hoods should be cleaned by professionals.
3. True
4. False (p. 72) Class A fire extinguishers are used for fires caused by wood, paper, cloth, or plastic.
5. True
6. False (p. 69) Because a steam kettle's sides and bottom are heated, it heats food more quickly than a pot sitting on a stove.
7. True
8. False (p. 55) Seamless plastic or rubber parts on food service equipment are important in maintaining sanitation.
9. False (p. 72) A Class K fire extinguisher can also handle grease, fat, and cooking oil in commercial cooking equipment as well as a Class B extinguisher.
10. False (p. 61) Silicone bakeware is extremely versatile because one can bake in it as well as produce candy and chocolate products. In addition to maintaining its integrity up to 485°F, it can also be frozen.
11. True
12. False (p. 68) Induction burners are gradually gaining popularity as cook surfaces on buffet lines (omelet stations, for example) but also in bakeshops where excessive heat that results from the cooking process is undesirable for products such as chocolate that cannot handle extreme fluctuations in temperature.
13. False (p. 73) Kitchen designers must also pay attention to the volume of food the operation intends to produce.
14. True

4G. Putting It All Together

1. Alexis Soyer is considered by many to be the father of the modern celebrity chef because he was a flamboyant, talented, and egocentric showman. Although he was a renowned chef in terms of the foods he prepared, he was also known for his kitchen designs, which were ahead of their time. The designs helped create a more healthy environment for the employees to work in while also increasing function and flow for service. Part of his design included using the most modern cooking equipment available and linking the classical brigade system employed in a particular kitchen to the flow and design in order to maximize efficiency.
2. The food should be fully heated to an internal temperature of 165°F before being placed in the carrier. Depending on how long the food will be stored in the carrier, a heat source may be needed to maintain the internal temperature of the food. One should take care to regularly check the internal temperature of the food product to ensure that it is kept above the temperature danger zone before serving.

3. Food should be stored and handled in a completely different area from any type of chemical. As a result, some clear-cut safety measures include never storing cleaning supplies or other chemicals with or near foods; never storing chemicals in a container that originally held food, and never storing food in a container that once held a chemical; and finally, keeping chemicals and cleaners in properly labeled containers.

CHAPTER 5 ANSWER KEY

5A. Terminology
Answers will not be provided in answer key. All answers can be found in text.

5B. Knife Safety
1.   Use the correct knife for the task at hand.
2.   Always cut away from yourself.
3.   Always cut on a cutting board. Do not cut on glass, marble, or metal.
4.   Place a damp towel underneath the cutting board to keep it from sliding as you cut.
5.   Keep knives sharp; a dull knife is more dangerous than a sharp one.
6.   When carrying a knife, hold it point down, parallel and close to your leg as you walk.
7.   A falling knife has no handle. Do not attempt to catch a falling knife; step back and allow it to fall.
8.   Never leave a knife in a sink of water; anyone reaching into the sink could be injured or the knife could be dented by pots or other utensils.

5C. Cuts of Vegetables
1. $\frac{1}{8}$ inch × $\frac{1}{8}$ inch × 1 to 2 inches
2. $\frac{1}{4}$ inch × $\frac{1}{4}$ inch × 2 inches
3. $\frac{3}{8}$ inch × $\frac{1}{2}$ inch × $\frac{1}{2}$ inch
4. $\frac{1}{8}$-inch × $\frac{1}{8}$-inch × $\frac{1}{8}$-inch dice
5. $\frac{1}{4}$-inch × $\frac{1}{4}$-inch × $\frac{1}{4}$-inch dice
6. $\frac{3}{8}$-inch × $\frac{3}{8}$-inch × $\frac{3}{8}$-inch dice

Similarities: 1.   Brunoise comes from a julienne.   2.   Small dice comes from a bâtonnet.

5D. Fill in the Blank
1.   knife tip; wrist
2.   back/tip; rocking
3.   away; metal; glass; marble
4.   heel; coarsest; finest
5.   root

5E. Dicing an Onion
1.   Remove the stem end with a paring knife, keeping the root intact. Peel off the outer skin without wasting too much.
2.   Cut the onion in half through the stem and root.
3.   Cut thin lines from the root toward the stem end, without cutting through the root.
4.   Make as many cuts as possible through the width of the onion without cutting through the root.
5.   Cut slices perpendicular to the other slices, producing diced onion.

5F. Chapter Review
1.   False   (p. 78) One must exert more effort using a dull knife, therefore increasing the chances of injury.
2.   True
3.   False   (p. 79) A steel is generally used to straighten the edge of a knife.
4.   False   (p. 84) An allumette has different dimensions that more resemble a julienne, only cut from a potato.
5.   False   (p. 79) Only water should be used to moisten the stone.
6.   True
7.   True
8.   True

5G. Putting It All Together

1. It takes much practice to perfect one's knife skills to the point where the resulting foods are both beautiful and produced quickly. However, once those skills are mastered, they can be a true way of distinguishing your foods from those of your competitors. Combined with a skill for purchasing only the best ingredients, properly handling them, applying cooking methods in a masterful way, and presenting the final dish with great attention to detail, executing excellent knife skills shows a chef's desire to produce only the very best foods for the clientele.

2. Hand-washing, rinsing, and sanitizing knives after contact with *each* food is vital in order to prevent cross-contamination. The very definition of cross-contamination—transmitting characteristics including bacteria from one food to another via contact by hands, knives, and cutting board—means that the washing and sanitation process must be carefully monitored in order to prevent it from occurring.

CHAPTER 6 ANSWER KEY

6A. Terminology
Answers will not be provided in answer key. All answers can be found in text.

6B. Discovering Tastes
1. d
2. h
3. g
4. a
5. f
6. c
7. b
8. i

6C. Categorizing Flavorings

Herbs:
1. cilantro
2. oregano
3. lavender
4. thyme
5. lemongrass

Spices:
6. paprika
7. coriander
8. ground mustard
9. capers
10. black pepper
11. garlic

6D. Herbs and Spices
1. a
2. c
3. b
4. d
5. d
6. a
7. c
8. b
9. d
10. a
11. b
12. c
13. d
14. c
15. b

6E. Short Answer
1. Japan
2. a. Taste buds   b. Back of throat   c. Roof of mouth
3. Saliva
4. a. At the top of the nasal cavity (the area within the head that collects the air that has been brought in through the nostrils)
   b. The area at the back of the throat contains receptors that take the aromas a "back way" up through the nasal cavity to the olfactory receptors. This greatly enhances our ability to observe the taste of a food or beverage once it has been placed in the mouth.
5. a. Season hot foods when they are hot and cold foods when they are cold because a food's temperature can affect how it tastes; foods served at warm temperatures offer the strongest tastes.
   b. A food with a thicker consistency will take longer to reach its peak intensity and will appear to have less flavor.
   c. A basic taste can be balanced or enhanced by using a small quantity of an opposing taste added to it. For example, lemonade that is too sour can be balanced by adding a small amount of sweetener. In the process the sour taste seems less extreme and is more palatable, and the sweetness adds a welcome taste as long as the lemonade hasn't been oversweetened.
   d. A moderate amount of fat in a food can help moderate the release of flavor compounds as the food is chewed and mixed with saliva. Too little fat and the flavors may disappear too quickly; too much fat may inhibit the sense organs' ability to absorb the flavor compounds to the fullest of their ability.

e. Another sense that humans possess, the ability to see, can play a tremendous role in our enjoyment of food even before we've taken a bite. A mere glimpse of a food can tell us a lot about color, texture, and portion size and can help us identify ingredients that may be appealing to us. Generally, as the color level of a food increases to match normal expectations, our perception of taste and flavor intensity increases as well.

6. Although each work scenario poses its own challenges, working in a nursing home may be a welcome change for some chefs. Doctor-prescribed diets create a special challenge for the chef, who often works hand-in-hand with a dietitian to create nutritious, satisfying meals that maximize the changing nutritional needs of aging clients. The mere fact that most of the clients are aging and therefore have a decreased ability to taste and smell means that the chef must strategize ways to flavor foods that will create interest while still meeting dietary requirements.

7. See page 116 (still and sparkling wines).

8. In an attempt to reduce the amount of hard liquor consumed in the United States, Thomas Jefferson, quite a French wine enthusiast, encouraged Americans to plant European wine grapes (*Vitis vinifera*) in an effort to increase wine production and offset the alcoholic beverages being consumed. As *Vitis vinifera* grapevine cuttings were brought back and forth between Europe and America, a destructive vine louse from American called phylloxera took hold in Europe. By the late 1800s many of the *Vitis vinifera* vineyards in France and elsewhere were destroyed, and numerous French vintners left their country for a career elsewhere.

9. The basic guidelines are as follows; descriptions are found on page 121.
    a. Match tastes.
    b. Match strengths.
    c. Match opposites.
    d. Match origins.

10.

Country	Common Flavors
China, general	General: Soy sauce, rice wine, fresh ginger Northern: Miso and/or garlic and/or sesame Southern: Sweet, sour, and hot Western: Black beans, garlic
Eastern Europe	(Jewish) Chicken fat and onion
Eastern and Northern Europe	Sour cream and dill or paprika or allspice or caraway
France	General: Olive oil, garlic, and basil or wine and herb or butter and/or sour cream and/or cheese plus wine and/or stock North: (Normandy) Apple, cider, Calvados South: (Provence) Olive oil, thyme, rosemary, marjoram, sage, plus tomato as a variation
Greece	Tomato, cinnamon or olive oil, lemon and oregano
India	Northern: Cumin, ginger, garlic Southern: Mustard seed, coconut, tamarind, chile
Italy	General: Olive oil, garlic, basil Northern: Wine vinegar, garlic Southern: Olive oil, garlic, parsley, anchovy, tomato
Japan	Soy sauce, sake, sugar
Mexico	Tomato and chile or lime and chile
Spain	Olive oil, garlic, nut or olive oil, onion, pepper, tomato
Thailand	Fish sauce, curry, chile

6F.   Chapter Review

1. True
2. True
3. False   (p. 109) Use less dried herbs than you would fresh herbs in a recipe. Loss of moisture in the dried herbs strengthens and concentrates the flavors.
4. True
5. True
6. True
7. False   (p. 113) Distilled vinegar is made from grain alcohol.
8. False   (p. 110) Salt can be tasted easily but not smelled.
9. True
10. True
11. False   (p. 103) Spices have been used therapeutically, cosmetically, medicinally, and ritualistically as well as for culinary purposes.
12. False   (p. 94) This is a myth created by the misinterpretation of a German article written in the 1800s. You can in fact taste all taste compounds everywhere on your tongue.
13. True
14. True
15. False   (p. 110) Although limited in flavoring application, basil and dill work wonderfully as toppings on savory breads and bagels.
16. True
17. False   (p. 116) Chianti is not one of the more popular red grape varietals.
18. True
19. True
20. False   (p. 117) They may have a certain rich, complex flavor with cherry and raspberry undertones; they will not be identical beverages. Differences in the conditions under which the grapes were grown or the techniques the vintners used to make the wines will create noticeable differences between them.
21. True
22. True
23. False   (p. 119) When selecting wines to use as flavorings, choose only wines that have a nice enough flavor that you would consider drinking them as a beverage. In other words, find wines to cook with that are flavorful and add a complementary flavor without being overly expensive; do not use wines just because they're called cooking wines and they're inexpensive.
24. True
25. True
26. True
27. False   (p. 128) Creole cooking is found in the southern Atlantic rim, resulting from the confluence of the Columbian exchange, the Atlantic slave trade, and the European age of exploration. As a result, Creole food is found in Brazil, the Caribbean, Cuba, the West Indies, coastal Mexico, and the southern United States, as well as other places.

6G. Putting It All Together

1. The chef could try a variety of things. First, if the guest wants to make a more drastic change, the chef could recommend a vegetarian dish, which would be naturally low in cholesterol because of the lack of animal products. To create a meaty texture and flavor, the chef could use ingredients that are naturally high in amino acid glutamates and therefore possess an umami taste profile: mushrooms, highly reduced vegetable stock, soy sauce, tomatoes, and perhaps a small amount of cheese. Third, the chef could suggest that the guest first adjust to eating smaller portion sizes of meats and to choose meats that are lower in cholesterol. For example, red meats in general are much higher in cholesterol than white meats and some fish.

2. The cuisines of this warm, even hot part of the world are characterized by fresh local ingredients (available, in many cases, year-round) from both land and sea. The foods of this region are influenced by many countries with a wide range of history and practices: Greece, Turkey, Syria, Lebanon, Egypt, Jordan, Israel, North Africa, Spain, southern France, southern Italy, Sicily, and Sardinia. Bold flavors, often available seasonally, are prepared using simple and quick cooking techniques. Many of these countries are still based on an agrarian and fishing lifestyle, and therefore those ingredients abound. The goal with the preparation of the foods is to prepare a historically accurate dish that highlights the quality of the ingredients used. Olive oils, a plethora of vegetables and fish, tree nuts, fruits—fresh and dried, citrus, dried beans and grains, yogurt and cheese, grapes and wine, and a variety of aromatics are commonly used.

CHAPTER 7 ANSWER KEY

7A. Terminology
Answers will not be provided in answer key. All answers can be found in text.

7B. Comparing Creams
1. e   3. b
2. d   4. a

7C. Cheese Identification
1. e   6. a   11. d   16. j
2. g   7. s   12. c   17. i
3. b   8. l   13. p
4. m   9. r   14. n
5. f   10. q   15. h

7D. Milk Products
1. c   9. a
2. a   10. b, c
3. a   11. d
4. c   12. c
5. d   13. c
6. b   14. d
7. b   15. c
8. c

7E. Chapter Review
1. True
2. False   (p. 135) Margarine is not made from animal products and therefore does not contain cholesterol.
3. True
4. False   (p. 132) By law, all Grade A milk must be pasteurized before retail sale.
5. True
6. True
7. True
8. False   (p. 168) Yogurt is not automatically a health food; it is only as healthful or low in fat as the milk from which it is made.
9. False   (p. 135) Margarine is not a dairy product and is included in this chapter only because it is so commonly used as a substitute for butter. It is actually made from animal or vegetable fats or a combination thereof. Flavorings, colorings, emulsifiers, preservatives, and vitamins are added before it is hydrogenated.
10. False   (p. 145) Processed cheese food contains less natural cheese and more moisture than regular processed cheese. Often vegetable oil and milk solids are added to make the cheese food soft and spreadable.
11. True
12. True
13. True
14. False   (p. 133) Milk, as well as all perishable foods, should be refrigerated at 41°F or below.
15. True
16. True
17. False   (p. 136) The FDA allows the manufacture and distribution of raw milk cheeses in the United States as long as they are aged more than 60 days at a temperature not less than 35°F.
18. True

7F. Putting It All Together

1. European-style whole butter would provide a creamier texture as a final addition to the poulette sauce because of its higher fat content. As you learned in this chapter as well as in Chapter 6, Flavors and Flavorings, fat creates a smoother texture that coats the tongue for an improved mouth feel. Therefore, the larger amount of fat found in European-style butter compared to traditional American-style butter would result in a richer, creamier sauce. You will learn more about this process, called a final liaison, in Chapter 10, Stocks and Sauces.

2. Because cholesterol is a lipid found only in animal products, such as milks and creams, when the fat is removed from a dairy product to create a lower-fat version, the new version becomes naturally lower in cholesterol as well as fat. You will learn more about cholesterol and fats in Chapter 23, Healthy Cooking.

CHAPTER 8 ANSWER KEY

8A. Terminology
Answers will not be provided in answer key. All answers can be found in text.

8B. Short Answer
1. Use one hand for dipping the food into the liquid ingredients and the other hand to dip the food into the dry ingredients.
2. a. Prepare the batter.
   b. Pat the food dry and dredge it in flour if desired.
   c. Dip the item in the batter and place it directly in the hot fat.
3. a. Fat: $2.15
   b. Water: $0.43
   c. Milk solids: $0.11
4. a. Work patterns
   b. Tool/equipment needs
5. a. Assemble the mise en place.
   b. With your left hand, place the food to be breaded in the flour and coat it evenly. With the same hand, remove the floured item, shake off the excess flour, and place the floured item in the egg wash.
   c. With your right hand, remove the item from the egg wash and place it in the bread crumbs or meal.
   d. With your left hand, cover the item with crumbs or meal and press lightly to make sure the item is completely and evenly coated. Shake off the excess crumbs or meal and place the breaded item in the empty pan for finished product.
6. a. Fat: 12.8 oz.
   b. Water: 2.56 oz.
   c. Milk solids: 0.11 oz.

8C. Multiple Choice
1. b   6. c
2. a   7. c
3. d   8. a
4. a   9. b
5. d   10. a

8D. Chapter Review
1. True
2. False   (p. 157) Beer batters contain beer for leavening as well as for flavor.
3. False   (p. 150) Front-of-the-house personnel, such as waiters, must prepare mise en place that may include cutting drink garnishes, folding napkins, polishing flatware/silverware, and refilling salt and pepper shakers, to name a few.
4. False   (p. 151) A food's weight does not always equal its measurement in volume.
5. False   (p. 153) Ghee contains the clarified fat and milk solids together, and the milk solids are allowed to brown to enhance flavor. Milk solids are removed when making classical clarified butter.
6. True
7. True
8. False   (p. 156) Breaded foods are usually cooked by deep-fat frying or pan-frying.
9. True
10. False   (p. 153) The bread was likely too fresh as opposed to being stale. You should have used 2- to 4-day-old bread instead of fresh bread to make the fresh bread crumbs.
11. True
12. True

8E. Putting It All Together

1. A tamis is a piece of equipment composed of a metal ring that has a mesh on one side of the opening. Foods such as bread crumbs are placed in the tamis, and moving the equipment back and forth in a shaking motion sifts the bread crumbs, resulting in a fine and more consistently shaped and sized crumb.

2. Raw meats of any kind should be stored on the lower shelves in the refrigerator, below any raw produce, dairy, and other ingredients that may be considered ready to eat.

CHAPTER 9 ANSWER KEY

9A. Terminology
Answers will not be provided in answer key. All answers can be found in text.

9B. Cooking Methods

Cooking Method	Medium	Equipment
ex: *Sautéing*	*Fat*	*Stove*
1. Stewing	Fat, then liquid	Stove (and oven), tilt skillet
2. Deep-frying	Fat	Deep-fryer
3. Broiling	Air	Broiler, salamander, rotisserie
4. Poaching	Water or other liquid	Stove, oven, steam-jacketed kettle, tilt skillet
5. Grilling	Air	Grill
6. Simmering	Water or other liquid	Stove, steam-jacketed kettle, tilt skillet
7. Baking	Air	Oven
8. Roasting	Air	Oven
9. Steaming	Steam	Stove, convection steamer
10. Braising	Fat, then liquid	Stove (and oven), tilt skillet

9C. Smoking Points
1. f
2. i
3. h
4. a
5. b
6. g
7. c
8. d

9D. Multiple Choice
1. a
2. d
3. c
4. a
5. c
6. b
7. d
8. d
9. a
10. b, d
11. a
12. c

9E. Short Answer

1. **Braising**
   a. Larger pieces of food
   b. Brown, then simmer/steam
   c. Cooking liquid covers ⅓–¼ of the food
   d. Cooking time is longer

   Stewing
   a. Smaller pieces of food
   b. Brown or blanch, then simmer/steam
   c. Cooking liquid completely covers the food
   d. Cooking time is shorter

2. a. The food must be placed in a basket or on a rack to allow for circulation of the steam.
   b. A lid should cover the steaming unit to trap steam and allow heat to build up.

3. a. Cut, pound, or otherwise prepare the chicken breast.
   b. Heat a sauté pan and add enough fat to just cover the pan's bottom.
   c. Add the chicken to the sauté pan in a single layer, presentation side down. Do not crowd the pan.
   d. Adjust temperature as needed to control browning; flip when half cooked.
   e. Turn the chicken breast.
   f. Cook until done.

4. a. Cut, trim, or otherwise prepare the food to be poached.
   b. Bring an adequate amount of cooking liquid to the desired starting temperature. Place the food in the liquid.
   c. For submersion poaching, the liquid should completely cover the food.
   d. For shallow poaching, the liquid should come approximately halfway up the side of the food. Cover the pan with a piece of buttered parchment paper or a lid.
   e. Maintaining the proper temperature, poach the food to the desired doneness in the oven or on the stove top. Doneness is generally determined by timing, internal temperature, or tenderness.
   f. Remove the food and hold it for service in a portion of the cooking liquid or, using an ice bath, cool it in the cooking liquid.
   g. The cooking liquid can sometimes be used to prepare an accompanying sauce or reserved for use in other dishes.

9F. Matching

1. e   2. c   3. b   4. a   5. d   6. g

9G. Chapter Review

1. False (p. 164) Heat is generated quickly and uniformly throughout the food. Microwave cooking does not brown foods, however, and often gives meats a dry, mushy texture, making microwave ovens an unacceptable replacement for traditional ovens (for cooking).
2. True
3. False (p. 264) A wood-fired grill is an example of the radiation heat transfer method.
4. False (p. 23) Chapter 2: 165°F internal temperature
5. True
6. False (p. 167) In broiling, the heat source comes from above the cooking surface.
7. False (p. 172) Deep-frying is an example of a dry-heat cooking method.
8. True
9. False (p. 170) Stir-frying is a variation in technique to sautéing, but it does not necessarily use any additional fat.
10. False (p. 175) A court bouillon should be used when poaching or simmering foods.
11. True
12. True
13. True
14. False (p. 23) Chapter 2: 165°F internal temperature
15. False (p. 173) Battered foods that will stick to the wire frying baskets are usually cooked using the swimming method.
16. True
17. False (p. 173) Filling the wire frying basket while it is hanging over the hot fat allows unnecessary salt and food particles to fall into the fat, shortening its life.
18. True

9H. Putting It All Together

1. Just as different metals are more efficient at conducting heat than others (for example, copper is better at conducting heat than stainless steel), foods cook at different rates in different media. So water (liquid) is a more efficient cooking medium (and therefore a better conductor of heat) than air, a gas. However, compared to these two media, nearly all metals are superior conductors.
2. The purpose of braising is to tenderize a tough cut of meat, and therefore the first way to determine doneness is to insert a braising fork into the center of the piece. If is the fork can be inserted and removed without resistance, the meat is tender and ready to serve. The second determining factor is whether the meat has reached an internal temperature of 165°F, the upper end of the temperature danger zone; if the meat is at this level of doneness, it is also safe to consume.

CHAPTER 10 ANSWER KEY

10A. Terminology
Answers will not be provided in answer key. All answers can be found in text.

10B. Stock-Making Review
White stock: reference page 188.
Brown stock: reference page 190.
Fish stock: reference page 191.

10C. Mother Sauce Review

	Mother Sauce	Thickener	Liquid
1.	Béchamel	White roux	Milk
2.	Velouté	Blond roux	White chicken/veal/fish stock
3.	Espagnole	Brown roux	Beef stock
4.	Tomato	Tomato purée	White stock
5.	Hollandaise	Emulsion	Butter

10D. Small Sauces

	Mother Sauce	Ingredients Added
1.	Béchamel	Scalded cream, lemon juice
2.	Béchamel	Cheddar, Worcestershire sauce, dry mustard
3.	Béchamel	Gruyère, Parmesan, scalded cream, butter
4.	Béchamel	Heavy cream, crayfish butter, paprika, crayfish meat
5.	Béchamel	Onion, sweated, cook and strain sauce
6.	Chicken/veal velouté	Lemon juice, liaison
7.	Chicken velouté	Cream
8.	Fish velouté	Diced shallots, dry white wine, butter, parsley
9.	Fish velouté	Heavy cream, cayenne pepper, lobster butter, lobster coral
10.	Fish velouté	Mushroom, liaison, strained
11.	Chicken/veal velouté	Sauce allemande, tomato paste, butter
12.	Chicken/veal velouté	Sauce allemande, heavy cream, mustard, horseradish
13.	Chicken/veal velouté	Sauce allemande, mushroom, shallots, cream, lemon juice, parsley
14.	Chicken velouté	Sauce suprême, glace de volaille, red pepper butter
15.	Chicken velouté	Sauce suprême, onion, butter, paprika, strained
16.	Chicken velouté	Sauce suprême, glace de volaille
17.	Espagnole	Demi-glace, red wine, shallots, bay leaf, thyme, black pepper, butter, sliced poached beef marrow
18.	Espagnole	Demi-glace, mushrooms, shallots, white wine, diced tomatoes, parsley
19.	Espagnole	Demi-glace, white wine, shallots, lemon juice, cayenne pepper, tarragon
20.	Espagnole	Poivrade sauce (with bacon trimmings added to mirepoix), red wine, dash of cayenne
21.	Espagnole	Demi-glace, Madeira wine or ruby port
22.	Espagnole	Demi-glace, red wine, shallots, strained
23.	Espagnole	Demi-glace, truffles
24.	Espagnole	Demi-glace, shallots, white wine, white wine vinegar, cornichons, tarragon, parsley, chervil
25.	Espagnole	Demi-glace, mirepoix, bouquet garni, vinegar, white wine, crushed peppercorns, butter, strained
26.	Espagnole	Demi-glace, onion, white wine, Dijon mustard, sugar, sliced pickles
27.	Tomato sauce	Onion, celery, garlic, bay leaf, thyme, green pepper, hot pepper sauce
28.	Tomato sauce	Mushroom, cooked ham, cooked tongue
29.	Tomato sauce	Mushroom, onion, sliced black or green olives

Mother Sauce	Ingredients Added
30. Hollandaise	Shallots, tarragon, chervil, crushed peppercorns, white wine vinegar, cayenne pepper; tarragon garnish
31. Hollandaise	Béarnaise sauce, tomato paste, heavy cream
32. Hollandaise	Béarnaise sauce, glace de viande
33. Hollandaise	Infused with saffron
34. Hollandaise	Orange juice, orange zest (blood oranges are traditional)
35. Hollandaise	Heavy cream

10E. Short Answer

1.
   a. Start the stock in cold water.
   b. Simmer the stock gently.
   c. Skim the stock frequently.
   d. Strain the stock carefully.
   e. Cool the stock quickly.
   f. Store the stock properly.
   g. Degrease the stock.
2. Hollandaise sauce: reference page 208.
3.
   a. Incorrect temperature of eggs and/or butter.
   b. Butter added too quickly.
   c. Egg yolks overcooked.
   d. Too much butter added.
   e. Sauce not whipped enough.
4. Thickening agents: reference page 195.

10F. Matching

1. d, k, n   4. c, g, m
2. b, i, l   5. e, h, o
3. a, f, j

10G. Chapter Review

1. True
2. False (p. 197) To prevent lumps when making sauces, add cold stock to hot roux or room-temperature roux to hot stock.
3. False (p. 198) Temperatures over 185°F will cause the yolks to curdle.
4. True
5. True
6. True
7. False (p. 198) Tempering gradually raises the temperature of a cold liquid, such as a liaison, by adding hot liquid.
8. True
9. True
10. False (p. 191) Fish stock should simmer for only 30 to 45 minutes.
11. False (p. 196) Antonin Carême is credited with developing the modern system for classifying hundreds of sauces.
12. True
13. True
14. False (p. 228) A nage is derived from a court bouillon.
15. False (p. 193) A china cap is the most appropriate piece of equipment.
16. True
17. True
18. False (p. 185) Beef bones are generally from an older animal and contain less collagen protein from cartilage and other connective tissue than veal bones or chicken bones, which in today's food service industry tend to come from a younger animal.

19. False   (p. 192) Vegetable stocks are not produced using bones as an ingredient and therefore contain no collagen protein, thereby resulting in a thinner body than meat stocks.

10H. Putting It All Together

1. Because fat is lighter than liquid, it will naturally rise to the surface of the stock. If the fat is of animal origin, it will solidify into a mass that is impenetrable by air. The lack of ready access to air, one of the elements bacteria need to survive, slows the growth of bacteria and may cause the stock to have a slightly longer shelf life provided the stock is stored at suggested temperatures.

2. Hot, freshly strained stock should be poured into clean, shallow metal containers and then chilled in an ice bath, stirring periodically during the cooling process. The stock should cool to 70°F (21°C) within 2 hours, then cool to 41°F (5°C) or below within 4 hours. Cover and refrigerate; store cooked food above raw. Because the stock should be cooled in shallow containers (generally less than 4 inches deep), a cooling wand may not be an effective tool.

    Cooling wands, which may vary in size but generally tend to be 2 feet long at a minimum, are generally designed to be frozen and then inserted into a deep container of cooling foods, such as a 5-gallon (or larger) storage bucket. Because the depth of the cooling food is so great, it will take a longer time to cool in an ice bath than if it is in a metal container that is 4 inches deep or less. As a result, the cooling wand can expedite the cooling process by being inserted into the center of the deep container, therefore reaching the center of the cooling food product that may not otherwise have been penetrated as quickly by the sole use of an ice bath. (See Chapter 2, Food Safety and Sanitation, for more details.)

CHAPTER 11 ANSWER KEY

11A. Terminology
Answers will not be provided in answer key. All answers can be found in text.

11B. Short Answer
1. Broth preparation: reference page 235.
2. Consommé ingredients and procedure: reference page 239.
3. a. Consommé was allowed to boil, or it was stirred after the raft formed.
   b. Stock was not degreased.
   c. Poor-quality stock.
   d. Onion brûlée omitted.
4. a. Thoroughly chill and degrease the consommé.
   b. Lightly beat four egg whites per gallon of consommé and combine with the cold consommé.
   c. Slowly bring the consommé to a simmer, stirring occasionally. Stop stirring when the egg whites begin to coagulate.
   d. When the egg whites are completely coagulated, carefully strain the consommé.
5. a. Never add cold milk or cream to a hot soup.
   b. Add milk or cream just before service.
   c. Do not boil soup after milk or cream has been added.
   d. Use béchamel or cream sauce instead of milk or cream to finish cream soups because the presence of roux or other starch helps prevent curdling.
6. Cream soup ingredients and preparation: reference page 242.

11C. Soup Review
1. Seven common categories of soup: reference page 234.
2. a. Beef broth and beef consommé:
      Commonalities: Both have the same base—beef stock.
      Differences: Beef broth uses meat and vegetables to give it a fuller flavor, and consommé uses clearmeat.
   b. Cream of mushroom soup and lentil soup:
      Commonalities: Both may use a stock to form the base, and both may finish the soup with cream.
      Differences: Cream of mushroom soup is thickened with roux, and lentil soup is thickened with a purée of the vegetables.
   c. Gazpacho and cold consommé:
      Commonalities: Both are cold soups.
      Differences: Gazpacho uses uncooked ingredients, and cold consommé uses ingredients that are cooked, strained, and cooled before service.

11D. Chapter Review
1. True
2. True
3. True
4. False   (p. 238) A consommé is a clarified broth.
5. False   (p. 241) Cream soups are thickened with a roux or other starch.
6. True
7. False   (p. 248) Cold soups should be served at 41°F/4°C or below.
8. False   (p. 238) If the consommé is insufficiently clear, a clarification can be performed.
9. False   (p. 248) The cold temperature at which the soup is served dulls the soup's flavor, and therefore more seasoning is required.
10. True
11. True
12. False   (p. 247) Not all chowders contain milk or cream.
13. True

14. False   (p. 22) Thick soups do scorch easily, but the food safety challenge is properly cooling and reheating the thick products as quickly as possible; both processes take longer with the thicker consistency.

15. True

16. False   The conversion factor would be 0.375.

17. True

18. True

19. False   (p. 294) Vichyssoise contains three potentially hazardous foods: potatoes, chicken stock, and heavy cream.

20. True

11E. Putting It All Together

1. A chef must be certain that the raw ingredients to be used in the production of the soup have been sourced from a reputable supplier and stored at the proper temperature. Once the product has arrived in-house, it should be washed thoroughly to remove contaminants, soil, and pesticides. The utmost care in handling the food product must be taken so as to prevent cross-contamination because the soup will never be cooked, therefore eliminating the opportunity to kill food-borne pathogens. Finally, the chef must work quickly during preparation and service in order to keep the ingredients out of the temperature danger zone as much as possible. The finished product must be stored and served below 41°F.

2. Conduct the final seasoning of hot soups when they are hot and cold soups when they are cold (and at the serving temperature so that seasoning is accurate). Because warm foods amplify flavors more readily, extra care must be taken to adjust the seasoning of a cold soup to make sure it is perfect.

3. The cost of the ingredients to produce New England–Style Clam Chowder is significantly higher than those for Chilled Cherry Soup. The more costly ingredients for the chowder are the clams, salt pork, and cream. Although most chefs would not consider these ingredients expensive, one must also consider that the labor and time needed to mise en place the ingredients (including dicing the vegetables) and prepare the chowder is fairly significant compared to the cherry soup. Time will also be consumed cooking the soup, and because it contains cream, added care will be needed to make sure it does not scorch.

    In contrast, Chilled Cherry Soup contains fairly inexpensive ingredients compared to New England–Style Clam Chowder. Aside from the champagne, which could be fairly costly if the chef chooses a good-quality wine to complement the delicate flavors of the fruit in the soup, and the crème fraîche, the number of costly ingredients is significantly lower and the labor and time required to produce the soup is noticeably less. Although pitting the cherries will take time, this can be done by just about any staff member in the kitchen and requires no particular skill level to perform. Holding the soup chilled is not technically difficult compared to the chowder.

CHAPTER 12 ANSWER KEY

12A. Terminology
Answers will not be provided in answer key. All answers can be found in text.

12B. Fill in the Blank
1. good
2. low, long
3. firm, non-red
4. flour
5. carryover, retain
6. larding
7. connective tissue
8. bacteria, parasites
9. tough
10. against

12C. Matching
1. d   2. e   3. f   4. b   5. c

12D. Cooking Methods
Reference pages 278–296.

12E. Chapter Review
1. False   (p. 276) Fresh meats should be stored at 30°F–35°F.
2. False   (p. 272) Green meats are meats that are frozen before rigor mortis has had an opportunity to dissipate.
3. True
4. True   The USDA stamp ensures only that the meat is processed in a sanitary way.
5. False   (p. 274) USDA Prime cuts are used for the finest establishments.
6. False   (p. 274) Yield grades apply only to lamb and beef.
7. True
8. True
9. False   (p. 276) Meat will hold in a vacuum package for 3 to 4 weeks under refrigeration.
10. True
11. False   (p. 274) The marbling in the meat is the principal factor in determining meat quality.
12. True
13. True
14. True
15. False   (p. 275) USDA inspection ensures only that the meat was handled in a sanitary fashion.
16. True
17. False   (p. 289) Because of its vast size, a steamship round should be removed from the oven at approximately 125°F to take into account carryover cooking.
18. False   The conversion factor is 2.5.
19. False   (p. 277) A whole stuffed chicken is not such a lean cut of meat that it needs lardoons of fat inserted into its center in order to add flavor and moisture. If anything, a whole stuffed chicken needs to be trussed in order to maintain its shape and even cooking—or even barded.
20. True
21. False   (p. 277) The standards state that grass and forage shall be the only feed source consumed for the lifetime of the animal except for the milk consumed before weaning. Therefore, animals that are fed any grain at all, even just before slaughter, cannot be labeled exclusively as grass-fed.
22. False   (p. 277) The meat of grass-fed animals is leaner than that of animals that eat grain.
23. True

12F. Putting It All Together

1. The time/temperature principle applies to all areas of food service, from the time an animal is slaughtered to the time the food is plated and presented to the guest. If a primary supplier does not follow HACCP procedures properly, then a chef's job is far more challenging because he or she has an even smaller window of time to work with the food to prepare it for the guest and still keep it safe for human consumption. Providing the primary supplier follows HACCP properly, the chef should have a maximum of 4 hours to work with the food, but the less time taken, the better.

2. The text does not recommend consuming these meats rare because at this temperature one cannot ensure that harmful bacteria have been killed, and therefore eating them may harm the consumer. Considering past risks of trichinosis in pork in particular, pork should be cooked to a minimum internal temperature of 145ºF, depending on the cut.

3. *Au jus* refers to serving a roasted piece of meat, poultry, or game with the natural pan drippings that result from the cooking process. The juices may be strained before serving but are not thickened.

CHAPTER 13 ANSWER KEY

13A. Terminology
Answers will not be provided in answer key. All answers can be found in text.

13B. Primal Cuts of Beef
1. Chuck
2. Rib
3. Short loin
4. Sirloin
5. Round
6. Brisket and shank
7. Short plate
8. Flank

13C. Cuts from the Round

	Subprimal/Fabricated Cut	Cooking Process/Use
1.	Inside (top) round	Roast
2.	Eye of round	Braise
3.	Outside (bottom) round	Braise
4.	Knuckle or tip	Roast
5.	Leg or round bone	Simmering—stocks, soups, and consommés

13D. Matching I
1. c   2. e   3. a   4. b

13E. Cuts of Beef and Applied Cooking Methods

	Cooking Method	Subprimal/Fabricated Cut	Primal Cut
1.	Combination (braise/stew)	Chuck	Chuck
2.	Combination (braise)	Shank	Brisket, shank
3.	Dry heat (broil/grill/roast/sauté)	Strip loin	Short loin
4.	Dry heat (broil/grill/roast)	Ground beef	Chuck
5.	Combination (braise)	Flank steak	Flank
6.	Moist heat (simmer)	Brisket	Brisket, shank
7.	Dry heat (broil/grill/roast)	Tenderloin	Short loin
8.	Dry heat (broil/grill)	Flank steak	Flank
9.	Dry heat (broil/grill/roast)	Tenderloin	Short loin
10.	Dry heat (roast)	Steamship/top round	Round
11.	Combination (braise)	Top round	Round
12.	Dry heat (broil/grill)	Skirt steak	Short plate
13.	Combination (stew)	Stew meat	Chuck
14.	Combination (braise/stew)	Ground beef	Chuck
15.	Dry heat (broil/grill/roast/sauté)	Strip loin	Short loin

13F. Multiple Choice
1. b
2. c
3. d
4. a
5. a
6. c
7. a: 2; b: 1; c: 3

13G. Matching II
1. b, e, g
2. c, d, h
3. a, f, i

13H. Chapter Review

1. True
2. False   (p. 302) The chuck has a high proportion of connective tissue, which makes it more flavorful than the tenderloin.
3. True
4. False   (p. 304) *Prime rib* refers to the fact that the rib is made up of the majority of the primal cut from which it comes.
5. True
6. True
7. True
8. False   (p. 304) Pastrami is made by curing and peppering the brisket.
9. True
10. False   (p. 304) Grinding the shanks is appropriate, but the meat is typically used in soups and stocks.
11. False   (p. 323) Four pounds of meat is needed because you're not increasing the yield of the total recipe, only the size and number of portions that result.
12. True
13. True
14. False   (p. 307) Although beef's full flavor does go well with strong flavors, more tender cuts can also go well with more subtly flavored sauces, such as béarnaise sauce or a red wine reduction.
15. True

13I. Putting It All Together

1. Trussing, barding
2. No, it would not make good financial sense to braise a strip loin. First of all, as a chef you will be paying good money for a strip loin because it is a tender piece of meat with good marbling and therefore will be in high demand on your menu. You will not want to perform such a long, drawn-out cooking process on such a cut, partially because of what it costs you in time and money to braise and partially because you don't need to. In most restaurants a good-quality steak is in high demand, and in order to make the most money from that entrée you want to have minimal processing of that product so that your profit margin is greater. If you were determined to braise, you would be better off spending less money on a piece of meat that would benefit from the braising process because the resulting product would benefit and would be flavorful. Because your food cost was less on the latter braised product, your profit margin will be greater than if you had used strip loin.

CHAPTER 14 ANSWER KEY

14A. Terminology
Answers will not be provided in answer key. All answers can be found in text.

14B. Primal Cuts Identification
Answers will not be provided in answer key. All answers can be found in text on pages 328–331.

14C. Primal Cuts of Veal
1. Shoulder
2. Rib
3. Loin
4. Leg
5. Foreshank and breast

14D. Cuts of Veal and Applied Cooking Methods

	Cooking Method	Subprimal/ Fabricated Cut	Primal Cut
1.	Combination (stew)	Cubed veal	Shoulder
2.	Dry heat (broil/grill/roast)	Rib eye	Rib
3.	Combination (braise)	Breast	Foreshank, breast
4.	Dry heat (broil/grill/sauté)	Loin chops	Loin
5.	Combination (stew)	Cubed veal	Shoulder
6.	Combination (braise)	Sweetbreads	Offal
7.	Combination (braise)	Kidneys	Offal
8.	Dry heat (broil/grill)	Ground veal	Shoulder
9.	Combination (braise)	Ground veal	Shoulder
10.	Dry heat (broil/grill/roast/sauté)	Veal tenderloin	Loin
11.	Dry heat (roast/sauté)	Top round	Leg
12.	Dry heat (broil/grill/sauté)	Calves' liver	Offal
13.	Combination (braise)	Hindshank/foreshank	Leg/foreshank, breast
14.	Dry heat (roast/sauté)	Leg	Leg

14E. Short Answer
1. a. Remove the shank.
   b. Remove the butt tenderloin.
   c. Remove the pelvic bone.
   d. Remove the top round.
   e. Remove the shank meat.
   f. Remove the round bone and knuckle.
   g. Remove the sirloin.
   h. Remove the eye of round.
2. a. Top round
   b. Eye round
   c. Knuckle
   d. Sirloin
   e. Bottom round
   f. Butt tenderloin

3.
Primal Cut	Subprimal/ Fabricated Cut	Menu Example
Rib:		
a.	Hotel rack	Roast veal with porcini mushrooms
b.	Rib chops	Braised veal chop with risotto
c.	Rib eye	Broiled rib eye with chipotle sauce
Loin (any three of the following would be appropriate answers):		
	Veal loin	Roasted veal loin with wild mushrooms
	Loin chops	Sautéed veal chops with mushroom sauce
	Boneless strip loin	Roasted veal loin sauce poulette
	Veal tenderloin	Sautéed tenderloin with garlic and herbs

4.   Reference page 328.

14F. Matching I
1. f   2. a   3. b (d is appropriate for breast only)   4. e   5. c

14G. Matching II
1. b, e   2. a, d   3. c, f

14H. Chapter Review
1.   True
2.   True
3.   False   (p. 336) Sweetbreads are pressed to improve their texture.
4.   False   (p. 334) Émincé should be cut across the grain.
5.   True
6.   True
7.   True
8.   True
9.   False   (p. 328) Restricting their movement prevents their muscles from toughening.
10. True
11. True
12. False   (p. 328) Veal shoulder would be better ground or cubed and cooked using a combination cooking method.
13. True
14. False   (p. 328) It is braised to break down the tough meat found in the foreshank.
15. True

14I. Putting It All Together
1.   Veal are usually male because they are more expendable as livestock. A farmer will keep as many female cows through adulthood as possible because they are more valuable for reproducing young and producing milk. One male cow can serve as stud to hundreds of female cows, limiting the number that are needed on a farm at any one time.
2.   Because veal comes from a younger and more tender animal, the length of the cooking time involved in braising or stewing veal is considerably shorter than that for beef. With veal's mild flavor, braising and stewing will tenderize the meat but will also make its flavors more complex than if it had been cooked using a dry-heat cooking technique such as sautéing or grilling.

CHAPTER 15 ANSWER KEY

15A. Terminology
Answers will not be provided in answer key. All answers can be found in text.

15B. Primal Cuts Identification
Answers will not be provided in answer key. All answers can be found in text on pages 350–353.

15C. Primal Cuts of Lamb
1. Shoulder   4. Leg
2. Rack   5. Breast
3. Loin

15D. Subprimal or Fabricated Cuts

	Primal Cut	Subprimal/Fabricated Cut	Cooking Methods
1.	a.	Chops	Broil/grill
	b.	Diced/ground	Stew/grill
2.	a.	Chops	Broil/grill
	b.	Lamb rack	Roast
3.	a.	Chops/boneless roast	Grill/roast
	b.	Medallions/noisettes	Sauté
4.	a.	Lamb leg (bone-in)	Braise
	b.	Boned leg	Roast
5.	a.	Breast	Braise
	b.	Lamb shanks	Braise

15E. Cuts of Lamb and Applied Cooking Methods

	Cooking Method	Subprimal/Fabricated Cut	Primal Cut
1.	Broil/grill/roast	Loin chops	Loin
2.	Stew	Diced lamb	Shoulder
3.	Broil/grill/roast/sauté	Lamb loin	Loin
4.	Stew	Diced lamb	Shoulder
5.	Broil/grill/roast/sauté	Frenched lamb rack	Hotel rack
6.	Combination (braise)	Breast	Breast
7.	Dry heat (broil/grill/roast/sauté)	Lamb rack	Hotel rack
8.	Dry heat (roast)	Lamb leg	Leg

15F. Short Answer
1. Reference page 354.
2. Reference page 355.
3. Reference page 356.

15G. Chapter Review
1. False   (p. 350) Lamb primals are not classified into a forequarter and hindquarter as with beef, or a foresaddle and hindsaddle as with veal.
2. True
3. True
4. False   (p. 352) Even though lamb is consumed young and tender, the shank is always a relatively lean, tough cut of meat and therefore should be cooked using long, moist cooking methods.
5. True
6. True
7. False   (p. 332) The chine bone runs through the primal lamb rack.
8. True
9. True

10. False   (p. 354) Frenching can be done on bones of other animals such as veal or pork.
11. False   (p. 366) 15 portions
12. False   (p. 352) The rib eye comes from the rack.
13. True
14. True
15. True
16. False   (p. 352) Although lamb is usually slaughtered young, its fat still maintains a strong flavor (compared to other meats), and therefore it is usually accompanied by strong flavors such as garlic and resinous herbs such as rosemary, mint, and oregano. Acidic ingredients may also accompany the meat because they help balance the strong flavor of the fat.

15H. Putting It All Together

1. Even though lamb from Australia and New Zealand accounts for 50 percent of the lamb sold in the United States, most lamb produced in the United States is actually consumed there. Even though fewer Americans purchase lamb to prepare at home, sales figures for meals containing lamb in restaurants show that Americans like eating it perhaps more than they like preparing it. The larger size of American lambs likely has to do with how they are raised. If American lambs are fed primarily grain and not grass, like their competition, it would suggest that the animal is less mobile during its short life, lacking the need to forage for its food. This, and also strong animal husbandry practices in America, accounts for fewer animals produced, but their larger size helps make for a better yield.

2. With knowledge and practice, a chef should easily be able to break down the hotel rack in-house, thereby saving a fairly significant amount of money per pound on a highly desirable cut of lamb. A chef will know whether this savings is significant enough to continue the practice, or whether his or her time and money are too valuable. Can the chef break down the hotel rack for less money, and if so, how much less?

CHAPTER 16 ANSWER KEY

16A. Terminology
Answers will not be provided in answer key. All answers can be found in text.

16B. Primal Cuts of Pork
1. Boston butt
2. Loin
3. Fresh ham
4. Shoulder
5. Belly

16C. Subprimal or Fabricated Cuts

Primal Cut	Subprimal/ Fabricated Cut	Cooking Methods	Cured & Smoked	Fresh
1.	Boston butt	Broil/grill/sauté	X	X
2.	Pork back ribs	Steam, then grill		X
	Pork loin chops	Broil/grill		X
	Pork tenderloin	Sauté/roast/braise/broil/grill	X	
	Pork loin	Roast/braise		X
3.	Fresh ham	Roast/boil	X	X
4.	Spare ribs	Simmer, then grill	X	X
	Bacon	Sauté/grill	X	
5.	Picnic shoulder	Bake	X	X

16D. Cuts of Pork and Applied Cooking Methods

	Cooking Method	Subprimal/Fabricated Cut	Primal Cut
1.	Dry heat (roast)	Fresh ham	Fresh ham
2.	Moist heat (simmer)	Boston butt	Boston butt
3.	Dry heat (broil/grill/sauté/roast)	Pork tenderloin	Loin
4.	Combination (braise)	Pork loin	Loin
5.	Combination (steam, then grill)	Spare ribs	Belly
6.	Dry heat (roast/bake)	Picnic shoulder	Shoulder
7.	Dry heat (sauté)	Bacon	Belly

16E. Short Answer
1. Reference page 376.
2. a. Shoulder
   b. Shoulder hock
   c. Boston butt—cottage ham
   d. Spare ribs—belly
   e. Pork belly—bacon
   f. Fresh ham

16F. Matching
1. d   2. f   3. a   4. b   5. c

16G. Chapter Review
1. False   (p. 374) The Boston butt is located in the forequarter.
2. True
3. True
4. False   (p. 374) The foreshank is called the shoulder hock.
5. False   (p. 375) Center-cut pork chops are the choicest chops from the primal loin.
6. False   (p. 375) Canadian bacon is made from the boneless pork loin.
7. True

8. False   (p. 372) Hogs are bred to produce long loins.
9. False   (p. 374) Picnic ham is made from the hog's primal shoulder.
10. True
11. False   (p. 372) A variety of cooking methods are usually applied to pork.
12. False   (p. 374) Spareribs are cut from the belly.
13. True
14. False   (p. 375) These things may occur, but by definition a suckling pig is simply a very young, very small whole pig used for roasting or barbecuing whole.

16H. Putting It All Together

1. Although pork is a good source of protein and B vitamins, it is not as good a source of iron as lamb. In addition, pork is much more marbled with fat than lamb, as well as possessing an outer layer of fat on the cuts. In general pork is higher in fat, especially saturated fat, than lamb. The fat on lamb is found more on the outside of the cuts, making it easier to trim away before cooking. It is also common for numerous pork cuts to be preserved by curing and/or smoking. Although more low-sodium pork products are available today, pork provides an excessive amount of sodium, requiring consumers to pay more attention to creating balance in their diet elsewhere and decreasing the total amount of preserved pork products they consume.

2. Pork ribs contain a relatively small amount of meat (muscle) combined with an equal amount of fat. The nature of how the animal grows and moves around suggests that the muscles along the rib cage are working muscles, making the meat more tough. (Think about your own rib cage and how much the muscles surrounding it work to move your torso from one side to the other all day long.) As a result, the moist-heat cooking method of steaming or boiling is first used to break down the tough muscle fibers of the meat while simultaneously flavoring it with the cooking liquid. This process also helps render out some of the fat so that the ribs are more palatable. Many people also finish ribs by grilling them at the end of the cooking process, usually with some acidic sauce or rub such as barbecue sauce, which further helps tenderize and flavor the meat. The dry-heat cooking method used at the end helps caramelize the remaining sugars in the pork, adding to its palatability.

CHAPTER 17 ANSWER KEY

17A. Terminology
Answers will not be provided in answer key. All answers can be found in text.

17B. Short Answer
1. Reference page 410.
2. Similarity: Overused muscles are more tough than underused ones.
   Difference: Red meat has marbling; poultry does not.
3. Reference pages 399–400.
4. Reference page 399.
5. Reference pages 395–396.
6. Reference pages 426–446.
7. a. Be sure all work surfaces and equipment are clean.
   b. Avoid getting poultry juices in contact with other food.
   c. Anything coming in contact with raw poultry should be sanitized before it comes in contact with any other food.
   d. Cooked foods should never be placed in containers that were used to hold the raw product.
   e. Kitchen towels used to handle poultry should be sanitized before being reused in order to prevent cross-contamination.
8. Reference page 468.

17C. Matching
1. b   2. e   3. a   4. f   5. c

17D. Fill in the Blank
1. protein, myoglobin   3. roaster duckling, dark, fat
2. 165°F, 170°F   4. white wine, lemon juice, herbs, spices, barbecue

17E. Multiple Choice
1. c   2. b   3. a   4. b

17F. Chapter Review
1. False   (p. 394) Poultry fat has a lower melting point than other animal fats.
2. True
3. True
4. False   (p. 404) Poultry that is left too long in an acidic marinade may take on undesirable flavors.
5. False   (p. 394) The cooking time for dark meat is longer.
6. False   (p. 400) Poultry should be frozen at 0°F/–18°C or below.
7. False   (p. 394) The skin color of poultry is related to what it is fed.
8. True
9. False   (p. 395) Older male birds have less flavor than older female birds.
10. False   (p. 398) Overcooking foie gras will cause it to melt away.
11. False   (p. 396) A young pigeon is known as a squab.
12. False   (p. 398) The gizzard is the bird's second stomach.
13. False   (p. 395) A capon is a castrated male chicken.
14. False   (p. 394) Poultry is placed into classes based on age and tenderness.
15. True
16. False   (p. 397) Ostrich is best cooked medium rare to medium.
17. True
18. False   (p. 404) Discard the marinade once it has been used.
19. False   (p. 397) Chefs use a magret, which comes from the Moulard or Mullard breed.
20. True
21. True

22. True
23. True
24. False   (p. 416) The weight measure of clarified butter is not equal to the volume.
25. True
26. True
27. True
28. False   (p. 397) Ratite meat is usually cooked medium rare to medium.

17G. Putting It All Together

1. There are several things a chef needs to consider when planning a menu and costing recipes:

    Customer demand: Duck is all dark meat and contains large amounts of fat. As a result, a chef must know his or her customers' tastes very well in order to put this entrée on the menu. Prepared skillfully, duck can be a delicious addition, providing it is something the guests desire.

    Yield: One 4-pound duck will yield two adult servings, whereas a 4-pound roasting chicken will serve four people. The bone-to-meat ratio is much higher for duck than chicken, and therefore a chef needs to plan accordingly when ordering ingredients for production and planning mise en place.

    Food cost: The cost per pound for duck is often higher than for chicken. Combine this with the fact that the chef will get only two portions out of each duck compared to four from a chicken, and the food cost for the base ingredient is already higher because the chef is paying more per pound for something that yields less meat.

    Ultimately the chef wants to make sure duck will be an entrée that customers will order on a regular basis so that he or she can ensure that it will be worth the effort to prepare and stock the perishable ingredients required. If the dish will not make money for the establishment, there is no sense putting it on the menu.

2. Because chicken is fairly mild in flavor, so should be the flavors used in the marinade. Once a chicken is broken down into its parts (breast, leg, and wing), most marinating should take no more than a couple of hours to infuse adequate flavor. Choices of ingredients to use in the marinade are numerous, although a few are provided here:

    Acid: lemon juice, white wine, rice wine vinegar, sherry
    Oil: canola oil, corn oil, olive oil
    Seasoning: basil, sage, garlic, scallion, thyme, soy sauce, mild mustard

CHAPTER 18 ANSWER KEY

18A. Terminology
Answers will not be provided in answer key. All answers can be found in text.

18B. Short Answer
1. a. Sausages
   b. Forcemeats
   c. Pâtés
2. Reference page 455.
3. Reference page 451.
4. Reference page 455.

18C. Multiple Choice
1. b   5. d
2. c   6. c
3. b   7. a
4. a

18D. Chapter Review
1. True
2. True
3. False   (p. 452) Mature boar is 1 to 2 years old.
4. False   (p. 450) Wild game can be served only by those who hunt and share their kill.
5. True
6. False   (p. 454) Game is lower in fat and higher in protein and minerals than other meats.
7. False   (p. 451) There is no marbling in venison flesh.
8. False   (p. 455) Large animals are available only precut into subprimals or portions.
9. True
10. True
11. True
12. False   (p. 450) The type, age, and cut of the game animal will determine its tenderness and therefore the cooking technique that should be employed. Most game meat contains little marbling of fat and therefore must be cooked lightly (medium rare to medium) to maintain moisture.
13. True
14. False   (p. 455) Traditionally wild game was usually marinated before preparation, but today, with the availability of young, tender farm-raised animals, marinating is no longer a necessity.
15. True
16. True
17. True
18. False   (p. 450) Because game can have a stronger flavor, tart fruits such as raspberries, cranberries, apricots, tart peaches, plums, and pears tend to create more flavor balance than mellow, milder fruits. In addition, citrus juices, flavored vinegars, and wines balance the flavor of game particularly well, also because of their acidity.
19. True
20. False   (p. 451) Beefalo is considered the meat of the future because it is a crossbreed between domestic cattle and bison, it is more tender than beef, and it has lower cholesterol as well.

18E. Putting It All Together
1. As with lean beef, and provided the cut of the bison is tender (such as strip loin, sirloin, or tenderloin), any dry-heat method should work well, such as sautéing, grilling, or broiling. However, if the bison is lean and from an area of the animal where the muscle was well developed, such as the shank, shoulder, or round, then a moist-heat or combination cooking method would be more appropriate.
2. The midsection or loin area tends to be most tender across all the various animals.

3. Many spices that have a pronounced flavor, such as caraway, fennel, mustard, cumin, juniper, and garlic, would work well (depending on which country's cuisine you're preparing), and herbs with pronounced flavors such as sage, thyme, lavender, rosemary, and basil would also hold up well to game. How did you do? Were your guesses similar?

CHAPTER 19 ANSWER KEY

19A. Terminology
Answers will not be provided in answer key. All answers can be found in text.

19B. Multiple Choice
1. b	5. d	9. c	13. d
2. d	6. b	10. d	14. c
3. c	7. a	11. c	
4. a	8. d	12. c	

19C. Market Forms of Fish
1. Whole or round
2. Drawn
3. Dressed or pan-dressed
4. Butterflied
5. Fillet
6. Steak
7. Wheel or center cut

19D. Short Answer
1. a. They cook evenly.
   b. They cook quickly.
2. a. Translucent flesh becomes opaque.
   b. The flesh becomes firm.
   c. The flesh separates from the bones easily.
   d. The flesh begins to flake.
3. a. Shallow poaching
   b. Sautéing
   c. Broiling
   d. Baking
4. **Oily**
   a. Trout
   b. Salmon
   Lean
   c. Bass
   d. Snapper
5. a. Scallops
   b. Lobster
   c. Shrimp
   d. Crab
6. a. Baked stuffed shrimp
   b. Oysters Rockefeller
   c. Baked stuffed lobster
7. a. They are naturally tender.
   b. They cook relatively quickly.
8. Eyes, gills, fins and scales, smell, texture, appearance, movement

19E. Chapter Review
1. False (p. 476) Only fish processed under Type 1 inspection services are eligible for grading.
2. False (p. 476) Fish and shellfish inspections are voluntary and are performed in a fee-for-service program.
3. True
4. True
5. True
6. False (p. 475) Maine lobsters have meat in both their tails and their claws and are considered superior in flavor to all other lobsters. Spiny lobsters primarily have meat in the tail.
7. False (p. 472) Atlantic hard-shell clams are also known as quahogs.
8. True
9. False (p. 498) En papillote is actually an example of steaming.
10. False (p. 476) In general, shellfish has less cholesterol than lamb and other meats.
11. True
12. True
13. False (p. 468) The only market form in which monkfish is sold is the tail (fillet).
14. False (p. 468) Surimi is very low in fat and relatively high in protein. Because of processing techniques, however, it has more sodium and fewer vitamins and minerals than the real fish or shellfish it replaces.
15. True
16. True

17. False   (p. 500) Poached items get their seasonings from the cooking medium, such as a court bouillon.
18. True
19. True
20. False   (p. 489) It prevents sticking and helps leaner fish retain moisture.
21. True
22. True

19F. Putting It All Together

1. Referring to information provided in this chapter and your knowledge of principles of cookery from Chapter 9, you should realize that the most commonly used cooking methods for seafood—broiling, grilling, poaching, sautéing, and steaming—add little or no fat. Granted, a chef could choose to pan-fry or deep-fat fry fish and shellfish, but numerous preparation options help the chef naturally keep this category of ingredients healthful, highly nutritious, and delicious.
2. Based on knowledge gained from the chapters on professionalism, food safety and sanitation, menus and recipes, and knife skills, a chef must consider:
   a. the food service operation's ability to use the bones and trim that cutting a whole fish produces.
   b. the employees' ability to fabricate fillets, steaks, or portions (including shucking shellfish). This includes considering the level of staffing and the time required for employees to complete this task.
   c. storage facilities and adherence to HACCP standards.
   d. the product's intended use.
      Even though fish fabrication is relatively simple, these are all things that need to be considered.

CHAPTER 20 ANSWER KEY

20A. Terminology
Answers will not be provided in answer key. All answers can be found in text.

20B. Multiple Choice
1. d	5. b, c, d, f	9. a	13. c
2. b	6. c	10. c	14. d
3. b	7. a	11. b	15. a
4. d	8. b	12. b	

20C. Egg Identification
a. Germinal spot   b. Shell   c. Yolk   d. White   e. Air cell   f. Chalaza

20D. Coffees and Teas
1. a. Body   3. Robusta
   b. Smell   4. 2, 6
   c. Acidity   5. coffee
   d. Flavor   6. tea
2. Arabica   7. Black, green, oolong

20E. Chapter Review
1. True
2. False   (p. 534) Shell color has no effect on the quality (grade), flavor, or nutrition.
3. False   (p. 542) When preparing French-style omelets, the eggs are cooked without a filling, then tightly rolled onto a plate for service. The finished omelet can then be cut and filled as desired.
4. False   (p. 547) The cooking surface should be 375°F.
5. False   (p. 537) The egg whites should be brought to room temperature to maximize the volume when whipping.
6. False   (p. 535) Eggs should be stored at temperatures below 45°F and at a relative humidity of 70 to 80 percent.
7. False   (p. 536) Egg substitutes have a different flavor from real eggs and cannot be used in recipes in which the eggs are required for thickening.
8. False   (p. 535) Egg whites contain more than half of the protein and riboflavin, but no cholesterol.
9. False   (p. 547) The pancakes should be golden brown and bubbles should be forming before they are flipped.
10. True
11. True
12. True
13. False   (p. 538) Custards are baked, not poached.
14. True
15. True
16. False   (p. 547) Grids of waffle irons should be seasoned well and never washed. The heat of the iron keeps it sanitary.
17. True
18. False   (p. 535) Egg whites coagulate at a lower temperature than yolks, so when preparing an egg-white omelet, adjust your cooking time and temperature accordingly.
19. False   (p. 548) Crepes are a type of pancake; however, they are thin, delicate, and unleavened.
20. True
21. False   (p. 555) Green tea is yellow-green in color with a bitter flavor, but it is not fermented at all.
22. False   (p. 553) To make caffè latte, mix one-third espresso and two-thirds steamed milk without foam.
23. True

24. True
25. False   (p. 554) A variety of cultures have been flavoring their coffees long before the United States was even a country. For example, toasted barley, dried figs, and spices are common flavoring ingredients, and the French have been adding ground chicory root to their coffee for its added bitterness. In America we enjoy coffees that are flavored, often with aromatic oils that add chocolate, vanilla, spice, or raspberry flavors, to name a few.
26. True
27. True
28. False   (p. 534) Because each shelled whole large egg weighs 1.6 ounces and you need the equivalent of three eggs in your recipe, you should measure 4.8 ounces of the pasteurized egg product.
29. False   (p. 536) A soufflé may also be a savory preparation.
30. True
31. True

20F. Putting It All Together

1. Whole eggs—particularly the yolk, which contains the fat and cholesterol—do not have as much cholesterol as researchers once feared. Like everything else, eggs should be eaten in moderation, and the saturated fat in the egg yolk should be of equal concern. However, the American Heart Association suggests that it is acceptable to consume up to four egg yolks per week as part of a balanced diet. Of course, if one commonly eats a four- to five-egg omelet several times per week, perhaps it is time to consider cutting back. One way of doing this is to use fewer egg yolks and more egg whites, which contain no fat or cholesterol and are a great, economical source of high-quality protein. Don't forget to include in the computation of how many eggs eaten per week those that are "hidden ingredients" in baked goods, sauces, pastas, and other common foods.

2. There are many things a chef can do to keep this high-protein, potentially hazardous food product safe for human consumption:

    a. Keep all raw eggs consistently refrigerated until needed for preparation. Refrigerate at 41°F or below.

    b. Work cleanly and neatly in order to prevent cross-contamination.

    c. Keep eggs and egg mixtures well chilled over an ice bath when working with them at room temperature. For example, when cooking eggs to order, keep them on ice. Containers of cracked and whisked eggs for omelets and scrambled eggs should be brought out of refrigeration in small quantities and stored in a container that is fully submerged in an ice bath in order to keep it well chilled. Stir often to ensure that the center of the egg mixture is as cold as the outer edges. If few egg orders are being placed, return the eggs or egg mixture to formal refrigeration.

    d. Wash and sanitize cooking implements often. For example, do not use the same dirty spatula to make omelets during a 2- or 3-hour service. Switch out spatulas on a regular basis to ensure cleanliness.

    e. Cook eggs completely, so that yolks and whites are firm. Because eggs tend to carry salmonella, thorough cooking is one of the best ways to prevent the bacteria from being transferred to the guest.

    f. Serve hot, freshly cooked eggs and egg products at the proper temperature and immediately.

CHAPTER 21 ANSWER KEY

21A. Terminology
Answers will not be provided in answer key. All answers can be found in text.

21B. Multiple Choice

1. b	4. c	7. c	10. b	13. d
2. c	5. a	8. d	11. d	14. a, c
3. b	6. c	9. b	12. b	

21C. Product Identification

1. i	4. h	7. g	10. l	13. n
2. b	5. a	8. d	11. c	14. o
3. f	6. j	9. m	12. e	15. p

21D. Chapter Review

1. True
2. False   (p. 606) Puréed vegetables are usually prepared by baking, boiling, steaming, or microwaving.
3. False   (p. 710) Winter squash is generally not braised or stewed and is better cooked by baking, steaming, or sautéing.
4. True
5. True
6. True
7. True
8. True
9. False   (p. 579) They are usually stored at 40°F–60°F.
10. True
11. False   (p. 593) Red and white vegetables such as red cabbage, beets, and cauliflower contain flavonoids.
12. False   (p. 594) Testing the texture, looking for an al dente consistency, is generally the best determination of doneness.
13. False   (p. 590) The ripening process of vegetables proceeds more rapidly in the presence of ethylene gas.
14. True
15. False   (p. 591) The FDA classifies food irradiation as an additive.
16. False   (p. 570) This technique is recommended when eggplant is going to be fried.
17. False   (p. 572) A chipotle pepper is a jalapeño that has been smoked.
18. False   (p. 591) The heat required in the canning process causes the contents of the can to lose nutrients and the texture to soften.
19. True
20. True
21. False   (p. 608) Pickling uses an acid, usually vinegar, to prevent spoiling as well as to flavor the food.
22. True
23. True
24. True
25. False   (p. 604) Vegetables are generally tender; braising and stewing may be performed to obtain an exceptionally flavorful final product.
26. False   (p. 582) When soaking dried beans, allow 3 cups of cold liquid for each cup of dried beans.
27. True
28. True

21E. Putting It All Together

1. Some simple rules to help you to remember how to get the most out of vegetables:
    a. Eat a variety of vegetables; the more colorful your plate, the better range of nutrients you're consuming.
    b. Choose fresh vegetables whenever possible, and wash them thoroughly before preparation. If fresh are not available, then select frozen. If frozen are not available, then choose canned vegetables as a last resort.
    c. Eat a variety of vegetables to help ensure that you're getting a variety of fiber (both soluble and insoluble) in your diet.
    d. Prepare vegetables with their peels intact whenever possible in order to preserve their nutritional content.
    e. Cook vegetables as lightly as possible, if at all, in order to maximize their nutritional value.

2. The information on color presented in Chapter 6, Flavors and Flavorings, primarily talked about the appeal of vibrant and varied colors in the final presentation of food. As diners we form a certain opinion about how a food will taste simply based on how it looks. Chapter 23, Healthy Cooking, talks about the same thing but in a more in-depth way. This chapter explains how various vegetables and the pigments they contain react positively and negatively to reactions to acids and alkalis that may or may not be present during a cooking process. The effects on the vibrancy of the pigments are also related to the concept of what happens when a vegetable is overcooked.

CHAPTER 22 ANSWER KEY

22A. Terminology
Answers will not be provided in answer key. All answers can be found in text.

22B. Short Answer
1. a. Wrapping the potato in foil causes it to steam instead of bake, and the skin will be soggy.
   b. Microwaving also causes steaming to occur and causes the skin to be soggy.
2. a. Italian risotto   b. Spanish paella   c. Japanese sushi
3. To allow the pasta ample space to move freely and so that the starches that are released don't cause the pasta to become gummy and sticky
4. This gives the dough a rich, yellow color, and the dough is more resilient to the machinery during high-scale production. It also produces pasta that has a lightly pitted surface, causing the pasta to absorb sauces well.
5. a. Duchesse + tomato concassée = marquis
   b. Duchesse + chopped truffles and almond coating, deep-fried = Berny
   c. Duchesse + pâte à choux = dauphine
   d. Dauphine + grated Parmesan, piped and deep-fried = lorette
6. a. Ribbon   b. Tubes   c. Shapes
7. a. Simmering   b. Pilaf   c. Risotto
8. a. The water softens the noodle strands.
   b. The bundles begin to separate.
   c. The noodles cook more evenly.

22C. Multiple Choice
1. b	4. d	7. b	10. a	13. d
2. c	5. c	8. b	11. a	14. c
3. d	6. b	9. b	12. a	

22D. Chapter Review
1. True
2. True
3. True
4. False (p. 639) Semolina flour, although it makes the dough more yellow, also makes it tougher and more difficult to work with. When making pasta, that is okay, because it gets rolled very thin and the pasta needs to have some strength.
5. True
6. False (p. 627) A yam is botanically different from both sweet and common potatoes. Although it is less sweet than a sweet potato, it can be used interchangeably.
7. False (p. 628) Potatoes should be stored between 50°F and 65°F.
8. False (p. 628) Waxy potatoes are best for these applications.
9. True
10. True
11. True
12. True
13. False (p. 638) The standard ratio for cooking rice is two parts liquid to one part rice.
14. True
15. False (p. 639) Generally, cracked wheat and bulgur cannot be substituted for one another in recipes.
16. True
17. False (p. 638) What makes rice a potentially hazardous food product is its neutral pH and high protein.
18. False (p. 640) One cup of dried quinoa yields 2 cups cooked.
19. False (p. 648) Dumplings are defined as a small mound of dough cooked by steaming or simmering, usually in a flavorful liquid.

20. True
21. False   (p. 629) Potato and grain dishes are indeed potentially hazardous foods, but they should first be heated to 165°F and then held for service at 135°F.
22. True
23. True

22E. Putting It All Together

1. Potentially hazardous foods (PHFs) are so called because they contain protein and have a neutral pH and high water content. The reason for such a heavy reminder of the dangers of PHFs in these two chapters is that it is easy to forget about this concept when talking about vegetables and carbohydrates. Many chefs have no problem relating the PHF definition to meats, eggs, seafood, and dairy products, but they often forget that vegetables, potatoes, grains, and pastas can possess the same nutritional component of protein, making them equally susceptible to high rates of bacterial growth if not properly handled. Because bacteria feed on protein and need moisture and a neutral pH to thrive, all they need is temperatures within the temperature danger zone and the conditions are perfect for growth and reproduction, thereby making vegetables, potatoes, grains, and pastas equally susceptible to causing food-borne illness.

2. As explained in the earlier answer, potatoes are a potentially hazardous food product. Potatoes also grow in soil that may be fortified with manure and other contaminants that may not be favorable to the human body when consumed. When a chef fails to wash and sanitize a potato before baking, then wraps it in aluminum foil, he or she is creating an environment where anaerobic bacteria can not only survive, but thrive. Botulism, for example, is not hindered by the application of heat and thrives in environments void of oxygen (whereas most bacteria require oxygen to survive). Wrapped inside the aluminum foil and containing a minimum water content of 60 percent, the potato provides plenty of oxygen and food for the bacteria to reproduce. The same thing can happen with a sealed container of rice pilaf or mashed potatoes being held warm in an oven during service. Chefs need to be incredibly aware of everything they do in the kitchen in order to ensure that food is safe for human consumption.

CHAPTER 23 ANSWER KEY

23A. Terminology
Answers will not be provided in answer key. All answers can be found in text.

23B. Short Answer
1. a.   Use proper purchasing and storage techniques in order to preserve nutrients.
    b.   Offer a variety of foods from each tier of the food pyramid so that customers have a choice.
    c.   Offer entrées that emphasize plant instead of animal foods.
    d.   Offer dishes that are considerate of special dietary needs, such as low fat or low salt.
    e.   Use cooking procedures that preserve rather than destroy nutrients.
2. a.   Ordering appetizers instead of entrées to control quantity of food
    b.   Requesting half orders or splitting a full order
    c.   Asking that dressings and sauces be served on the side
    d.   Asking that a different cooking method be used
3. a.   Reduce the amounts of the ingredient(s).
    b.   Replace the ingredient(s) with a substitute that will do the least to change the flavor and appearance of the dish.
    c.   Eliminate the ingredient(s).
4. a.   Religious beliefs
    b.   Emotional aversion to inflicting pain on animals
    c.   Environmental concerns
    d.   Health concerns
5. a.   Use grains and beans to add texture and satiation.
    b.   Take advantage of meaty vegetables and soy products as main attractions.
    c.   Compose dishes with an eye to balancing color.
    d.   Balance texture on the same plate.
    e.   Layer flavors for complexity of taste.
    f.   Create a vegetarian pantry stocked with ingredients that help enhance plant-based cooking.
    g.   Seek inspiration from ethnic cuisines in which vegetarian food is traditional.
6. First, a server or chef should ask the guest what type of vegetarian he or she is, because one cannot simply assume that a guest who claims to be vegetarian eats only vegetables and grains. The chef needs to ask specific questions to delineate the parameters for a meal that he or she will prepare to accommodate the vegetarian guest's diet. Because the chef is already preparing a special meal for the guest (which could result in an excellent experience at that restaurant), the chef may also want to ask if there are ingredients or ethnic cuisines the guest dislikes, or whether he or she is allergic to anything. By asking these types of questions, the chef creates a list of ingredients/options that he or she can work with in creating a unique vegetarian dish that meets the nutritional needs of the guest while being satisfying as well. Although doing this takes extra effort, the chef is more than likely to turn a potentially onetime guest into a regular patron who will likely tell his or her friends about the excellent meal and great attention to detail in service.
7. Soy milk, tofu, miso, tempeh, textured soy protein, seitan, various analogous food products

23C. Roles of Nutrients in Health
1. e   3. c   5. b   7. d
2. g   4. f   6. a

23D. Essential Nutrients
1. d   6. c
2. b   7. a
3. a   8. b
4. c   9. b
5. d   10. d

23E. Parts of a Food Label
a. Serving size
b. Calories from fat
c. Daily values
d. Percentage of daily value
e. Recommended Daily Intake or RDI
(see text for the description of each section of the food label)

23F. Chapter Review

1. False — (p. 695) According to the United Soybean Board, soy protein is the only plant protein that is equivalent to animal protein, and it is a rich source of phytochemicals as well.
2. False — (p. 696) Once opened, soy milk must remain refrigerated and has a shelf life of only 5 to 7 days.
3. True
4. True
5. False — (p. 695) Although tossed salads may be garnished with meat, tofu, legumes, cheese, nuts, or seeds as part of a special order, they do not generally contain these ingredients. Vegetarians who are conscientious about getting adequate protein in their diet may need to order these ingredients specifically.
6 True
7. False — (p. 695) Eggs are consumed by ovo- and lacto-ovo-vegetarians, but not vegans.
8. False — (p. 686) RDI stands for Recommended Daily Intake.
9. True
10. True
11. False — (p. 685) A chef is not required to meet the recommendations of the Food Guide Pyramid, but rather the pyramid is provided as a guide for consumers so they are aware of the numerous options for making healthy food choices.
12. False — (p. 682) Dietary cholesterol is found only in foods of animal origin.
13. True
14. True
15. False — (p. 689) Not all artificial sweeteners can be substituted for sugar when preparing baked goods. For instance, aspartame breaks down when heated and therefore cannot be used to sweeten foods that will be cooked.
16. True
17. False — (p. 681) Dietary fibers are considered complex carbohydrates.
18. True
19. True
20. False — (p. 682) Although people are usually instructed to lower their cholesterol levels when they become too high because they are a risk factor for heart disease, a certain amount of cholesterol in the diet can actually be good because of the role cholesterol plays; it is a regulatory substance that aids in bodily functioning. However, because our body produces its own supply of cholesterol, that which we consume in our foods is usually extra and can easily evolve into being far more than our body needs.
21. False — (pp. 683–684) Vitamins and minerals provide no caloric value to the body and yet are considered essential nutrients because they are important to the body in generating energy from the foods we eat.
22. True
23. False — (p. 682) Although butter is solid at room temperature, it has not been hydrogenated to get to that state; it is a fat that is largely made up of saturated fatty acids, thus resulting in its solid characteristics.
24. False — (p. 697) Cooking does temper tempeh's flavor, but it should be cooked because of the type of live culture it contains.

25. False   (p. 696) Although tofu can come in a variety of textures based on the amount of calcium sulfate added to the soy milk, it never quite takes on the texture of cooked textured soy protein or seitan, referred to by many as "wheat meat."

26. True

23G. Putting It All Together

1. Like beef, veal is a major source of protein as well as niacin, zinc, and B vitamins. Veal has less marbling than beef, but because the animal is so young and its activity has been limited, the meat is still tender. Because of the decreased marbling, once visible fat is trimmed, veal is lower in fat and calories than comparable beef cuts. It is also leaner than many cuts of pork and poultry. Because cholesterol is found in the fat, with its lower fat content veal is also a bit lower in cholesterol.

2. Tofu may be bland, but because of this it is an extremely versatile vegetarian ingredient that can be used in a plethora of dishes. It can be flavored in a variety of ways, including marinating before cooking or incorporating it in a dish, such as a stir-fry, where it picks up flavors from a variety of ingredients. As a result it should be seen as the ultimate plant-protein-rich ingredient that can take on whatever flavor the chef desires.

3. First of all, one needs to consider the dish in which substitution is taking place. For example, while making a veal stew, one can understand the texture the veal has upon completion of the stewing process (depending on the cut used in the recipe) and use that knowledge to choose the vegetarian protein ingredient that will most closely match the texture of the veal. The veal will be quite firm once cooked, so textured soy protein or seitan will probably most closely match the texture of veal. Although the chef cannot find a substitute for the marbling of fat in the grain of the veal that lends flavor and tenderness, at least he or she can use a protein that has a similar firm texture. There is something very psychologically satisfying about having a meatlike texture in your food, particularly if you originally ate meat and are just adapting to being a vegetarian. In addition, including other vegetable ingredients containing free glutamates, such as mushrooms, tomatoes, and soy sauce, will add a savory or meatlike flavor to enhance the final characteristics of the adapted vegetarian stew.

CHAPTER 24 ANSWER KEY

24A. Terminology
Answers will not be provided in answer key. All answers can be found in text.

24B. Multiple Choice

1. b	4. c	7. c	10. d
2. b	5. d	8. d	11. b
3. c	6. a	9. b	12. a

24C. Short Answer

1.
   a. Cheese and other high-fat dairy products
   b. Most meats (especially if high in fat)
   c. Most emulsified dressings
2.
   a. The gas causes the greens to wilt   b. Accelerates spoilage
3.
   a. Buttermilk   c. Herbs   e. Vegetables
   b. Vinegar   d. Spices
4.
   a. Bring mise en place up to room temperature.
   b. In the bowl of an electric mixer, whip the egg yolks until frothy.
   c. Add seasonings to the yolks and combine.
   d. Add a small amount of liquid from the recipe and combine.
   e. Begin whipping on high speed and slowly drizzle in oil until emulsion starts to form.
   f. After the emulsion forms, slow the mixer and add the oil a bit faster.
   g. When the mayonnaise is thick, add a small amount of the liquid from the recipe. Alternate this process with the oil until all is incorporated.
   h. Taste, adjust seasonings, and refrigerate immediately.
5.
   a. Liqueur   c. Yogurt
   b. Fruit purée   d. Sweetener, such as honey

24D. Chapter Review

1. True
2. True
3. False   (p. 716) Tender greens such as butterhead and baby lettuces benefit from hand tearing, whereas hardy greens such as romaine and cos can be cut with a knife.
4. True
5. False   (p. 719) Although tossed salads should be dressed at the last possible moment, it is to prevent the greens from becoming soggy.
6. False   (p. 715) Generally, softer-leaved lettuces tend to perish more quickly in storage than crisper-leaved varieties; however, iceberg is not a soft-leaved lettuce.
7. True
8. True
9. False   (p. 719) The standard ratio of oil to vinegar in a temporary emulsion is 3:1.
10. True
11. True
12. False   (p. 715) Roses and zinnias are poisonous; chefs should be certain of the edibility of a bloom before using it to enhance food presentations.
13. True
14. False   (p. 727) A conversion factor of 9.17 yields 55 portions.
15. True
16. False   (p. 722) Use pasteurized egg yolks and keep ingredients and finished mayonnaise-based products below 41°F at all times.
17. True

18. False   (p. 732) The croutons would stay crisp longer as a canapé base if they were sautéed in clarified butter or olive oil. The cooking method used to make the canapé should be chosen based on how the crouton will be used.

24E. Putting It All Together

1. A chef has no formal obligation to offer vegetarian or low-fat items, such as salads or salad dressings, for his or her guests' dining pleasure. However, from the standpoint of professionalism discussed in Chapter 1 and from the nutritional perspective in Chapter 23, Healthy Cooking, the chef should get to know his or her clientele and do everything within reason to try to appease them. Success in today's food service industry depends on repeat customers, so if a chef can discover what his or her clientele desire or need and strive to make them happy, then the chef as well as the establishment at which the chef is employed will benefit greatly.

2. Salad Niçoise is dressed with a vinaigrette, so most people would automatically assume that it is a healthful dining choice in and of itself. However, everything we eat must be taken in moderation, and based on the nutritional analysis of the salad, the quantity of the ingredients (particularly the salad's garnishes) could be decreased in order to create a more healthful option. For example, 2 ounces of olive oil is rather heavy for a single serving of dressing. A whole tomato in addition to a variety of salad greens (4 to 6 ounces), 4 ounces of cucumber, 2 ounces of green beans, a whole hard-boiled egg (average weight 2 ounces), a couple of artichokes, 2 ounces of potato, green bell peppers, 4 ounces of tuna (which is a very oily fish), and 1 ounce of olives could be considered an excessive amount of food, even for a dinner salad. If you add up the total ounces in a single portion, a conservative estimate is 30 ounces; that's almost 2 pounds of food! This recipe might be good for an occasional splurge, but salads (and their portion size) need to be assessed before we can automatically rate them as a healthful dining option.

CHAPTER 25 ANSWER KEY

25A. Terminology
Answers will not be provided in answer key. All answers can be found in text.

25B. Short Answer
1. a. Bananas   c. Apples
    b. Tomatoes   d. Melons
2. A grayish cast or color on the fruit.
3. **Vitamin C:** Citrus, melons, strawberries
    Vitamin A: Apricots, mangoes, kiwis
    Potassium: Bananas, raisins, figs
4. Process the fruit into:
    a. sauces   c. jellies
    b. jams   d. preserves
5. a. Irradiation   d. Acidulation
    b. Canning   e. Drying
    c. Freezing
6. a. Apples   c. Pears
    b. Bananas   d. Peaches
7. a. Apples   d. Bananas
    b. Cherries   e. Pineapples
    c. Pears

25C. Fill in the Blank
1. Poaching   4. Grapes
2. apples   5. batter
3. pumpkins, melons, cucumbers

25D. Product Identification
1.	b	4.	h	7.	k	10.	n	13.	c
2.	e	5.	i	8.	j	11.	a	14.	l
3.	d	6.	g	9.	f	12.	m	15.	o

25E. Chapter Review
1. True
2. True
3. False   (p. 770) Sulfur dioxide is added to prevent browning and extend the shelf life.
4. False   (p. 770) Freezing is generally one of the worst preserving methods for preserving the natural appearance, because all fruits are 75 to 95 percent water, which seeps out of the fruit when it defrosts.
5. False   (p. 768) The highest grade is U.S. Fancy.
6. True
7. True
8. False   (p. 766) Papayas are also referred to as pawpaws.
9. True
10. True
11. False   (p. 760) Red Delicious apples are best for eating raw.
12. False   (p. 765) Although stone fruits are commonly dried or made into liqueurs and brandies, mangoes are not a stone fruit.
13. True
14. False   (p. 766) Meat tenderizers contain enzymes similar to those found in pineapples and the seeds of kiwis and papayas.
15. True

16. True
17. False   (p. 772) Fruits laid in a pan and sprinkled with a strudel topping and then baked are called crisps or crumples.
18. False   (p. 750) Berries must fully ripen on the vine, as they will not ripen further after harvesting.
19. True
20. False   (p. 760) Fruits with sturdy skins, such as apples and pears, work well for stuffing and baking.
21. True
22. True
23. False   (p. 771) Organically grown or not, fruits should have labels removed and should be washed thoroughly before use, particularly because so many of them are eaten raw.

25F. Putting It All Together

1. Citrus juices are highly acidic and play the role of the acid in a marinade, tenderizing food but also adding flavor at the same time. Bacteria need a neutral pH in order to survive and thrive, so when an acidic element is present, it will at the very least slow the bacterial growth down significantly. The oil in the marinade will also form a layer on top, preventing further incorporation of oxygen, which most bacteria also need to thrive.
2. Raw; many nutrients, especially vitamin C, begin to diminish when heat is applied.
3. Organic production of food was introduced in Chapter 1, Professionalism, presenting it as an option for chefs to consider when sourcing their ingredients and planning their menus. Organically produced produce is grown more naturally, and although it may not be the prettiest, the taste is often superior. Heirloom produce, including fruits, offers chefs another option when they look to include the freshest, most original, and highest-quality ingredients on their menus. Although the growing population of our planet benefits from high-volume farming methods that provide a consistent food supply, the quality and characteristics of produce can be lost, particularly when we consider how long the food sits in refrigeration before it is consumed. Although not every chef will take advantage of the resurgence of heirloom varieties, it is a wonderful option for chefs to be able to explore the possibilities.

CHAPTER 26 ANSWER KEY

26A. Terminology
Answers will not be provided in answer key. All answers can be found in text.

26B. Short Answer
1. hot, cold
2. protein
3. hands
4. purées, butter, mayonnaise
5. bound
6. open-faced
7. Reference pages 793–794.
8. Thanks to the sandwich grill referred to as the panini grill, which has a heated hinged lid, grilling sandwiches so that they're toasted on both top and bottom has become a quick, uncomplicated process, thereby adding to the popularity of grilled hot sandwiches.

26C. Multiple Choice
1. a
2. c
3. d
4. a
5. a

26D. Matching
1. e   2. b   3. a   4. c   5. f

26E. Chapter Review
1. False   (p. 789) Unlike butter, vegetable purées do not provide a moisture barrier between the bread and fillings.
2. True
3. False   (p. 789) Butter, mayonnaise, and vegetable purées are classified as spreads.
4. True
5. True
6. False   (p. 794) For sit-down service, hamburgers are often served open faced for a more attractive presentation.
7. True
8. False   (p. 795) A gyro is made with thinly sliced, rotisserie-cooked lamb wrapped in pita with onions and cucumber-yogurt dressing.
9. False   (p. 790) Keep cold foods cold (below 41°F) and hot foods hot (above 140°F).
10. False   (p. 795) Thinly sliced corned beef, not roast beef, is used in a Reuben.
11. True

26F. Putting It All Together
1. Sandwiches are extremely popular but like many other American meals can easily become nutritionally unbalanced. First, according to the nutritional guidelines provided by the Food Guide Pyramid, a traditional sandwich made with two pieces of bread actually represents two portions from the grains food group, not one. Therefore, a person trying to eat according to the pyramid must either eat only half the sandwich or opt for an open-faced sandwich instead. A chef could also choose ingredients, particularly the sandwich meats, that contain a reduced level of fat and sodium. If the diner is consuming the entire sandwich, then the portion size of the main component (meat, for example) should be reviewed to ensure that it does not exceed 4 ounces. Vegetables, which are often used as a garnish, should be used generously as they provide valuable vitamins, minerals, and fiber. Finally, the spread or dressing could be reviewed to determine whether it is a low-fat, low-sodium option.

2. Many of the ingredients in a sandwich are potentially hazardous food products because of the high percentage of protein they tend to contain. As a result, the chef should follow HACCP standards closely, being sure to monitor time/temperature practices related to mise en place, assembly of the order, and proper packing of foods "to go" by using ice packs that will maintain the temperature of the foods below 41°F.

CHAPTER 27 ANSWER KEY

27A. Terminology
Answers will not be provided in answer key. All answers can be found in text.

27B. Short Answer
1. a. Basic forcemeat
   b. Country-style forcemeat
   c. Mousseline forcemeat
2. Add small quantities of crushed ice, bit by bit, to the machine while it is grinding.
3.

Galantine	**Ballotine**
a. Uses whole chickens, ducks, etc.	Uses poultry legs
b. All bones are removed	All bones are removed
c. Cavity of bird is filled with forcemeat	Cavity of leg is filled with forcemeat
d. It is wrapped in skin, plastic, cheesecloth	Cooked without wrapping
e. It is poached	It is poached or braised
f. Always served cold	Usually served hot

4. a. Keep a precise ratio of fat to other ingredients.
   b. Maintain temperatures below 41ºF during preparation.
   c. Mix ingredients properly.
5. a. To glaze, preventing drying out and oxidation of food
   b. To cut into a decorative garnish
   c. To add flavor and shine
   d. To bind mousses and salads
   e. To fill cooked pâtés en croûte

27C. Multiple Choice
1. a
2. c
3. a
4. a
5. d
6. b
7. c
8. b
9. d
10. d

27D. Matching
1. f
2. i
3. e
4. d
5. b
6. a
7. g
8. c
9. j

27E. Chapter Review
1. False (p. 817) Mousseline forcemeats can be made out of only meats, poultry, fish, or shellfish.
2. False (p. 824) The best type of mold to use is a collapsible, hinged, thin metal pan.
3. True
4. False (p. 811) Eggs and egg whites are used as a primary binding agent in some styles of forcemeats.
5. True
6. False (p. 811) When marinating forcemeat ingredients before grinding, the trend today is to marinate them for shorter periods to let the natural flavors of the ingredients dominate.
7. True
8. True
9. False (p. 830) A fresh ham is made from the pig's hind leg.
10. False (p. 812) If testing a forcemeat's texture shows that it is too firm, a little cream should be added to fix the problem.
11. True
12. True
13. False (p. 821) Chopped chicken liver should be eaten within a day or two of its preparation, whereas rillettes will keep for several weeks under refrigeration.

14. True
15. True
16. True
17. False   (p. 821) Vegetable mousses are cold preparations made by combining puréed vegetables with béchamel and whipped cream and binding with aspic.
18. True
19. True
20. True
21. False   (p. 831) Although pork products are certainly the most commonly cured meats, others are cured as well, including beef, turkey, duck, and chicken.

27F. Putting It All Together

1. Meatloaf and meatballs both contain similar ingredients. Although we don't usually think of these common, everyday recipes as forcemeats, they are—minus the fact that we don't emulsify the mixture. In general the concept of garde manger and forcemeats tends to be new, unfamiliar, and even daunting to the young cook, but if we realize that we already understand the basics of forcemeats through the recipes we have made before, it may seem a little easier to learn the simple technique of emulsification and how its application can create such a completely different dish.
2. Common recipes for meatloaf and meatballs often contain a panada, but as laypeople we don't usually realize that we already understand this seemingly complicated principle; it's actually quite simple!

CHAPTER 28 ANSWER KEY

28A. Terminology
Answers will not be provided in answer key. All answers can be found in text.

28B. Short Answer
1–8. Reference pages 853–854.
9.   a.   Fish
        b.   Rice
        c.   Seasonings
10.   Reference page 848.
11.   Reference page 849.
12.   Reference page 855.
13.   Reference page 895.
14.   Reference page 849.
15.   Reference page 854.

28C. Multiple Choice
1. d   2. b   3. c   4. b   5. d

28D. Fill in the Blank
1. brochettes
2. pan-fried, deep-fried
3. three, five; four, five
4. 1
5. Meatballs
6. Lamb satay

28E. Matching
1. d   2. c   3. a   4. e

28F. Chapter Review
1. False   (p. 848) Appetizers are usually the first course before the evening meal.
2. True
3. True
4. False   (p. 854) Caviar should be served in the original container or a nonmetal bowl on a bed of crushed ice.
5. False   (p. 848) Canapés with bread bases tend to become soggy, so spreading butter on the base prevents this.
6. False   (p. 849) Canapés are best made as close to service as possible.
7. True
8. True
9. False   (p. 855) Rice wine and other seasonings are added to short-grain rice.
10. False   (p. 856) Filled pastry shells should be assembled at the last possible moment and then served immediately to prevent them from becoming soggy.
11. True
12. False   (p. 859) Phyllo dough is a dough made of flour, water, oil, and eggs that is stretched paper thin. Hors d'oeuvre made with phyllo dough have several layers of thin, flaky dough surrounding the filling, providing a very different textural experience than appetizers made with puff pastry.
13. True
14. True

15. False   (p. 861) Hors d'oeuvre may be presented on platters; however, presentation styles have become more diverse in the past few years. Variety is the key when planning hors d'oeuvre service, choosing three or four different types of each hot and cold style. Visual interest can provide a certain excitement over the course as well, so plan to present the selection in different ways: on platters, on spoons, in edible cups (such as a fried tortilla), or in small varied glassware.

28G. Putting It All Together

1. Both stuffed, fried wontons and rumaki are potentially hazardous foods because of their high protein content. Because they are being prepared in large quantities to serve a large number of guests over the considerable period of 2 hours, the chef needs to consider not only making sure the quality of the food is perfect, not under- or overcooked, but also how far in advance he or she can cook the food and hold it for service. Rumaki is made with chicken livers, which become very grainy and bitter when overcooked; fried wontons can easily become soggy if held too long, because of the accumulation of moisture that will make the crisp wonton wrapper become limp. The chef needs to consider that these hors d'oeuvre need to be cooked nearly to order in the kitchen rather than cooked as one big batch and held hot (250°F or higher) until needed for service. This ensures that the food is not only safe to serve but also enjoyable to consume.

2. Sushi is a particularly tricky hors d'oeuvre to serve, particularly on a buffet. Because of the protein found in the seafood, which is raw and ready to eat, and the protein in the sticky steamed rice, it is potentially hazardous because if it is not stored properly and consumed immediately, it could easily become a breeding ground for bacteria, causing food-borne illness. The chef should set up a preparation station for the cook assigned to the station, either on the buffet line or in the back of the house, where he or she can keep the seafood well below 41°F and the rice cool but not cold. Preparation of the sushi in large quantities well before opening of the buffet and chilling it in the walk-in is not an option because although it keeps the seafood cold and out of the temperature danger zone, the starch in the rice becomes very firm and gummy. Those who appreciate sushi properly prepared know that although the seafood should be kept ice cold and cut to order, the rice should be at room temperature in order to maintain a delicate and appropriate texture.

CHAPTER 29 ANSWER KEY

29A. Terminology
Answers will not be provided in answer key. All answers can be found in text.

29B. Matching
1.	d	4.	b	7.	a
2.	i	5.	c	8.	j
3.	f	6.	e	9.	g

29C. Multiple Choice
1.	d	5.	d	9.	d	13.	a
2.	b	6.	a	10.	a	14.	c
3.	c	7.	d	11.	d	15.	a, d
4.	b	8.	d	12.	b		

29D. Short Answer
1.
   a. Melt the chocolate in a container made from copper, aluminum, or heatproof glass.
   b. Finely chop or grate the chocolate to ensure uniformity of melting.
   c. When using a double boiler, the water temperature should not exceed 140°F and the container holding the chocolate should not touch the water.
   d. Watch the melting chocolate carefully and stir regularly.
   e. Remove the melting chocolate from the heat source when it reaches 115°F, because carryover cooking will occur. Continue to whisk as the temperature of the chocolate rises to 120°F.
   f. Melt the chocolate uncovered to prevent condensation buildup.

2.

	Unsweetened	**Bittersweet/Semisweet**
a.	Virtually inedible as is	35 percent chocolate liquor
b.	No sugar added	Sugar added
c.	No flavorings added	Flavorings added
d.	No emulsifiers added	Emulsifiers added

3.
   a. The process slowly raises and lowers the temperature of melted chocolate, preventing bloom.
   b. Tempering causes chocolate to dry rapidly to a hard and shiny appearance.
   c. The chocolate shrinks as it dries, enabling it to be released from molds.

4.
   a. Springform pans   d. Petit fours molds
   b. Tartlet pans   e. Various spatulas
   c. Piping tools

5.
   a. A lack of mixing and/or kneading of the dough
   b. If a formula contains too much fat in relation to the flour, the excessive fat has a tendency to coat the strands of gluten, preventing their development.

29E. Chapter Review
1. False   (p. 885) Self-rising flour is all-purpose flour with salt and baking powder added.
2. False   (p. 884) Glutenin and gliadin are the proteins, which form gluten when introduced to moisture and manipulated.
3. True
4. False   (p. 894) Unsweetened chocolate is 100 percent chocolate liquor.
5. True
6. True
7. True
8. False   (p. 884) Flour derived from this portion of the endosperm is finer than other flours.
9. True
10. False   (p. 886) Unopened flour should be stored in the manner described, except it is also very important to store it away from strong odors.
11. True

12. True   In addition to these qualities, unsalted butter tends to be preferred because it is generally fresher than salted butter.
13. True
14. True
15. False   (p. 890) Most bakeshop ingredients combine completely with liquids, but fats do not.
16. False   (p. 891) Oils may not be substituted for solid shortenings in recipes.
17. True
18. False   (p. 893) The white coating is actually vanillin, and the bean can still be used.
19. False   (p. 895) Do not substitute milk chocolate in any product that must be baked, as the milk solids tend to burn.
20. False   (p. 893) The refining process for chocolate varies from country to country. For example, Swiss and German chocolate is the smoothest, followed by English chocolates. American chocolate has a noticeably more grainy texture.
21. True
22. True

29F. Putting It All Together

1. The first challenge is to think what in the bagel makes it chewy. Think about it: What element of flour makes it elastic? The elasticity is caused by the protein, also known as gluten, which is made more elastic the more the dough is kneaded. The second challenge is to go to your descriptions of the different flours available. Which ones contain the most gluten? Bagels are most commonly made from bread flour, but occasionally chefs will use a blend of bread flour and high-gluten flour to increase chewiness.

2. No, your pastry chef is incorrect. First of all, the pastry chef is not likely to have a composite flour blend in the kitchen, nor is she likely to have all the ingredients needed for a composite flour blend in the correct proportions. Second, because composite flour does not contain the same gluten-forming protein of all-purpose (wheat) flour, the resulting chocolate chip cookie will not be as appealing as the original unless the pastry chef has had the time to experiment and adjust the cookie formula to be wheat-free. Composite flour cannot be substituted measure for measure for wheat flour and achieve the same results.

CHAPTER 30 ANSWER KEY

30A. Terminology
Answers will not be provided in answer key. All answers can be found in text.

30B. Short Answer
1. The bitter or soapy flavor, and sometimes yellow coloring, is often caused by too much baking soda that may not have been properly mixed into the batter.
2. Baking soda can release carbon dioxide only to the extent that there is also an acid present in the formula. If the soda/acid reaction alone is insufficient to leaven the product, baking powder is needed for additional leavening.
3. Batters and dough that may sit for some time before baking often use double-acting baking powder, which has a second leavening action that is activated only with the application of heat.
4. The higher fat content in the creaming method shortens the strands of gluten and therefore makes the final product more tender.
5. Softening the fat makes it easier to cream with the sugar and therefore creates better aeration.
6. Overmixing the batter
7. A scone is seen by many as a rich biscuit that also has butter and eggs in it. It is speculated that biscuits, at least the American form, contain a less expensive type of fat, such as lard, and omit the eggs.
8. a. Biscuits
   b. Shortcakes
   c. Scones

30C. Chapter Review
1. False   (p. 908) All-purpose flour is used in all of these methods.
2. True
3. True
4. False   (p. 906) Baking powder already contains both an acid and a base, and therefore only moisture is needed to induce the release of gases.
5. False   (p. 906) All quick breads use chemical leavening agents, and because they don't need to ferment, like yeast-leavened doughs, they are considered "quick."
6. True
7. False   (p. 909) Fats used in the muffin method should be in the liquid form.
8. False   (p. 913) The leavening agent was there, so the assumption should be that the oven temperature was too low.
9. True
10. False   (p. 906) Batters and dough made with single-acting baking powder should be baked as soon as they are assembled and mixed together.
11. False   (p. 906) Baking soda releases carbon dioxide gas if both an acid and moisture are present; heat is not necessary for leavening to occur.
12. False   (p. 907) Shortcakes are made using the biscuit method.
13. True
14. False   (p. 909) Muffin and quick-bread batters are similar, and therefore their baking methods are interchangeable as long as the baking time is altered.
15. True
16. False   (p. 908) Makeup is the cutting, shaping, and forming of dough products such as biscuits or scones before they are baked.

30D. Putting It All Together
1. The question is really based on common sense but also reminds us of the importance of weighing certain ingredients, but measuring others by volume. In this scenario, blueberries weigh more because of their water weight, whereas pecans are lighter.

2. The two ingredients that occur in the greatest quantity are the flour and the butter, in nearly a 1:1 ratio—that's a lot of butter! Butter breaks up the strands of gluten in the flour, giving the baked product flavor and tenderness. The sugars that caramelized as the product bakes may provide a faint firmness as it browns in the oven, but it crumbles in our mouth as we bite into it.

CHAPTER 31 ANSWER KEY

31A. Terminology
Answers will not be provided in answer key. All answers can be found in text.

31B. Multiple Choice

1. c	4. b	7. d	10. a
2. d	5. b	8. a	
3. c	6. a	9. c	

31C. Short Answer

1. a. The yeast, liquid, and approximately half of the flour are combined to make a thick batter known as a sponge, which is allowed to rise until bubbly and doubled in size.
   b. Then the salt, fat, sugar, and remaining flour are added. The dough is then kneaded and allowed to rise again. This creates a different flavor and a lighter texture than breads made with the straight dough method.
2. The organism is considered dormant because virtually all of the moisture has been removed, which helps increase the shelf life, among other things.
3. a. Product size
   b. The thermostat's accuracy
   c. Crust color
   d. Tapping the loaf on the bottom and listening for a hollow sound
4. a. Croissants
   b. Danish pastries
   c. Non-yeast-leavened pastry
5. Halve the specified weight of compressed yeast when substituting dry yeast in a formula.
6. Combine all ingredients and mix.
7. a. Scale ingredients.   f. Round portions
   b. Mix and knead dough.   g. Makeup: Shape portions.
   c. Ferment dough.   h. Proof products.
   d. Punch down dough.   i. Bake products.
   e. Portion dough.   j. Cool and store finished products.
8. a. 190°F–210°F   b. 180°F–190°F

31D. Chapter Review

1. True   More specifically, though, it occurs just after fermentation.
2. False   (p. 924) Salt's primary role in bread making is conditioning gluten, making it stronger and more elastic.
3. True
4. True
5. False   (p. 931) Underproofing results in poor volume and texture.
6. True

7. True
8. False   (p. 925) Active dry yeast contains virtually no moisture.
9. True
10. False   (p. 926) Prior to commercial yeast production, bakers relied on starters to leaven their breads. Today starters generally provide consistency and reliability.
11. True
12. False   (p. 928) Overkneading is rarely a problem.
13. False   (p. 924) Yeast is very sensitive to temperature, but it prefers temperatures between 75°F and 95°F.
14. True
15. True

16. False   (p. 924) All yeasts are destroyed at 138°F.

17. False   (p. 928) The fermentation process starts when the dough is finished mixing and continues until the dough is baked and reaches a temperature of 138°F and the yeast dies. This explains why the kneading, fermenting, and punching-down steps in the process are so important. Provided the formula is accurate and the ingredients used are correct, the gluten in the bread dough must be developed to its maximum ability to capture the gases produced from fermentation, because no more rising will take place during the baking process (for the most part). Once bread goes into the oven and reaches an internal temperature of 138°F, the yeast dies and the ingredients of the dough are baked into the shape/structure they hold at that point. Therefore a dough that is under- or overproofed will not improve in quality when it goes into the oven; the quality is "frozen in time," and the resulting finished product will possess the same quality, usually rather dense, with the addition of the baking and resulting browning that occurs during the cooking process.

18. True   The retarder exposes the dough to cooler temperatures, which in turn slows down the yeast activity and the fermentation process, thereby helping the flavor become more complex.

19. False   (p. 933) The doneness of a loaf of bread (providing the oven temperature is within the proper range) can also be determined by a uniform, rich, burnished gold to brown crust color. When done, the loaf will also sound hollow when tapped on the bottom.

20. True

21. False   (p. 937) Although most people around the world think that croissants were invented by the French, they were invented by Hungarian bakers in celebration of Budapest's liberation from Turkey in 1686. In spite of this, croissants have become a common (and favorite) baked good served in many Parisian sidewalk cafes.

31E. Putting It All Together

1. Most breads that the American public loves to consume are made from flour that is milled from wheat. Even though all-purpose flour, cake flour, pastry flour, bread flour, and high-gluten flour don't have the word *wheat* in their name as whole-wheat flour does, they are all still derived from the same grain, and therefore no, a person allergic to wheat could not eat bread as most Americans know it.

    Alternative flours, such as soy, rice, potato, tapioca, sorghum, and cornstarch, can be used to make bread for those who are allergic to wheat. Unfortunately, these flours contain no gluten to capture the gases produced during the fermentation process of yeast, and therefore an ingredient called xanthan gum must be added to the formula. Even with this addition, the resulting bread is considerably more dense than traditional wheat breads, and many people with this allergy have a difficult time enjoying breads in the same way that they once did.

2. In the process of assembling and mixing ingredients for a formula of bread dough, the yeast is brought to the perfect temperature (usually by mixing with a liquid of the proper temperature: 75°F–95°F) to ensure activity, given food to eat (sugar), and then mixed with the remaining ingredients, which includes flour. As fermentation progresses, gases are produced. Mixing and kneading the dough develops the strands of gluten (making the protein increasingly elastic), which enables the dough to capture the gases produced, allowing the bread to rise (almost the same way a balloon captures our breath as we blow into it). The bread is then rounded and shaped, proofed to allow the fermentation process to be completed, and then baked to capture the dough in its light, airy form and to make it edible.

CHAPTER 32 ANSWER KEY

32A. Terminology
Answers will not be provided in answer key. All answers can be found in text.

32B. Short Answer
1. a. Chiffon   b. Cooked juice   c. Cream
2. a. Cream   b. Chiffon   c. Cooked juice   d. Cheesecake
3. a. Baked fruit   b. Custard
4. a. To make lattice coverings
   b. To make pie top crusts
   c. To make prebaked shells later to be filled with cooked fillings
5. It is a rich, nonflaky dough that is sturdier than flaky or mealy dough because of the addition of egg yolks and the blending of the fat.
6. When the crust has a potential of becoming soggy, as in the making of custard and cooked fruit pies
7. You have better control because you can feel the fat being incorporated and therefore prevent overmixing.
8. It is cooked before baking.
9. The ratio of sugar to egg whites
10. a. Vol au vents   c. Feuilletées
    b. Napoleons   d. Bouchées
11. a. Ratio of ingredients in dough
    b. Oven temperature
    c. Pan coating

32C. Multiple Choice
1. d   4. c
2. b   5. d
3. b   6. c

32D. Chapter Review
1. True
2. False   (p. 970) Strawberries, pineapples, and blueberries would be more appropriate.
3. True
4. True
5. False   (p. 967) A typical ratio for crumb crusts consists of one part melted butter, two parts sugar, and four parts crumbs.
6. True
7. False   (p. 962) Pâte sucrée should be used specifically rather than flaky and mealy doughs because it is less flaky, and because of the addition of the egg yolks, it is still tender but strong enough to withstand the removal of the tart pan during service.
8. False   (p. 984) If crisp cookies are stored in the same container as soft cookies, the crisp cookies will absorb moisture from the soft cookies, ruining their texture. Also, if strongly flavored cookies, such as spice cookies, are stored with mildly flavored cookies, such as shortbreads, their flavors will be commingled.
9. True
10. False   (p. 970) A cooked juice filling should be combined with a prebaked or crumb crust.
11. False   (p. 972) Baked fruit pies may be stored at room temperature until service.
12. True
13. False   (p. 965) An American gâteau refers to any cake-type dessert.
14. True

32E. Putting It All Together

1. The pie dough may take on a rancid flavor, particularly if it is made with a nonhydrogenated fat. In addition, a chef must consider weather conditions where he or she works. For example, a geographic location that regularly maintains a relatively high humidity level (perhaps 20 percent or greater) will cause the baked pie dough to become soggy, losing its distinctive crunch and texture.

2. Cream and custard fillings, even once baked, are potentially hazardous foods. Therefore they must be stored at a temperature below 41°F until service. The potential moisture in the refrigerator, the condensation that is created on the pie/pie crust when bringing it from a cold temperature to a warm one and back again, and the inherent moist quality of the filling mean that the crust of a custard- or cream-filled pie is more likely to become soggy as a result. The shelf life to maintain quality of the overall pie (provided it is refrigerated as directed) is realistically 1 to 2 days even though it is still safe to eat after 4 to 6 days.

CHAPTER 33 ANSWER KEY

33A. Terminology
Answers will not be provided in answer key. All answers can be found in text.

33B. Basic Cake Mixes
Butter cake: reference page 1010.
Genoise cake: reference page 1012.
Spongecake: reference page 1014.
Angel food cake: reference page 1015.

33C. Matching I—Ingredients
1. f
2. a
3. e
4. c
5. d
6. g

33D. Matching II—Frostings
1. d
2. f
3. b
4. e
5. a
6. g

33E. Cake Mix Categories
1. b
2. b
3. a
4. b
5. a
6. a
7. a
8. b
9. a
10. a

33F. Short Answer—Frostings
1. Simple buttercream: reference page 1023.
2. Italian buttercream: reference page 1024.
3. French buttercream: reference page 1025.

33G. Fill in the Blank
1. decreased, whipped, 2
2. appearance, touch, a cake tester should come out clean
3. 325, 375
4. decorator's
5. flour, shortening, oil
6. air cells, the proper texture

33H. Chapter Review
1. False   (p. 1021) All cakes should be cooled away from drafts or air currents that could cause them to collapse.
2. True
3. True
4. True
5. False   (p. 1015) Angel food cake is usually not frosted but may be topped with fruit-flavored or chocolate glazes, fresh fruit, fruit compote, or whipped cream.
6. True
7. False   (p. 1037) The results from package mixes are consistent and acceptable to most customers.
8. False   (p. 1011) High-ratio cakes require emulsified shortenings to absorb the large amounts of sugar and liquid in the formula.
9. True

10. False   (p. 1022) A compote is not an icing, although it may top or accompany a cake.
11. True

33I. Putting It All Together

1. The chef does not need to be concerned with many detailed food safety issues when mixing and baking a butter cake, angel food cake, spongecake, chiffon cake, or other type of cake. As long as the ingredients are properly stored and handled and no contamination occurs from chemicals or hazardous objects, the process is pretty straightforward. If the cake is one that contains many potentially hazardous food ingredients, such as cheesecake, then much closer controls must be followed, including storing the cake at 41°F or below and protecting the cake from cross-contamination until served.

    In the case of butter cakes, angel food cakes, spongecakes, chiffon cakes, and other similar cakes, the chef needs to be most aware of food safety once the cake is baked. Because it is a ready-to-eat product from this point until service, care must be taken to prevent cross-contamination during the storage, slicing, and decorating stages. The same principles apply to the icing. As long as the icing or frosting contains no potentially hazardous foods such as milk, cream, eggs, or cream cheese, it may be stored, covered, for several days at room temperature without cause for concern.

2. The food service establishment needs to determine whether it has the time needed for production, the talent required to produce a variety of desserts, the work and storage space, the equipment, and the customer demand for house-baked products. If these questions are answered and making desserts in-house seems economically advantageous, it could help the establishment create a niche in the marketplace.

CHAPTER 34 ANSWER KEY

34A. Terminology
Answers will not be provided in answer key. All answers can be found in text.

34B. Short Answer
1. Sanitary guidelines for eggs: reference page 1049.
2. Vanilla custard sauce: reference page 1049.
3. Ice cream: reference page 1063.
4. Baked soufflés: reference page 1055.
5. Sabayon: reference page 1052.
6. Mousse: reference page 1060.
7. Dessert assembly: reference page 1067.
8. Precautions for ice cream: reference page 1062.

34C. Fill in the Blank
1. Zabaglione
2. mousseline, meringue
3. chiffons, crèmes Chantilly
4. whip to better volume, more easily incorporated

34D. Chapter Review
1. False   (p. 1065) A coulis sauce may be cooked or uncooked.
2. True
3. True
4. True
5. True
6. True
7. False   (p. 1064) The sorbet may be soft and syrupy because of too much sugar in the formula.
8. False   (p. 1050) Several steps can be followed to repair a curdled vanilla custard sauce.
9. False   (p. 1064) A sherbet contains milk and/or egg yolks for creaminess.
10. True
11. True
12. False   (p. 1055) In spite of its French name, crème brûlée was most likely invented in Great Britain.

34E. Putting It All Together
1. The process of adding the whipped egg whites to the other ingredients, particularly the chocolate base, involves using a long thin straightedge, such as that on a large rubber spatula, to incorporate the light, airy egg whites into the heavier base ingredients. This is done by scooping the whipped egg whites on top of the base in the bowl, then using the thin edge of the spatula, cutting through the two from one side of the bowl to the other, scooping up from the bottom to the top, and repeating as the bowl is turned and until the two mixtures are blended lightly. By doing this with the thin edge of the spatula as opposed to the wide side of the spatula, and with a very specific movement, the chef is less likely to beat the air cells out of the egg whites, therefore keeping them in place to use as leaveners during the cooking process.
2. A mousse generally has a light and airy texture, yet a refined flavor, such as chocolate. If you've never had mousse before, in some ways it is an elegant version of pudding. The text gives the chef the option of whether to add gelatin because the chef knows how the mousse will be served to the guest. If gelatin is added, it is still used in small proportions in relation to the other ingredients because even if the mousse contains gelatin, it should still have a smooth, light, and airy texture (caused by the inclusion of whipped cream in the recipe). The texture of the mouse should not be rubbery. The gelatin simply helps keep the air molecules in the mousse until the dessert is consumed. So as an example, if a chef is serving the chocolate mousse in a martini glass topped with a mixture of seasonal berries, generally speaking gelatin would not be required as the glass itself would hold the mousse in place until it is

consumed. However, if the mousse needs to be piped or is used as a filling between thinly sliced layers of a chocolate genoise, the chef may choose to add a very small amount of gelatin to the mousse as he or she is making it so that the mousse is slightly more firm, helping maintain the structure of the assembled cake once it is frosted and decorated.

3. As with similar questions in this study guide, the answer really comes down to balancing the time, talent, and resources available to produce the product in-house. What makes this question different is that a wide variety of quality ice creams, sherbets, and sorbets are available from retailers, which requires the chef to determine whether it's worth the effort for a food service establishment to produce its own. If ice cream is a signature item that guests drive from miles around to the restaurant to enjoy as a primary dessert, or if the establishment creates custom flavors that accompany signature desserts that the restaurant is widely known for, then perhaps it is worth the investment. On the contrary, if ice cream is used only as a small garnish on a handful of desserts that sometimes sell but not consistently, then the decision is much simpler. A large ice cream machine, one that has a self-contained refrigeration unit, takes up a significant amount of space in a kitchen and can also be fairly expensive to purchase, considering it can produce only a fairly limited array of desserts, and so it is an unjustified expense in the latter scenario.

CHAPTER 35 ANSWER KEY

35A. Terminology
Answers will not be provided in answer key. All answers can be found in text.

35B. Fill in the Blank
1. Hippen masse
2. shape, color
3. size
4. focal
5. cold

35C. Short Answer
1. a. Cutting   b. Molding
2. a. Flavor   d. Color
   b. Moisture   e. Texture
   c. Flow
3. a. Height
   b. Texture
4. a. To show the chefs' attention to detail
   b. To provide visual appeal
   c. To ensure even cooking of the product
5. a. Strike a balance between overcrowding and leaving empty gaps on the plate.
   b. Choose a focal point.
   c. Make sure the plate's composition flows naturally.
4. a. To create height
   b. To add a new shape
   c. To keep the plate neat and clean

35D. Chapter Review
1. True
2. False   (p. 1080) The food should always be the focal point of any plate.
3. True
4. False   (p. 1088) Small plates are elegantly prepared small portions of foods that were once reserved for the start of the meal but now may be grouped in combinations of three or four to replace the traditional appetizer and entrée.
5. True
6. False   (p. 1087) A squeeze bottle would be a good choice of equipment for preparing sauce drawings.
7. False   (p. 1086) An equally important concept is that the sauces need to be thick enough to hold a pattern, and all sauces used in the drawing need to be the same viscosity.
8. True
9 True
10. False   (p. 1086) Plate dusting may also be used in pastry presentations.
11. True
12. False   (p. 1080) Equally important is to decorate the presentation quickly so the food on the plate is served at its proper temperature.
13. True
14. False   (p. 1088) Although the chef must consider a balanced presentation between color, texture, height, flavor, and temperature, he or she must also be careful that the plate does not become overcomplicated to assemble. When portions are small, customers will order more dishes, which means more plates to send out from the kitchen.

35E. Putting It All Together

1. The chef will need to ensure that the recipe for the food is perfect and tested before service so that when the time comes to shape the food for the plate presentation, there is no delay. He or she also needs to make sure that the cook who will be shaping, cooking, and plating the quenelles to order is proficient at the skills involved. Stove top space must be adequate to ensure that one burner can be dedicated to keep the poaching liquid (court bouillon) at the proper temperature during the entire service. Finally, the service team must be proficient at cooking food to order and plating it quickly and efficiently so that hot food is served hot and cold food is served cold.

2. There are several things the chef must consider once he or she has determined that the kitchen equipment line and space is conducive to *à la minute* plating and that the kitchen staff is willing and able to complete the plating efficiently and effectively for each order. Common rules to focus on might include the following:

   a. Cost of garnish must be considered and/or limited, based on both the time required and the cost of the ingredients. Garnishes not only must complement the plate's flavors and enhance the presentation, but also must be kept within budgetary constraints.

   b. The plating process must be efficient so that hot foods are served piping hot and cold foods are served ice cold. If the proper focus is not kept, it is easy to let priorities slip and take too long to plate the food. In the process of excessive handling, we also run the risk of cross-contaminating the finished food product before it is consumed by the guest.

CHAPTER 36 ANSWER KEY

36A. Terminology
Answers will not be provided in answer key. All answers can be found in text.

36B. Short Answer
1. a. Dishes featuring different principal ingredients
    b. Foods cooked by different cooking methods
    c. Foods with different colors
    d. Foods with different textures
2. Buffet presentation: reference page 1101.
3. a. Use a double-sided buffet.
    b. Use a single-sided buffet, divided into two, three, or more zones, each of which offers identical foods.
    c. Divide the menu among various stations, scattered throughout the room, each station devoted to a different type of food.
4. a. Choose foods that hold well.
    b. Cook small amounts of delicate foods.
    c. Ladle a small amount of sauce in the bottom of the pan before adding sliced meats.
    d. Keep chafing dishes closed whenever possible.

36C. Multiple Choice
1. c   2. b   3. d   4. c   5. c

36D. Chapter Review
1. True
2. False   (p. 1095) Costs are a consideration, but the principal factors limiting a menu are the client's desires and the chef's imagination.
3. False   (p. 1096) The buffet should be in an area with easy access to both the kitchen and the dining tables.
4. True
5. True
6. False   (p. 1105) Portioning of foods with potentially dripping sauces will be easiest for guests if the product is placed at the front of the table.
7. False   (p. 1104) Try to avoid too much dead space on a buffet by filling in with decorations and props.
8. True
9. False   (p. 1106) Spaghetti will not hold particularly well on a buffet, and it also may be messy to serve—especially if topped with a sauce.
10. True
11. True
12. True
13. False   (p. 1109) Typically servers or chefs are placed only at stations where foods are prepared or carved to order.
14. True

36E. Putting It All Together
1. The Italian banquet that developed in concept during the Renaissance period (1450–1600) was the first of its kind, and therefore foods that were prepared for it were quite experimental compared to today. The practice of cooking foods to make them more palatable and safe to eat was in its infancy, so you can imagine that the fanciful preparation of foods was experimental at best. Because the concept of sanitation had not fully been defined at the time, food safety practices were pretty much nonexistent. Banquets often lasted for days on end, and because refrigeration and the mechanical production of ice did not occur until the 1900s, you can imagine that the time/temperature concept was grossly abused—

in both preparation of foods and service of them on the buffet.

　　Take a step forward in time to the modern buffet in America, France, Belgium, or any handful of developed countries, and you'll find quite a different picture, as outlined in the text. Our cooking profession has come a long way in a relatively short period of time, not the least of which is in the study of sanitation practices and how we as chefs can ensure that food is safe to consume.

2.　Assign kitchen or dining room staff, professionally dressed in pristinely clean and pressed uniforms, to serve the food to guests. Such a practice:

　　a.　ensures prompt service and a steady flow of traffic on the buffet.

　　b.　helps prevent guests from serving themselves, ensuring better portion control and preventing cross-contamination from using one service utensil for two or more food items.

　　c.　helps ensure that the buffet table is carefully monitored; the presentation of the whole table stays neater and fresher with staff readily available, and guests are less likely to play with the display or get unusually close to it, perhaps sneezing or coughing on it.

NOTES

NOTES

NOTES

339

NOTES

NOTES

NOTES

NOTES

NOTES

NOTES

NOTES

NOTES

NOTES